The Rise
of the
Computer
State

The Rise of the Computer State

David Burnham

Foreword by Walter Cronkite

Random House · New York

Portions of this work were previously published in *The New York Times*.

Grateful acknowledgment is made to the following for permission to reprint previously published material:

Channels of Communications: From "Twists in Two-Way Cable" by David Burnham. First published in *Channels of Communications,* June/July 1981. Reprinted by permission of the publisher.

W.H. Freeman and Company: Excerpt from *Computer Power and Human Reason* by Joseph Weizenbaum, 1976. Reprinted by permission of the publisher.

Hiroshi Kashiwagi: Excerpt from "A Meeting at Tule Lake." Copyright © 1980 in *Ayumi*. Reprinted by permission of the author.

Random House, Inc.: Specified excerpt from *Dr. Seuss's Sleep Book* by Dr. Seuss. Copyright © 1962 by Dr. Seuss. Reprinted by permission of Random House, Inc.

Science: Excerpt from "Some Moral and Technical Consequences of Automation" by N. Weiner, *Science,* Vol. 131, pp. 1355–1356, May 6, 1980. Copyright © 1960 by the American Association for the Advancement of Science.

Library of Congress Cataloging in Publication Data
Burnham, David, 1933–
The rise of the computer state.
Includes index.
1. Privacy, Right of—United States. 2. Computers—
Access control. I. Title.
JC596.2.U5B87 1983   323.44′83′0973   82–42808
ISBN 0-394-51437-8

Manufactured in the United States of America
98765432
First Edition

To my daughters, Sarah and Molly

Foreword
by Walter Cronkite

In 1948 George Orwell wrote what turned out to be his final work, the classic *1984*. It drew a picture of a chilling future in which the world had fallen under the sway of three great totalitarian governments.

The country that comprised what had been Western Europe, Britain and the United States was called Oceania and was ruled by Big Brother. The state was all and to serve it, loyally and unthinkingly, its citizens had been divested of all pretense of privacy, and hence liberty.

Books, movies, plays—everything was censored, of course. History was rewritten to suit current propaganda needs. Thought police monitored behavior patterns to detect possibly deviant attitudes. Sophisticated listening devices tuned in the most intimate conversations.

And perhaps the most effective means of control was the two-way television set that looked into every room at office, factory or home. The individual never was free from the surveillance of the security forces.

And yet Orwell, with his vivid imagination, was unable to foresee the actual shape of the threat that would exist in 1984. It turns out to be the ubiquitous computer and its ancillary communication networks. Without the malign intent of any government system or would-be dictator, our privacy is being invaded, and more and more of the experiences which should be solely our own are finding their way into electronic files that the curious can scrutinize at the punch of a button.

The airline companies have a computer record of our travels— where we went and how long we stayed and, possibly, with whom we traveled. The car rental firms have a computer record of the days and distances we went afield. Hotel computers can fill in a myriad of detail about our stays away from home, and the credit card computers know a great deal about the meals we ate, and with how many guests.

The computer files at the Internal Revenue Service, the Census Bureau, the Social Security Administration, the various security agencies such as the Federal Bureau of Investigation and our own insurance companies know everything there is to know about our economic, social and marital status, even down to our past illnesses and the state of our health.

If—or is it when?—these computers are permitted to talk to one another, when they are interlinked, they can spew out a roomful of data on each of us that will leave us naked before whoever gains access to the information.

This is the threat, with its many permutations, with which David Burnham deals here. His is not a polemic against the computers or those who program them, and there is full acknowledgment of the great benefits they can and are bringing to mankind. (For instance, we could not have gone to space without them, and they hold the potential for helping scientists conquer disease.)

But we must be vigilant against their misuse, either accidentally or intentionally. The alarm is raised here that, while we are only too aware now of the danger of losing everything in a nuclear holocaust, there also is a danger of losing it all in the green glow from a little phosphor screen.

Acknowledgments

To thank all who have assisted me is not possible. Sophy Burnham strongly encouraged me to undertake the wonderful independent adventure of writing this book. Walda Roseman was my first tutor in the many ways that changes in communications technology are affecting every facet of our lives. Marcia MacNaughton remains a constant friend, steadfast supporter and forthright critic. She long has been directly involved in the challenging struggle to understand and tame the forces of the communications revolution. Mae Churchill's insights into the workings of the great bureaucracies of our age have provided a constant reminder of the alertness required if we are to maintain the rights and privileges guaranteed by our Constitution. Joanne Omang's buoyant humor and loving good sense are an essential balance.

Fred Friendly and Sanford Jaffe, both with the Ford Foundation; Mary Milton of the Markle Foundation; and Elizabeth McCormack and Wade Greene, representing a member of the Rockefeller family, all offered early, informed and generous support. The Aspen Institute for Humanistic Studies—Joseph Slater, Michael Rice and Steve Strickland—provided me a happy place to work.

Robert Loomis of Random House constantly offered help and support that was invaluable. From the very beginning of my thinking about this book, my agent Robin Straus has been an extraordinarily good friend and thoughtful advisor.

Contents

The Rise of the Computer State

The Beginning

My story begins more than a century and a half ago; Napoleon had been dead for one year. James Monroe was the president of the United States. Baby Victoria was fifteen years from assuming her splendid throne. Charles Darwin would not publish his revolutionary thesis *On the Origin of Species* for another three and a half decades.

The year was 1822. In England a brilliant, cantankerous mathematician named Charles Babbage completed the construction of a model of a technically advanced adding machine that he called the difference engine. The British government, correctly assuming that the special power of this machine could greatly enhance the navigating skills of the world's leading maritime nation, decided to subsidize the difficult task of building a full-scale version of Babbage's device.

This nineteenth-century example of a government-supported research and development program went forward in a laboratory partially built by public funds. Babbage's craftsmen, however, found the challenge of building the necessary system of gears and cogs extraordinarily difficult.

Year after year Babbage continued the frustrating task of trying to transform the model of his difference engine into a full-scale reality. But he also began thinking about a far more ambitious invention. The mathematician first wrote about this new device in 1833. Historians now say that this second conception, which Babbage called the analytical engine, was the world's first universal digital computer.

From the high-technology perspective of the late twentieth century, Babbage's two devices look a good deal like each other. A replica of the experimental model of the difference engine at the Smithsonian Institution in Washington looks like the brass innards of a carefully crafted and very sturdy antique clock. Hundreds of brass spools, geared to each other and stacked on a series of metal shafts, rest on a thick oak frame. The drawings of the analytical engine suggest a similar but far more intricate machine.

The apparent similarity, however, is misleading. The model of the difference engine could do nothing but add numbers with complete accuracy. The analytical engine, as conceived by Babbage, was far more ambitious. With it, the operator could place instructions in the machine to later undertake a lengthy series of different mathematical functions. In today's language, the operator could program it. The analytical engine had a memory or "store" unit, as well as input, arithmetic, control and output units.

Unlike virtually all inventions of the first part of the Industrial Revolution, Babbage's second machine was not intended to increase the physical strength and mechanical ability of mankind. Instead, implicit in its plans lay a revolutionary method to examine and organize the universe, to increase the power of the mind. Now, fifteen decades after Babbage's fertile brain conceived the analytical engine, both the device itself and the thought processes that emerged from it have come to play a major, perhaps even dominant, role in how people earn their livings, teach their children, elect their leaders, play their games and wage their wars.

The significance of Babbage's conceptual achievement was understood by neither the British government nor most of his peers. But it was recognized and celebrated by one of his disciples. Her name was Ada Augusta, the Countess of Lovelace, and she was the brilliant daughter from the brief stormy marriage of Lord and Lady Byron.

Contemporary portraits show Ada to be a slight, beautiful woman with dark romantic eyes, a slim nose and a small, determined mouth. She was known as an excellent horsewoman, and in her later years was a compulsive gambler. There were even rumors, apparently unfounded, that she and her mentor, the brilliant Babbage, once worked together to develop the elusive dream of all gamblers, a sure-fire system to confound the bookies.

Mathematics was the second curious passion of Lady Lovelace, and with expert tutoring from Babbage, she had become a first-rank practitioner, unusually well trained for her time and sex. Partly because of this expertise, she came to understand Babbage's invention and believe that the analytical engine was a powerful instrument that ultimately would have an enormous impact on the world, its inhabitants and how they thought.

"If we compare together the powers and purposes of the Difference and of the Analytical Engines, we shall perceive that the capabilities of the latter are immeasurably more extensive than those of the former, and that they in fact hold to each other the same relationship as that of analysis to arithmetic," she wrote in an English scientific journal of 1842.

"The former engine is in its nature strictly mathematical, and the results it can arrive at lie within a very clearly defined and restricted range, while there is no finite demarcation which limits the power of the Analytical Engine. A new, a vast and a powerful language is developed," she said, a language "through which alone we can adequately express the great facts of the natural world, and those unceasing changes of mutual relationships which, visibly or invisibly, consciously or unconsciously, are interminably going on in the agencies of the creation we live amidst."

A little more than a hundred and twenty-five years after her death, the U.S. Defense Department paid tribute to the unique insights of this intelligent and passionate woman in a way both unusual and appropriate. The Pentagon named a computer language after her. With the help of Ada, a new language designed to replace eight separate languages being used by the three services in 1980, the experts said they hoped to increase the flexibility of the military while at the same time save the taxpayers about $1 billion a year.

In the middle of the nineteenth century, however, partly because of the failure to make the full-scale version of his earlier machine function, the inventor never tried to transform the intricate plans for his analytical engine into a working model. In fact it was not until the application of the vacuum tube to the concept of the computer at about the time of the beginning of World War II that the significance of the analytical engine began to match the promise claimed for it by the Countess of Lovelace. But during the century and a quarter that separated the conception of the computer from the first steps to make it a mechanical reality, the way of thinking inherent in Babbage's plans came to permeate many of the institutions of the industrial nations.

One of the most provocative critics to identify this process is Jacques Ellul, a French lawyer and World War II Resistance leader. Ellul coined the word *technique* to describe an approach to life that he feels has come to dominate the method of thought of the people, corporations and government agencies of much of the world.

Technique, Ellul has written, is the rational and unblinking search for increased efficiency and greater productivity. When technique is applied to machines, as it was at the beginning of the Industrial Revolution, it made sense. But as machines have come to play a larger and larger role in almost every aspect of our lives, technique has come to dominate the minds of corporate executives, government officials and just plain people as they go about planning their organizational and personal lives.

Streamlining a high-speed locomotive or airplane, Ellul suggests, is totally rational. But streamlining the management procedures of a hospital, the guidelines that determine when a policeman can make an arrest, or the way a law-school graduate takes a bar exam or an unemployed mother applies for public assistance for her child may have painful and unforeseen consequences.

Furthermore, some of the procedures adopted in the sacred name of efficiency directly conflict with the ethical standards and human values that have been developed by the great religious and philosophical movements of the world.

Ellul thus contends that the way of thinking implicit in Babbage's invention had become a potent force in many nations long before the middle of the twentieth century when the computer finally became an essential recruit in every army, every government agency, every police force, every corporation and every largish institution.

With the full blossoming of the computer in the decades since World War II, however, the velocity of the search for greater efficiency and productivity has accelerated at an incredible speed and the analytical engine has now become the central force of our civilization, the unique metaphor of our time.

In the rushed clutter of our daily lives, it is easy to lose sight of the combined power that the computer, the related telecommunication links and the computer's system of thinking have come to exert over almost every aspect of our lives. For the fish swimming in the ocean, the comprehension of wetness is impossible. Wet requires the contrast of dry. In the same way, it is hard for most Americans to appreciate the intricate layering of computerized networks that have been built up around each of our lives during the last twenty-five years. Abrupt violent changes, like the revolution in Iran, are easy to see. Incremental changes, stretching over decades, are harder to perceive.

The enormous benefits provided by this technology offer another kind of camouflage. The comforts and conveniences of the computer make thinking about its potentially negative effects something of an exercise in self-denial. Computers, after all, give the United States the largest and most sophisticated telephone system in the world. Computers allow firemen in some cities to receive reports on the number of tenants who live in the apartment house as they are rushing to put out the fire. Computers scan the records of millions of drivers in a few seconds and permit a state in the East to deny a license to an applicant from the West who has been convicted of drunken driving. Computers, built into the engines of our cars, increase fuel efficiency by precisely regulating the flow of gas into the carburetor. Lives saved. Time saved. Money saved.

The overwhelming influence of computers is hard to exaggerate. Linked computers have become as essential to the life of our society as the central nervous system is to the human body. Industries engaged in the processing of information by computers now generate about half of the gross national product of the United States. The Social Security Administration, AT&T, the Internal Revenue Service, the insurance industry, the Pentagon, the bankers and the federal intelligence agencies could not function without the computer. Access to a computer is one way to define class, with those who cannot or will not plug themselves into a terminal standing on the bottom rung of the social ladder.

One sign of just how deeply the computer has penetrated the psyche of America is a stanza from one of Dr. Seuss's books for children, a high-spirited examination of sleep in America that is calculated to entertain the four-year-olds, if not their parents.

> Counting up sleepers . . . ? Just how do we do it . . . ?
> Really quite simply. There's nothing much to it.
> We found how many, we learn the amount
> By an Audio-Te-ly-O-Tally-O Count.
> On a mountain, halfway between Reno and Rome,
> We have a machine in a plexiglass dome,
> Which listens and looks into everyone's home.
> And whenever it sees a new sleeper go flop,
> It jiggles and lets a new Biggel-Ball drop.
> Our chap counts these balls as they plup in a cup.
> And that's how we know who is down and who's up.

A jolly Big Brother alive in the blithely cute world of Dr. Seuss.

With incredible speed, after a gestation period of more than a hundred years, the offspring of Babbage's analytical machines are now changing the way we live: how we pay our bills, get our news and entertainment, earn our living, obtain a government handout, pay our taxes, obtain credit, make our plane and hotel reservations, inform the government of our views and even receive our love letters.

Most U.S. commentary on computers has tended to be laudatory, in part because of the widely shared perception that the machines are essential to the continued growth of the American economy. A few critics, nevertheless, have sought to examine the dark side of computers, often aiming their fire at the somewhat narrow question of personal privacy.

In response to these criticisms and the increased public awareness of government surveillance that grew out of the Watergate scandals of President Richard Nixon, Congress enacted a handful of narrowly drawn laws. One statute imposed restrictions on the use of personal information by federal agencies. Another permitted Americans to see and challenge the information collected about them by credit reporting firms. A third established a secret court that authorizes the FBI to install bugs and taps against espionage suspects.

Despite this flurry of legislative activity, Americans frequently discount the importance, in the phrase of one Supreme Court decision, of being left alone. "I have nothing to hide," many respectable citizens reply when asked whether they fear the increased intensity of all kinds of surveillance made possible by the computer. And they often seem unaware that personal privacy has been considered a valuable asset for many centuries and is not just a faintly hysterical fad of the age of technology.

"A wonderful fact to reflect upon that every human creature is constituted to be that profound secret and mystery to the other," Charles Dickens wrote in *A Tale of Two Cities*. "A solemn consideration, when I enter a great city by night, that every one of those darkly clustered houses encloses its own secret; that every beating heart in the hundreds of breasts there is, in some of its imaginings, a secret to the heart nearest it."

Privacy, however, is far more than the aesthetic pleasure of Charles Dickens. And the gradual erosion of privacy is not just the unimportant imaginings of fastidious liberals. Rather, the loss of privacy is a key symptom of one of the fundamental social problems of our age: the growing power of large public and private institutions in relation to the individual citizen.

This book examines how the widely acknowledged and heavily advertised ability of the computer to collect, organize and distribute information tends to enhance the power of the bureaucratic structures who harness the computer to achieve their separate and often worthy goals. This book also examines how the computer, as utilized by the institutions of our society, is affecting our values. Thus the book is not just about computers and data bases and computerized communication networks. It is about how large organizations use such systems and how these systems influence what we think is important.

One of the most brilliant and knowledgeable men to ponder these questions was Norbert Wiener, a child prodigy who earned his Ph.D. degree from Harvard University when he was eighteen and was a professor at the Massachusetts Institute of Technology for most of his life. Wiener, a mathematician, was a unique and enthusiastic pioneer in the development of computers and computer languages.

At the same time, however, he feared that computers ultimately would pose a serious threat to the independent spirit of mankind.

"We are the slaves of our technical improvements, and we can no more return a New Hampshire farm to the self-contained state it was maintained in 1800 than we can, by taking thought, add a cubit to our stature or, what is more to the point, diminish it," he wrote in 1954.

Asking us to open our eyes, Wiener argued that "progress imposes not only new possibilities for the future, but new restrictions. The simple faith in progress is not a conviction belonging to strength, but one belonging to acquiescence and hence to weakness."

Five years later, he turned his attention more directly to the computer. The occasion was a 1959 lecture to the Committee on Science in the Promotion of Human Welfare at a meeting of the American Association for the Advancement of Science. "It is my thesis that machines do and can transcend some of the limitations of their designers, and that in doing so they may be both effective and dangerous."

The scientist noted that over a limited range of operations machines already could act more quickly and precisely than humans. "This being the case, even when machines do not in any way transcend man's intelligence, they very well may, and often do, transcend man in the performance of tasks. An understanding of their mode of performance may be delayed until long after the task which they have been set is completed. By the very slowness of our human actions, our effective control of our machines may be nullified."

Wiener told the audience that in his view the computer presented a moral problem that paralleled one of the great contradictions of slavery. "We wish the slave to be intelligent, to be able to assist us in carrying out our tasks. However, we also wish him to be subservient. Complete subservience and complete intelligence do not go together. How often in ancient times the clever Greek philosopher, slave of a less intelligent Roman slaveholder, must have dominated the actions of his master rather than obeyed his wishes."

As machines become more and more efficient and operate at a higher and higher psychological level, Wiener went on, the catastrophe "of the dominance by machines comes nearer and nearer."

In part because of the great speed with which the computer was being plugged into almost every aspect of American life, Wiener worried about the unanticipated and unintended effects of these machines as much as those he could foresee.

Over and over again he would tell the story of "The Monkey's Paw," a parable about a shrunken relic from India that guaranteed any wish to the person holding it. When the old sailor in the story gives the paw to a friend, the sailor explains the incredible powers of the shriveled piece of blackened skin but then advises the friend against calling upon the genie because he always grants his wishes in an unexpected fashion. The friend naturally does not heed the warning. He asks the genie for a large sum of money. The wish is quickly fulfilled when a messenger arrives from an insurance company with a bundle of money and the sad news that the friend's son has just been killed in an accident.

What does the genie of the computer age have in store for our society? As the question was posed by Norbert Wiener, it seemed to have the quality of an unanswerable riddle. But the problem can be restated in a form more susceptible to resolution. In what concrete ways does the computer enlarge the power of public and private organizations over the individual citizen?

Computers and telecommunications enormously enhance the ability of organizations to collect, store, collate and distribute all kinds of information about virtually all of the 232 million people of the United States. Computers have allowed far more organizations to have far more access to far more people at far less cost than ever was possible in the age of the manual file and the wizened file clerk.

The computer thus has wrought a fundamental change in American life by encouraging the physical migration of information about the most minute details of our personal and public lives into the computerized files of a large and growing number of corporations, government bureaucracies, trade associations and other institutions. As recently as the end of World War II, much of this information would not have been collected at all, but would instead have been stashed away in our homes. Even when it was collected, it rarely was subject to casual inspection because of the considerable expense involved in paying the salaries of the clerks needed to retrieve any particular item. Computerization has now greatly reduced this economic disincentive to inspect the files.

The migration of information from the home to the organization has significant legal consequences. The Bill of Rights was added to the Constitution by Madison and his followers because they feared an overly powerful central government. One important safeguard of the Bill of Rights requires law-enforcement officials to persuade an independent judge that there is good cause for them to search a citizen's house before they are given a warrant to push down that citizen's front door.

Partly because Madison did not anticipate the computer and growth of large record-holding organizations, the shield of the Fourth Amendment was not extended to the third-party holders of records. The combined effect of the computerization of American life and the limited scope of the Fourth Amendment thus is a critical one. With a great deal of personal information jotted down on records physically stored in the house of citizens in the pre-computer age, law enforcement required a search warrant to obtain it. With the development of large computerized organizations such as hospitals, insurance companies and credit reporting companies, however, law enforcement now can obtain a great variety of information about an individual on the basis of an informal contact or a written request that is not reviewed by a judge.

In addition to allowing large organizations to collect large amounts of detailed information, computers and the linked telecommunication networks have considerably enlarged the ability of these organizations to track the daily activities of individual citizens.

Many computer scientists, government officials and business executives take comfort in the observation that during the last few years in the United States little concrete evidence has emerged suggesting current widespread abuse of these interlocked systems. But history tells us nothing if not that all bureaucracies seek to maximize their powers. The powerful warning of John Emerich Edward, better known as Lord Acton, has not lost its force since expressed in a letter to Bishop Creighton in 1887: "Power tends to corrupt; absolute power corrupts absolutely."

The most immediate example of this important lesson, which

optimistic Americans are already pushing from their minds, was the illegal and improper government surveillance of hundreds of thousands of citizens suspected of political activism during the last quarter of a century at the direction of three separate presidents. The Kennedy administration initiated a far-reaching effort to keep track of civil-rights activists such as Dr. Martin Luther King. This surveillance ultimately involved the placement of electronic bugs in the motels where King stayed as he moved about the country and the subsequent effort to peddle the secretly recorded material to newspaper columnists. During the Johnson administration, concern about race riots, civil-rights demonstrations and antiwar protests prompted the president to order the army to greatly enlarge its surveillance of citizens, almost all of whom were only exercising the right to speak their minds. The surveillance led to the creation of intelligence files on about 100,000 persons (including Catholic priests and one U.S. senator) and on an equal number of domestic organizations (for example, the National Organization for Women, the John Birch Society and the NAACP). President Johnson ordered the CIA to undertake a similar surveillance program of citizens even though it violated the law approved by Congress when the agency was initially established. During the Nixon administration, the president knowingly encouraged the White House staff to violate the law by obtaining the computerized tax files on individuals Mr. Nixon did not like. This action served as the basis for one of the proposed articles of impeachment drawn up against Mr. Nixon by the House Judiciary Committee shortly before he resigned.

Telecommunications equipment and computers have tended to centralize the power held by the top officials in both government and private industry. Computer experts often reject this complaint. They contend that the rapid growth in the use of personal computers by millions of American citizens will cancel out the increases in power flowing to the large organizations. This defense has a surface plausibility. But when the vast capital, expertise and manpower available to the large government and business organizations are compared to the capital, expertise and available working time of even the most favored individual, the personal computer does not appear to be a great equalizer. Furthermore, who controls what information is stored in the great data bases of the United States and who serves as the gatekeeper to most of the giant communication networks?

Is it reasonable to believe that a dedicated band of environmentalists, sending electronic smoke signals to each other via their home terminals, really will be able to effectively match the concentrated power of a giant oil company or committed government agency? Can it really be argued that the personal computers and word processors now being purchased for more and more corporate employees and government officials will enhance their personal freedom? Or will the equipment, while increasing individual output, also allow a level of automated surveillance unknown to any previous age? Certainly the large airlines have spent hundreds of millions of dollars installing computer terminals to help their clerks sell tickets. But how many of the airlines are installing terminals in the homes of stockholders, or even of members of the board of governors, to give them more information about the internal operations of the company so they can exercise more effective control?

Even Simon Nora and Alain Minc, the authors of a report prepared for the French government on the impact of computers on that country's citizens, were not entirely optimistic about this point. The new computerization, they said, could lead to greater local autonomy. "By contrast, however, it may constitute a powerful means of centralization: the network makes it easier to collect basic data and follow-up production operations in real time. In that case, the workers lose the limited degree of freedom they experience under intermittent supervision; they are even more integrated into the production process."

Max Weber, the brilliant German sociologist, discussed the question in terms of organizational power long before the great organizations of the world had equipped themselves with computers. "The bureaucratic structure goes hand in hand with the concentration of the material means of management in the hands of the master," he wrote in an essay published before World War I. "This concentration occurs, for example, in the development of big capitalist enterprises, which find their essential characteristics in the process. A corresponding process occurs in public organizations."

But massive data bases, the ability to track large numbers of individuals and the concentration of power are not the only contributions of the computer. It also increases the influence of the major bureaucracies by giving these organizations a method by which they can anticipate the probable future thoughts and activities of groups of people.

One bizarre example of this particular use of the computer involves about two thousand families in Pittsfield, Massachusetts, who have been tied into an automatic reporting system called Behaviorscan that keeps track of every single item the sample families purchase at their local supermarket. Simultaneously, the same families receive special test commercials on their home television sets. The families of course do not know which commercials are special and which are normal. But after the Behaviorscan system records the purchases of the test families, a central computer in Chicago checks for correlations between what they saw in their television ads and what they bought at their supermarket. The market researchers then use the information about the responses of the test families to predict the behavior of huge segments of the population.

Similar small experiments are now being conducted in at least half a dozen other cities around the United States. But will the experiments remain experimental? Remember that more and more supermarkets are purchasing computer checkout equipment capable of collecting exact information on the purchases of each customer. Also note that changes in banking procedures may soon mean that the payment for the weekly shopping trip will be achieved by an electronic system that will automatically transfer funds from the customer's account to that maintained by the supermarket.

Many computer experts, computer salesmen and computer users are not comfortable when questions are asked about this and other tasks assigned to the modern version of the analytical engine. For some of them, the technology has become an article of religious faith, part of the framework of their lives, the magic carpet that until very recently seemed to be carrying the United States to the heights of world power while providing most of its citizens with material wealth far beyond the dreams of their fathers. Furthermore, at least some of the scientists and engineers have been so intimately involved in operating the major institutions of the United States that they are unable to understand that a question directed at a government agency or corporation is not necessarily an attack on their integrity.

The defenders of the faith seem to fall back on four general defenses when confronted by questions about the efficacy of the computer and its potential impact on the American people.

The first and most favored response offered by the technologist is that the computer is simply a neutral machine that can be used for either good or evil. "It's not the computer that creates the problem, it's people," they frequently will say. This argument was explicitly embraced by IBM, the world's largest manufacturer of computers, in an advertisement that ran in a number of America's glossy magazines in 1982. The ad pictures a police lineup in which four shady-looking characters and a computer terminal are lined up for identification. "The computer didn't do it," the IBM headline boldly proclaims.

The assertion is irrelevant and misleading. The knife lying on the table can be picked up by a sculptor to transform his personal vision to the certainty of stone. Or the knife can be picked up by a hungry man to slice a chunk of life-giving bread. Or a murderer can grab it and stab the object of his hatred. The question is the intent of the person who picks up the knife, not its special quality of sharpness.

The absurdity of the IBM defense is nicely illustrated by General Motors, the giant automobile manufacturer who for many years fought legislative efforts to reduce the incredible slaughter on our highways by requiring that the insides of cars be made less hazardous. The standard position was that it was not poorly designed cars and highways that killed people, it was poor drivers. Though Ralph Nader ultimately helped GM and the other manufacturers see the light, the National Rifle Association still clings to the same position. "Guns don't kill people, people kill people," the NRA says.

In a very limited sense, of course, there is some truth in the current position of the NRA. But the complete truth is that thousands of times a year Americans pick up guns with the express purpose of killing someone. Similarly, as this book tries to demonstrate, there have been numerous occasions when people have chosen to use computers in ways that harmed society.

A second argument frequently raised by technologists has even less merit. People who question computers are nothing but Luddites, they say. Luddite was the name given a group of English weavers in the early part of the nineteenth century who smashed laborsaving textile machinery in protest against the lower wages and high unemployment they attributed to the new equipment. The charge of Ludditism is particularly irritating because many of those making it pride themselves on their analytic abilities while seeming to be unable to distinguish between an angry mob of violent weavers and those who ask whether the computer may not be used for malevolent purposes.

A third argument frequently advanced by Americans intrigued by the power of computers is the assertion that the people of the United States today experience more freedom than has ever been known before in the history of the world. To an unprecedented degree we can live and travel where we choose. In an extraordinary way we are blessed by an amazing range of material things—clothes, food and personal ornaments. Most important, perhaps, the mass migration of the American people from villages and farms to anonymous cities has created for many of us an amazing sense of privacy. Anyone who has lived on an island in Maine or an isolated town in Alabama and then experienced the exhilarating freedom of Los Angeles, Chicago or New York understands that the city gives the individual a splendid suit of armor against the wagging tongues and prying eyes of knowing neighbors. But society's escape from the tyranny of gossip is a separate subject, one entirely distinct from how the computer is increasing the power of large organizations in relationship to the individual.

A fourth defense involves questions of timing. Some computer experts in both government and industry acknowledge they are concerned about how computers might be harnessed by their bureaucracies in the distant future. But because they frequently spend most of their working days attempting to resolve the technical flaws of the current computer system, the experts find it hard to believe that the imperfect machine they are always patching could pose a threat to anyone. Thus at least some of the technologists are genuinely surprised when a critic sees potential problems in the operation of their creaky old systems.

A parallel problem is created by the perception that as fast as the computer has brought change to all aspects of our society, the pace of this change has been somewhat slower than predicted by the futurologists. "George Orwell predicted the coming of 1984 more than thirty years ago and nothing has happened yet," said one Justice Department computer designer. Whether the assumption of the official is correct is at least open for debate. Because the changes have not kept pace with the most dramatic predictions, however, the apologists have been able to minimize the significance of those alterations that have undoubtedly occurred.

This book attempts to focus a clarifying light on the implications of some of these changes. To make sense of the massed, powerful armies of organization that seek to channel the choices of every individual, I have chosen to examine the problem in terms of function rather than in terms of the principal actors in the drama. There are not separate sections of the book devoted to such organizations as the Internal Revenue Service, AT&T, the Social Security Administration and the credit reporting agencies. Instead, the activities of these and other larger organizations are described in chapters devoted to broad topics: the growth of large data banks, the concentration of power in fewer and fewer organizational hands, the benign and malignant surveillance that has become so important to the functioning of the United States, the alteration of our values.

Most of this book concerns procedures and processes and organizations and machines that exist today. Thus it largely concentrates on the present, not on some point in the unknowable future. One chapter, however, does examine how some of the processes and machines that currently are on the drawing boards might affect our society in the year 2020.

The one exception to the decision not to devote a chapter to an examination of a specific organization is the National Security Agency, a secretive and largely unknown bureaucracy whose particular powers could handily serve as a metaphor for the entire book. How does an organization that controls large amounts of information exert its power? Is the information it collects the ultimate source of power? How does an agency with this kind of power escape accountability?

This book was written in the spirit of the late Alan Barth, an editorial writer at the *Washington Post.* Alan Barth was a personally quiet man who wrote vigorous denunciations of the McCarthyists, racists and other individuals he felt threatened the sensible tolerance that has held the United States together for more than two hundred years. Barth had one abiding conviction. "The price of liberty," he wrote in his book by that name, is always "vigilance against constituted authority, against the force of order."

This book is devoted to Alan Barth's splendid rule.

Surveillance

The right to be left alone—the most comprehensive of rights, and the right most valued by civilized men.

—Louis D. Brandeis

Hiroshi Kashiwagi stood on the makeshift speaker's platform, the flatbed of a huge army truck. Painted in undulating camouflage patterns of tan and green and gray, the truck was out of place in the busy parking lot of the Tan Foran Shopping Center, just beyond the first range of hills south of San Francisco. Very few of the Sunday shoppers on that warm spring morning in 1981 stopped to hear the speaker's message.

But the small audience sitting in the folding chairs near the truck listened intently as Kashiwagi read his memorial poem "A Meeting at Tule Lake." Tule Lake was one of the ten internment camps established by the United States at the beginning of World War II to hold 112,000 Japanese Americans—a majority of them native-born citizens—driven from their homes in California, Oregon and Washington. And the Tan Foran Shopping Center where the audience gathered to hear the poet was of special interest too. Four decades before it had been a racetrack that had been swiftly converted into an emergency assembly area where 8,033 Japanese Americans from the San Francisco area were held behind barbed-wire fences until they were shipped to the permanent detention centers such as Tule Lake.

Kashiwagi, wearing blue jeans, a plaid shirt and a tan jockey's cap, read his poem with melodic intensity:

"We are driven inside . . .
For three years or more,
For three years or more.
To see again the barbed-wire fence,
The guard towers, the MPs, the machine guns,
The bayonets, the tanks, the mess halls, the latrine.
It's right to know the bitter cold of winter,
The dust storms. How can we forget the sand, the sand?
Biting into our skin, filling our eyes and nose and mouth and ears,
Graying our hair in an instant.
How can we forget the sand, the sand?
It's right to recall the directives, their threats and lies, the meetings,
the strikes, the resistance, the arrests, stockades, violent attacks,
murder.
Derangement. Derangement. Pain, grief, separation.
Departure. Informers, recriminations, disagreements.
Loyalty, disloyalty. Yes, yes. No, no, no. Yes."

Kashiwagi's passionate words on that sunny February afternoon marked the day thirty-eight years before when President Roosevelt signed Executive Order 9066, a regulation effectively authorizing the army to remove all people of Japanese ancestry from the West Coast. The president's order has long been recognized as setting in motion the single most massive civil-rights violation in the history of the United States. What has not been celebrated, however, is how an early version of the computer contributed to this dark moment.

First a brief outline of the incarceration itself. This extraordinary breach in the constitutional rights of 112,000 persons of Japanese descent frequently has been excused as a necessity of war. But the available evidence puts this reassuring assumption in doubt. J. Edgar Hoover, for example, contended that the Federal Bureau of Investigation could keep the relatively small number of serious Japanese suspects under direct surveillance and that the demand for the evacuation of all Japanese Americans was "based primarily upon public political pressure rather than upon factual data."

Curtis B. Munson, a respected troubleshooter in the State Department, was appointed by President Roosevelt several months before Pearl Harbor specifically to investigate the loyalty of Japanese Americans. His report, kept secret until well after World War II, concluded: "For the most part the local Japanese are loyal to the United States or, at worst, hope that by remaining quiet they can avoid concentration camps or irresponsible mobs. We do not believe that they would be at the least any more disloyal than any other racial group in the United States with whom we went to war."

Commander K. D. Ringle, intelligence chief for the Southern California Naval District, agreed with Munson's analysis. He said a mass evacuation was "unwarranted" and argued that the question of what to do about the Japanese people living in the United States had been "magnified out of true proportion because of the physical characteristics of the people."

The intelligence officer's concern about the impact of racial prejudice on the government's policy was valid. Consider the argument for forced removal by the young attorney general of California. "When we are dealing with the Caucasian race we have methods that will test the loyalty of them. . . . But when we deal with the Japanese we are in an entirely different field and we cannot form an opinion that we believe to be sound." The author of this openly racist remark later earned a reputation as one of America's most liberal judges after he was appointed Chief Justice of the U.S. Supreme Court. His name was Earl Warren.

President Roosevelt came down on the side of the U.S. Army and the local politicians such as Warren. On February 19, 1942, he signed an order authorizing the secretary of the army to establish "military areas" from which all persons who did not have permission to enter could be excluded as a military necessity. The first action under the executive order was the expulsion of the entire Japanese American community from Terminal Island near Los Angeles on February 25 through 27. Armed soldiers marched into the old fishing village and ordered all persons of Japanese ancestry to leave their homes. A substantial majority of the refugees were citizens of the United States who had been born here. A large number were infants, children and women. No hearings were held. No charges were brought.

The initial targets were the Japanese Americans living close to the

Pacific Ocean. But gradually the government campaign began to move inland. During the summer of 1942, the notices went up on the telephone polls around Fresno, California. A family named Okamura—three children, their parents and two grandparents—made hurried arrangements to leave their forty-acre farm.

"I was confused and terrified," recalls Raymond Okamura, then eleven years old. "I didn't know what was happening to us on the trip to Arizona. It took four days. We had to keep the shades down in the railroad car and the train was locked and guarded. When we finally got to the Gila Relocation Center, it was hot and windy. We believe the dusty windstorms there probably were the cause of my grandfather's death about two weeks after we got to the camp."

Okamura has a round, gently smiling face, short cropped hair, and a soft voice. He now lives in Berkeley with his wife and three children and works as a chemist with the California Health Department. He is obsessed by what the government did to his people. Okamura was the principal organizer of the memorial service at the Tan Foran Shopping Center. He also is the person who by persistent inquiry forced the Census Bureau, after forty years of evasion, to disclose the details of how it provided the army with material from the 1940 census to help in the roundup of the Japanese.

The Census Bureau data, recorded on punch cards that could be quickly tabulated by a kind of mechanical computer, was used in the roundup despite a provision in the bureau's legal charter that said "in no case shall information furnished under the authority of this act be used to the detriment of the person or persons to whom such information relates."

The Census Bureau's admission was made in a letter from Vincent Barabba, the director of the agency under both President Nixon and President Carter, in response to repeated inquiries from Okamura. The punch cards given the army, Barabba acknowledged, "provided sufficient geographical information to use for planning purposes in the evacuation program."

But the government official sought to obscure the significance of his admission by informing Okamura that the Census Bureau cards had "contained no names or other identifiers for individuals." This same point was emphasized by the bureau in 1980 during an intense advertising campaign designed to persuade the American people of the sanctity of information given the bureau just before its most recent census. In one television spot, in fact, the Census Bureau proudly proclaimed that at the beginning of World War II the secretary of war had tried to persuade the bureau to disclose the names and addresses of all Japanese Americans living on the West Coast.

"In spite of the national emergency—and the hysteria—the bureau's decision not to supply this information was upheld," the advertisement claimed.

Barabba's defense, while technically accurate, was misleading and irrelevant. First of all, on at least one occasion when under pressure from the military the Census Bureau *did* provide law-enforcement officials with the names and addresses of individuals. This happened during World War I when the Justice Department was trying to track down and prosecute young men who were dodging the draft.

Second, and most important, in the age of the computer, aggregate information can be just as dangerous as information that is attached to an individual's name. A young lawyer from Texas named Tom Clark was the Justice Department's coordinator of alien control at the beginning of World War II. Clark subsequently was named attorney general and then associate justice of the Supreme Court. In an interview that is part of the Earl Warren Oral Library Project at the University of California at Berkeley, Clark described how he used the Census Bureau's aggregate information to round up the Japanese. It is worth noting that Clark, unlike Warren, later expressed deep personal regret about his involvement in the mass incarceration.

The Census Bureau, Clark explained, "would lay out on a table various city blocks where the Japanese lived and they would tell me how many were living in each block. Then the army engineers prepared housing; we started with the Santa Anita racetrack and turned the stalls into nice apartments. The army would designate certain blocks where the Japanese lived. A processing station, as it was called, would then be opened up in the designated area, and all the persons of Japanese descent were directed to report to that station and to bring with them all electronic devices such as radios, as well as firearms and anything of that nature. On the day that the army selected for removal, these people would report to the processing station with their clothing, personal effects, etc., and the army would move them by bus or by train to the camp where they were to stay for the duration."

So much for the benign quality of aggregate information. A second defense offered by Barabba was that the Census Bureau had been authorized to do whatever was necessary for the war effort by the Second War Powers Act. The law in question was introduced on January 22, 1942, passed by Congress on March 19 and signed by President Roosevelt on March 27. "But the Census Bureau," Okamura observed, "started releasing information on Japanese Americans to other agencies as early as December 17, 1941, well before the bill was introduced and over three months before the law took effect."

In the fall of 1981, the National Commission on Wartime Relocation and Internment of Civilians held a hearing in Washington to examine the circumstances of the roundup forty years before. One witness was Calvert L. Dedrick, a white-haired, blue-eyed statistician and sociologist who had been in charge of the project that used census material to tell the army exactly how many Japanese lived within each of its evacuation areas.

Dedrick told the commission that early in 1942 he had organized a mapping unit, an analytical unit, a tabulating unit and what was "in effect a war room, where we kept the officers in charge up-to-date as to where people were, how many were moving back and forth under permits of one kind or another."

Now retired, the elderly gentleman was proud of his work for the army and insistent that it had not violated the law. One commission member, however, Judge William Marutani of the Pennsylvania Court of Common Pleas, was skeptical. In response to the judge's questions, Dedrick offered an analogy about a current situation that the judge did not find reassuring.

"The fact that there are so many Cubans living in Miami is a census fact, a statistical fact, and if something happens to the Cubans in Miami that is not our fault," Dedrick contended.

"Well, I don't want to prolong our discussion, but I cannot help but make one comment," Judge Marutani replied. "That perhaps if

I was a Cuban-American and the Census Bureau came around, and particularly if I lived in South Florida, I might leave the space blank or put something other than Cuban with this type of interpretation."

"Then, sir," Dedrick replied, "you would be in violation of federal law."

"Well, that would be better than being jailed for certain," the judge shot back.

When the Supreme Court of the United States reviewed the issue during the heat of World War II, however, a majority of the judges did not share Judge Marutani's feelings. By a margin of six to three, in a decision handed down in 1944, the Supreme Court held that the massed incarceration of the people of Japanese ancestry was constitutional. Justice Owen J. Roberts was one of the three dissenters. He wrote that the real purpose of the army regulation issued under President Roosevelt's executive order was to lock up the defendants "in a concentration camp." Justice Frank Murphy offered a second dissenting opinion. "Being an obvious racial discrimination, the order deprives all those within its scope of equal protection of the laws as guaranteed by the Fifth Amendment."

At the Tan Foran Shopping Center almost four decades later, the reedy sound of Japanese music and the nostalgic beat of such World War II hit tunes as Glenn Miller's "In the Mood" shared equal time in the loudspeakers set up by the memorial committee. Ray Okamura, despite his anger, remained guardedly optimistic. The only hope, he said, "is the attitude of the people in charge. This depends upon the public mood: whether the public will stand for certain actions. The people of California were fully aware that the Japanese Americans were being locked up. And they supported it. If the people had understood the true dangers, the general erosion of freedom implied by the mass evacuation of the Japanese Americans, it could have been halted."

In an extraordinarily complex world, however, understanding the dangers can be hard. It is not easy, for example, to understand how aggregate and statistical information can be used by a large organization to control and manipulate people. It also is hard to comprehend just how easy it is for a government agency or corporation to collect information for one purpose, often benign, and then use it for another purpose, sometimes malignant.

Consider the small but sophisticated computer General Motors has installed on the V8-6-4 model Cadillac automobile. "Your Cadillac," the 1981 owner's manual boasts, "is equipped with a digital fuel injection system which monitors the exhaust stream with an oxygen sensor. The oxygen sensor signals the control unit to adjust the air-fuel ratio as necessary."

The manual further notes that the "Check Engine" light in the instrument panel "is designed to warn you if the system has detected any faults. If the light comes on and stays on while driving, the car should be taken to a Cadillac dealer as soon as possible for system inspection and maintenance. If the light comes on and goes off, it is an indication that a temporary problem has cleared itself. While it is not as critical that the vehicle be brought in to a dealer for inspection immediately, the dealer may at a later date be able to determine what trouble had occurred and if any maintenance is necessary."

But *Electronics Engineering News,* a trade publication, discerned another possible motive in the tiny onboard electronic spy: to ascertain owner negligence over warranty claims. The publication noted that the computer allowed the dealer to determine how many times the car has been driven faster than 85 miles an hour and also how many times the engine was started after the "Check Engine" message first lit up on the dashboard.

GM was shocked. "Any suggestion that there is any equipment in our cars designed to spy on a driver is pure hogwash," said a Cadillac spokesman. "The computer is just to help mechanics repair cars, and the information it provides is used for that purpose only."

The slippery quality of GM's promise that information collected for one purpose will not later be used for other purposes is illustrated on a grand scale by the growing use of computer matching programs by federal, state and local governments.

"There is nothing new about matching," said Thomas McBride, the pipe-smoking inspector general of the Reagan administration's Labor Department and a leading advocate of this particular investigative technique. "You do it as a reporter; I did it when I was a prosecutor. I remember, for example, when I was a member of the special team investigating Watergate and I matched the lists kept by the president's secretary—Rose Mary Woods—against the federal campaign contributions roster. What is new, what is exciting, is that so much more information is now stored on computer tapes. This enables you to match a thousand names or a hundred thousand names against telephone numbers, social security numbers or whatever in a matter of seconds."

The systematic use of computers to detect fraud in certain programs of the federal government actually got started under President Carter. But with the election of President Reagan, computer matching has come into vogue. McBride, in fact, is a cochairman of a special presidential committee established to increase the use of the technique.

"There now are about sixty different federal programs that depend on the income level of the individual to determine eligibility," McBride explained. "Everything from weatherization grants to Head Start. There just isn't any question that this methodology should be widely applied, that it has an enormous potential for eliminating fraud or erroneous payments and saving the taxpayers billions of dollars each year."

McBride acknowledged that most of the programs so far have been aimed at the poor. "We're now trying to get some matches going that don't have this welfare tilt," he explained. "Disaster loans are one example. This is an area where benefits primarily go to business people, agri-business people, and where some quite wealthy people were into some pretty heavy double-dipping. Medical providers, like pharmacists, doctors and hospitals, are another area where big bucks can be saved. I'm quite sure there are a number of areas in the Pentagon where matching might be a big-ticket item."

The Labor Department official acknowledges there are dangers inherent in widespread computer matching. "Making sure that computer data bases are clean and accurate is very difficult. Social security, for example, is really a mess. Sure there is a real potential for abuse. That's why we need very careful controls. I certainly am not prepared to say, for example, that all federal and state programs managers should automatically get access to everyone's income-tax return. I think that would be going too far."

One of the fundamental principles of the Constitution is separation of powers. The theory was thought important because the members of the constitutional convention believed it essential to check the central power of the federal government by dividing it into three essentially equal and sometimes competing parts. But the increased sharing of information by all agencies of government gradually may be undermining the constitutional theory of checks and balances.

Despite the recognition of the hazards, the enticing search for greater efficiency, enhanced by the speed and the minimal cost of computer matching, continues at a furious pace. A few years ago, for example, a very large new law-enforcement program was started by Congress for the worthy purpose of reducing the fraud found in the federally financed but state-administered project to provide assistance to impoverished children.

Because much of this particular kind of fraud occurs after the fathers of the children have skipped out on the legal obligations to their families, Congress decided to establish a nationwide parent-locator system that would track down runaway fathers and force them to provide financial support to their families that otherwise would have been drawn from federal coffers.

With the active support of Senator Russell Long, then chairman of the Finance Committee, Congress passed a law in 1974 that required every state receiving funds under the Aid for Dependent Children program to set up some kind of investigative and enforcement service. The law also provided federal funds to meet 75 percent of the costs. Not surprisingly, the carrot and stick held out by Congress proved quite effective in persuading all levels of government to get cracking.

Consider California, for example, where the primary responsibility has been assigned to the state's fifty-eight district attorneys. Now focus on a cream-colored three-story office building in an industrial section of Los Angeles just off the freeway to Disneyland. This is the headquarters of the Bureau of Child Support of the Los Angeles district attorney's office. With 1,007 investigators, lawyers, technicians and clerks, the bureau now represents exactly half of all the men and women hired by the county of Los Angeles to prosecute all the thousands of different crimes that occur within its borders.

Robert Kiehl is one of this new breed of law-enforcement officers. For the last few months before our meeting, Kiehl had been working on developing a computerized system in which state tax refunds due men identified as runaway fathers are identified and automatically diverted to the support of their children. Just outside of Kiehl's office is a large poster showing a pretty young girl peering through some leaves in a lovely pastoral setting. The slogan printed under the picture: "KIDS NEED LOVE AND SUPPORT."

Kiehl is fifty-four and has a full gray mustache that dominates his mournful face. He speaks in the quiet monotone of many long-time government employees. "The seizing of tax refunds is just one aspect of our child support program, and a rather new one at that," he explained. "Here is how it works. Once we have a court order on a parent and there are delinquencies built up on that order for support of a child receiving public assistance, we send the name up to the Franchise Tax Board. They run the name through their computer. If the parent is due a refund, it is intercepted and used by the state to offset the support going to the child."

The program appears to be quite efficient. During its second year of operation, said Dan Hicks, an analyst with the California Department of Social Services, the district attorneys of the state's fifty-eight counties submitted the names of 117,000 parents for inspection by the computers of the Franchise Tax Board. The result: over $10 million in tax refunds were taken away from delinquent parents and given to the state to defray the costs of supporting needy dependents.

The refund-intercept program is just one way computers help the Los Angeles district attorneys force parents to meet their obligations to their children. With direct electronic links to the state Department of Motor Vehicles, the Employment Development Board, the criminal justice information system and other data banks, the county investigators have many ways of locating the parents—usually the fathers—who have left their children without support.

Richard Beall, the manager of the California Locator Service, explained how his office in Sacramento, largely funded by the federal government, helped the county prosecutors. "In those cases where the local district attorneys run out of leads, they will send us whatever information they have and we search the computerized files of the state, including the records of the Employment Development Board that receives employment earning slips that show where people work and how much they make. If no information pops up in the state files, we make an inquiry to neighboring states or the federal parent locator agency. Last year, we received 230,879 requests from the district attorneys—55,131 of which we shipped on to Washington. We were able to provide some kind of information such as an address in 62 percent of the cases," he said.

Louis Hays, the director of the Federal Child Support Enforcement Office, provided the perspective from Washington. "This year the whole program will result in support payments being made by about 1 million parents—400,000 who have applied to receive Aid for Dependent Children, 600,000 who have not," he said.

"During roughly the same time period, the states asked us for address information on 200,000 individuals. We put these names on magnetic tapes and periodically submitted them to the Internal Revenue Service, the Social Security Administration, the Defense Department, the Veterans Administration, and the National Personnel Record Center. Using their computers, the agencies search their records for information about the people whose names have been submitted by the states. Most of the states have terminals directly linked to us, and when we get a hit, which happens in about 60 percent of the cases, we send the information we have found back to the state."

Hays believes, however, that obtaining the home addresses and places of employment of runaway parents is the simple part of the problem. "You can locate people easily. You can go to court easily. But that doesn't mean you can make them pay," he said.

Hays gives every appearance of being an effective and highly efficient government executive. But he became uneasy when I asked him several questions about the possibility that his system might someday be turned against another target—say, civil-rights protesters organizing legal demonstrations.

"I balk at the implication in your question that parents have a right to avoid their responsibilities," he said. "And besides, the average state doesn't have a very sophisticated computer tracking system yet. I am not saying that we *never* could get to 1984. I'm just saying that the facts don't support such a premise at the present time."

Under a recent amendment to the federal tax law, the Internal Revenue Service has been authorized to follow the lead of California and withhold tax refunds going to parents whom the courts have determined are not making their child-support payments. For 1981 returns filed in 1982, the IRS used its computers to prevent the distribution of $168 million in refunds scheduled to go to 275,479 delinquent parents.

Just five years after Congress cracked the whip, law-enforcement officials at the federal, state and local level of government have built an expansive and expanding computerized telecommunications net that now is used to force fathers to meet their obligations to their children. Certainly runaway fathers are a social problem of great importance. But the recognition that abandoned children represent a difficult challenge to society does not necessarily mean that the law-and-order solution dictated by Congress is the most effective response. Several questions present themselves.

First, did the narrowly focused congressional decision limiting its concern to cracking down on welfare cheats head off other more fundamental legal reforms that might have actually improved the stability of American families?

Second, once a federally mandated tracking system is established that increases the power of county and state officials to trace the movements of one group of citizens, will the system inevitably come to be used for the surveillance of others who fall into disfavor?

Third, hasn't a partial enlargement of the original target group already occurred? Under the federal law, all women applying for aid for dependent children are required to help government investigators identify and locate missing fathers so they can be forced to provide child support. Most members of Congress find it hard to question any program that is sold to them as intended to reduce government waste.

But the law pushed through Congress by Senator Long of Louisiana contains a far broader mandate. It required the state and county offices to help any woman trying to locate the father of her children, even though she has no intent of applying for government assistance. That is why three out of five of the payments collected with the assistance of the federally backed enforcement program are made by persons whose children are not receiving federal aid.

The congressionally mandated requirement that the parent locator services help any woman who asks is an interesting precedent. If Congress has decided it is appropriate for the government to become intricately involved in one kind of private debt relationship, why not extend the service to help other creditors? This very point was made during a hearing of the House Information Subcommittee a few months before the bill authorizing the service was passed. "When you ask whether I would support the use of the social security number for the purpose of locating a deserting father, my response to that is yes," said Representative Edward Koch, now mayor of New York City. "If, on the other hand, someone said well, how about the use of the social security number to find the guy who took a car and failed to make his payments, to help the creditor find him, the answer is no. That would be an abuse of the system."

Ed Koch had identified a key hazard of the computer age. Once a government agency or corporation has invested its expertise and capital in creating a surveillance system to track a single segment of the population that society agrees needs watching, it is hard to resist the temptation to extend the surveillance to other classes. In addition to the almost irresistible pressure to increase the target groups of any system, however, there is a second important hazard: the incredible damage such systems can inflict on an individual when they contain incorrect information.

Consider, for example, the case of Michael Ducross, a Canadian-born Indian who lives in Huntington Beach, California, a small city halfway between Los Angeles and San Diego. At about 9:00 P.M. on March 24, 1980, Ducross, a slight, dark-complexioned man with a gentle smile and wire-rimmed glasses, decided he needed some groceries at the local supermarket. A few minutes later, he turned his 1976 Pinto into a shopping center near his apartment. Almost immediately the flashing red lights of a police car filled his rearview mirror. He had made an illegal left-hand turn.

The policeman, using his two-way car radio, asked for a check on Ducross. A clerk sitting in the Huntington police station punched Ducross's name and driver's license number into the terminal. The message was instantly flashed to the state capital in Sacramento. Nothing. Then 3,000 miles east to Washington and the FBI's computer-operated National Crime Information Center.

Pay dirt! Back across the continent came the answer. The computerized records of the FBI said Ducross was wanted because a decade before—on Christmas Eve of 1969—he had gone AWOL from the Marine Corps. Based on this lead, the police took Ducross to the brig at Camp Pendleton. After holding him for five months the Marine Corps dropped the charges, and he was set free to pick up the broken pieces of his life. Ducross says the government released him after it discovered he had never been AWOL because he had left the Marine Corps in 1969 under a special discharge program available to foreign citizens and Native Americans.

Thus did an error somewhere in the government's computerized records and surveillance system reach across a vast expanse of time and space to violently interrupt the life of a single Iroquois Mohawk Indian.

The growing number of privately operated surveillance systems also make errors. In 1977, Harvey Saltz, a former deputy district attorney in Los Angeles, formed a company called U.D. Registry, Inc., to warn landlords about unreliable tenants. Using a computer to store information obtained from legal charges filed by landlords in the courts, Saltz said he currently has compiled more than a million records about such disputes all over the Los Angeles area. Over 1,900 landlords pay Saltz an annual fee ranging from $35 to $60 and an individual search fee of $7.50 to determine whether the individuals who come to them for housing have had arguments with other landlords in the past.

But as Lucky Kellener, Barbara Ward and many other Los Angeles area residents have learned, such information retrieval systems are frequently capricious. Lucky Kellener, for example, paid his brother's rent in 1978. Some months later, when the brother was evicted, Kellener's name was inadvertently included in the papers filed in court. U.D. Registry transferred the incorrect listing to its computer, where Kellener was identified as an undesirable tenant. Three years after he paid his brother's rent, in December of 1981, the bearded Los Angeles lawyer decided he needed a larger apartment. "I went to three apartment houses but was turned away," Kellener said. "They kept saying things like 'Someone was here before you' or 'We'll get back to you'—you know, the brush-off."

After the third rejection, a landlord inadvertently let Kellener in on the dark secret. There was a computerized blacklisting service and his name was on it. "It's creeping McCarthyism," he said. "Actually, it's worse. McCarthy usually did his stuff out in the open. This operation does it under the table."

Barbara Ward is another victim. She recently moved to Los Angeles, rented an apartment, and found it was infested with cockroaches and rodents. When the landlord refused to deal with the infestation, she gave him thirty days' notice. He countered with an eviction notice. Ward went to court armed with county health records to support her case. The landlord did not show up. The judge ordered the case off the calendar. Several years later, however, she discovered she was unable to rent an apartment because U.D. Registry reported she had once been served with an eviction notice.

The problems of this kind of surveillance are manifest. In Kellener's case, there was a clerical error. In Ward's case the notation was correct—she *had* been served an eviction notice—but the implication that she was unreliable was untrue and the case subsequently was thrown out of court. In both cases the damage to individual reputations was especially serious because the people did not know that U.D. Registry existed and that it was transmitting false information about them.

The cases of Michael Ducross, Lucky Kellener and Barbara Ward all illustrate the impact of an essentially passive record-filing system when it can be searched by computer and its product can be distributed quickly and easily. But a very different kind of surveillance, one that involves the active creation of records, is also greatly enhanced by the computer.

From time to time, for example, the U.S. Army has undertaken intense surveillance of the political activities of American citizens. According to research by the writer Joan M. Jensen, this surveillance goes back at least to 1917 and the U.S. involvement in World War I. But the character of the army's intermittent intelligence-gathering activities underwent a fundamental change in the middle of the 1960s when President Lyndon Johnson became disturbed by both the civil disturbances that occurred after the assassination of Dr. Martin Luther King and the demonstrations of those opposed to the Vietnam War. With the assistance of the military's comparatively new system of computers, Johnson ordered the army to begin collecting intelligence that might help the federal government predict and prevent civil disturbances that might escape the control of state and local officials.

The program quickly developed into a monster. A few years later, Senator Samuel J. Ervin, the deeply conservative North Carolina lawyer who headed the Senate Subcommittee on Constitutional Rights, held hearings on the surveillance program. The army, he discovered, had already collected information on the political activities of an estimated 100,000 persons, including a number of congressmen, such as Representative Abner Mikva, and many members of such organizations as the American Civil Liberties Union, the American Friends Service Committee and the National Association for the Advancement of Colored People.

With very few directives to guide them, Senator Ervin said, army intelligence agents "monitored the membership and policies of peaceful organizations who were concerned with the war in Southeast Asia, the draft, racial and labor problems, and community welfare. Out of this surveillance, the army created blacklists of organizations and personalities which were circulated to many federal, state and local agencies who were asked to supplement the data provided. Not only descriptions of the contents of speeches and political comments were included, but irrelevant entries about personal finances, such as the fact that a militant leader's credit card was withdrawn. In some cases, a psychiatric analysis taken from the army or other medical records was included."

Senator Ervin found the information collected on the individual who did not support the avowedly liberal Johnson administration policies filed in at least four different military computers located in the headquarters of the Army Intelligence Command (Fort Holabird, Maryland), the Continental Army (Fort Monroe, Virginia), the Third Army Corps (Fort Hood, Texas) and the Pentagon. Not only was the army collecting large amounts of personal and political information, it also ordered its analysts to code the data so that the subjects could be listed in the computers according to various predetermined and arbitrary categories.

Ralph Stein, a young army analyst, told the Senate subcommittee about the frequently arbitrary coding system required by the army's computers. "To make the difficult decisions about what category a person belonged in, the analyst was required to examine reports and then resort to a special intelligence code. He had to apply various number combinations which indicated a person's beliefs or status. For instance, 134.295 indicated that a person was a non-Communist, while 135.295—a difference of one digit—indicated Communist party membership or advocacy of Communism."

Not surprisingly, official Washington insisted that the mass surveillance and computerized blacklisting undertaken by the U.S. Army was necessary and appropriate. The officials said it had not affected the constitutional rights of the American people to express their political opinions. Robert F. Froehke, an assistant secretary of defense from 1969 to 1971, was willing to acknowledge that some of the army activities did not "make much sense." But, he said, "we maintain there was no illegal activity." The simple act of watching someone, the official added, does not violate constitutionally protected rights unless there is "specific evidence that someone was deterred."

William H. Rehnquist, now an associate justice of the Supreme Court, but then an assistant attorney general in the Nixon administration, also rejected the contention that a person's right to free speech was stifled merely because his political activities were placed under surveillance.

"It may have a collateral effect such as that, but certainly during the time the army was doing things of this nature, and apparently it was fairly generally known that it was doing these things, it didn't prevent two hundred and fifty thousand people from coming to Washington on at least two occasions to protest the war policies of the president," Mr. Rehnquist testified. He added that in his opinion

there was no violation of the Constitution by government investigation and data-gathering unless some direct government sanction was
taken.

Some of the 100,000 subjects of the army's surveillance disagreed
with the official analysis. Abner J. Mikva is now a judge on the
United States Court of Appeals for the District of Columbia. During
the late 1960s he was a widely respected Democratic member of the
House of Representatives from Illinois. While Mikva was in Congress, army intelligence agents in Illinois began to attend some of the
public meetings held in his district, where they jotted down his views
on a number of the issues of the day. The agents subsequently recorded these jottings in the army's computerized file system.

"The objection to this program is not that a U.S. senator may have
been subjected to surveillance or that a special file was or was not
kept on him," Mikva explained. "The harm comes rather when the
ordinary citizen feels he cannot engage in political activity without
becoming a 'person of interest,' without having his name and photo-
graph placed in a file colloquially, if not officially, labeled 'subver-
sive.' "

At a Senate hearing in February of 1971, Mikva explained the
subtle ways that the army surveillance could influence the judgments
of a congressman. "The scenario might go like this," he said. "Those
who speak out strongly in opposition to the policies of those in power
are subjected to precautionary surveillance by the military. Constituents learn that their elected representative is under surveillance. The
inference is made, either explicitly or implicitly, that he must be
doing something wrong or at least questionable, and that suspicion
will be evident in the next election results. After all, who wants to
be represented by a man who is so disreputable that the army feels
that the national security requires that his activities be monitored?
. . . It is entirely likely that some elected officials will exercise greater
caution than they otherwise would in order to be sure that their
political future is not imperiled by a military spy."

At the time Mikva was describing how the army surveillance could
weaken the independence of Congress—and thus increase the power
of the president and the executive branch—the Illinois congressman
did not know the full extent of the secret spy system that had been

developed in the United States. Mikva was unaware, for example, that the National Security Agency regularly was reading virtually all cablegrams entering, leaving and transiting the country even though it was specifically prohibited by federal law. Mikva did not know that the same agency, which is the subject of a later chapter in this book, was routinely eavesdropping on the international telephone calls of such political activists as Jane Fonda. Mikva did not know that the Central Intelligence Agency had moved to gain information about and possible control of the computerized intelligence files maintained by the New York Police Department and a number of other local law-enforcement organizations. Mikva did not know that the CIA had established its own computerized surveillance program of political activists. Mikva did not know that Attorney General Ramsey Clark had approved the creation of the Interdivision Information Unit, a Justice Department computer that by 1970 was receiving 42,000 new reports a year from the Internal Revenue Service and the CIA about individuals and organizations "who may play a role, whether purposefully or not, either in instigating or spreading civil disorders, or in preventing or checking them."

With sufficient investment in manpower, each of these government surveillance programs could probably have been carried out without the assistance of computers. But the ability of computers to collect and collate large amounts of detailed information at a negligible cost makes the program hard to resist.

Without such general surveillance operations by American business, of course, the quick access to credit and the mobile life our society prizes would be impossible. Take the everyday business of renting a car, for example. Computers, such as the highly promoted Wizard of Avis, are essential to the rental agencies that each year guarantee properly qualified businessmen a low-mileage car within minutes of landing at airports all over the United States. By almost any measure of speed, efficiency and reliability, the service offered by these companies is astounding. But the system also means that each transaction of each customer requires a separate record that can be stored, modified and retrieved in a matter of seconds from terminals all over the United States.

It is the stated policy of the Federal Bureau of Investigation to obtain such records only as the result of an administrative summons. But a summons is available to an FBI agent upon request, and in most jurisdictions federal, state and local law-enforcement officers develop informal relations with a variety of such record holders that make even the modest restraint implicit in such a system easy to avoid. Easy access is guaranteed by the design of computerized credit and reservation nets such as those maintained by the car rental companies. Avis Rent-a-Car, for example, presently has more than 15,000 employees, most of whom are in close physical proximity to the 900 terminals around the country that connect to the company's central data base in Kansas City.

Such a network can be wonderfully handy for the police. But it also can be useful to other curious individuals. Peter Bronson is the pseudonym of a first-class reporter at the *New York Times.* Because he loves his wife, he told me this story with the understanding I would not disclose his name. A few years ago, while he was living in Washington, D.C., but doing a great deal of traveling for the paper, he became infatuated with a young woman who worked at the Avis desk in Atlanta. "One day I came to Atlanta after being out of Washington for about a week and I stopped by to see my friend," the reporter recalled. "The first thing she did was ask me what I had been doing in Los Angeles and Houston before coming to Atlanta. I'll tell you, her tracking of my movements shook me up. It turns out that when someone has your Wizard number it is very easy to find out where you have been renting cars anywhere in the country. I've quit seeing this lady, by the way."

The presumably benign computer surveillance request by our fast-paced economy, however, has played a determining role in matters of considerably more weight than a casual love affair. On August 9, 1974, Richard Nixon became the first president of the United States to resign from office. Nixon announced his resignation four days after he admitted what he had previously steadfastly denied: he and his aides had repeatedly sought to conceal the facts of the 1972 burglary of the Democratic National Headquarters at the Watergate Office Building in Washington, D.C.

Without doubt, the aggressive reporting of Carl Bernstein and Bob Woodward of the *Washington Post* and the work of reporters with several other publications contributed to Nixon's downfall. Many of the stories which ultimately showed that Mr. Nixon had lied in some of his statements to the American people were based on the information and insights provided by officials who demanded that their true identity not be revealed. At several crucial junctures, however, the independent evidence used to support or prove the involvement of the White House was generated by the computers that have become essential to modern life.

One of the first such critical discoveries was made by Walter Rugaber, a reporter with the *New York Times,* a few days after June 17, 1972, when Bernard Barker and four other men were arrested on charges of breaking into the Watergate office of the Democratic party. Rugaber obtained computerized telephone records from the telephone company showing that at least fifteen calls had been made between the Miami telephone used by Barker and his colleagues and the Washington campaign office of Mr. Nixon. The reporter wrote a story based on the records, and the White House credibility sustained its first serious wound.

The second important break provided by a computer came some months later when Woodward and Bernstein were attempting to untangle the activities of a young California lawyer named Donald Segretti. The two reporters had been told by Alex Shipley, then an assistant attorney general in Tennessee, that Segretti had offered him a job arranging dirty tricks to undermine the campaigns of the Democratic opponents of Mr. Nixon. Shipley, however, had no hard evidence to back up his account of Segretti's offer. Then Bernstein decided to check with an employee of a credit card company who had once promised he could deliver selected records if promised anonymity. The information contained in the computer files of an all-purpose credit card company is a far richer source of data than the computer of a car rental company. "Segretti, whose last name means secrets in Italian, had crisscrossed the country more than ten times during the last half of 1971, according to his credit card records, usually staying in a city no longer than a night or two," Woodward and Bernstein reported in their Watergate book, *All the President's Men.* "The stops had included Miami; Houston; Manchester, New Hampshire; Knoxville; Los Angeles; Chicago; Portland; San Francisco; New York; Fresno; Tucson; Albuquerque; and—repeatedly—Washington. Many of the cities were in key political states for the 1972 presidential campaign, mostly primary states. In New Hampshire, Florida, Illinois and, particularly, California, Segretti had moved from city to city, leaving his trail in territories where the Democratic primaries would be hardest fought. The travel records supported Shipley's account."

The high drama of Watergate, what has properly been called one of the most devastating political detective stories of the century, is in some ways misleading. The extraordinary circumstances surrounding the undoing of the most powerful man in the Western world takes away from the significance of the hundreds of millions of occasions each year that the American people are placed under various kinds of surveillance. Much of the surveillance is benign in the sense that it is an acknowledged and even necessary part of living in a highly mobile society where large bureaucracies provide credit and other services we all require. Some of the surveillance, however, is hidden and occasionally hurtful.

Hurtful or not, its scope is astounding. The five largest credit reporting companies in the United States maintain in their computers more than 150 million individual credit records. For most of the credit companies, the information contained on each individual includes a person's full name, social security number, address, telephone number, name of spouse, place of work, salary, other sources of income, names of credit grantors, complete payment history, arrest and conviction records, bankruptcies, tax liens and lawsuits. Some of this information is volunteered by persons seeking credit; some is collected by investigators.

The insurance industry is another major collector of personal information. Two out of three Americans have life insurance. Nine out of ten working Americans are covered by individual or group health insurance policies. Most of the registered automobiles and homes have insurance.

Americans now make more than a billion visits each year to physicians. In addition, more than a million individuals—5 percent of the population age sixty-five or over—live in nursing homes. Each of these contacts generates new records or adds new information to existing ones. Often they are made available to government or private investigators upon request. A few years ago, one of the largest and most aggressive credit investigating companies said that its agents are able to review all the personal records held by 90 percent of the accredited hospitals in the United States. Andrew Bailey, the director of medical records at the Stanford University Hospital in California, testified to the frequency of the requests for information about individual patients. He said he received an average of 30,000 such requests a year, 34 percent from third-party payers, 37 percent from other physicians, 8 percent in the form of subpoenas and 21 percent from other hospitals, attorneys and other psychiatrists.

The various industries that control and manipulate all this information are quick to assure the public it has nothing to fear. Similar assurances are voiced by the government agencies and private corporations who enjoy access to the massed files that individually and in combination can provide such precise portraits of virtually every individual in the United States. And few of the companies who manufacture and sell the computers that are increasingly used for various kinds of remote surveillance are willing to articulate the hazards.

Nevertheless, such hazards do exist, not only from the present arrangements of computers and communications networks but in an even more serious form in the steadily more powerful technologies now being developed in the laboratories of universities and corporations and in the brains of some of the most intelligent and powerful members of our society.

A few more examples, drawn only from the present, will illustrate how these hazards have become an integral part of American life. In September of 1976, an Ohio man named Bennie Bryant applied for a mortgage through the Hammond Mortgage Company. Before granting the mortgage, Hammond took the routine step of asking a credit company named TRW to run a check on Bryant. On September 28, TRW telephoned the mortgage company and said its forthcoming written report would show that Bryant had credit problems with four separate firms. Bryant, alerted by the mortgage company about the negative report, immediately complained to TRW that its information was not correct. Two days later, according to the federal judge who handled Bryant's later suit against TRW, the credit report was sent to the mortgage company "in its original form" and Bryant was denied the loan. "Subsequently, with a revision in the mortgage report and through the plaintiff's personal efforts, the loan was closed," the judge reported. In December of 1979, a federal jury ruled that TRW had not followed reasonable procedures to assure the accuracy of its report and awarded Bryant $8,000 in damages.

The giant computerized credit company, both during the trial before the jury and now in an appeal pending in the federal courts, has contended that Bryant's complaint is unjustified. As a matter of law, TRW argues, it has no obligation to determine the accuracy of the information it receives from businessmen about the bill-paying habits of individual consumers. "Put another way," said Avern Cohn, the federal district judge who handled the case, TRW contends "it was an error to allow the jury to consider whether there is an obligation on the defendant [TRW] to test the truthfulness and/or accuracy of the information it receives."

It is a fascinating argument for a company that currently is selling 35 million credit reports each year to 24,000 subscribers all over the country. A visit to the company's computer operations center in a single-story unmarked building about three miles from TRW's corporate headquarters in Anaheim, California, explains why TRW has so strenuously opposed being held accountable for the information it collects, reorganizes and then provides to its customers. Every month TRW receives computer tapes from thousands of companies describing the condition of the accounts of their customers. The small staff of TRW then uses its massed computers—the largest single commercial concentration of computers in the world—to lift the information from the tapes of the companies and compile it by alphabet and region so that the aggregate up-to-date data on approximately 90 million customers is ready for tapping by businessmen who want to know whether they should extend credit to a new customer. More than 200,000 times each business day, the subscribers type the name of such a customer into the terminal in their place of business. Within an astounding three seconds, the inquiry moves with the speed of light to Anaheim, the information is located in the company's massed computers, and a report is flashed back to the waiting businessman. Quite obviously the largely automated system developed by TRW would not be able to function were the courts to force TRW to check the accuracy of the underlying reports it receives from subscribers about individual consumers.

Even as the system operates at the present time, according to TRW lawyers, a significant number of reports with incorrect information are routinely transmitted to businessmen trying to determine the creditworthiness of their customers. Each year about 350,000 individual subjects become sufficiently upset to register a formal complaint with the company's consumer relations department about the accuracy of TRW reports. And each year as many as 100,000 of these contacts result in TRW changing the information in the computers. Because of the obscurity of the credit reports and the reluctance of all bureaucracies to correct errors, the question must be asked: How many incorrect entries are not noticed, and how many of those that are noticed go uncorrected?

One other problem must be examined concerning surveillance and TRW. The consumer credit reporting system of this corporation is operated by a single division, one small part of a huge conglomerate that is engaged in a broad range of high-technology industries for many different customers. One of the customers is the Central Intelligence Agency. Though this particular relationship is highly classified, it is known to involve the processing of computerized intelligence reports gathered by secret government satellites. TRW prides itself on the independence of its separate divisions, and there is no known instance where information that was supposed to stay in one division strayed to another. But the decision of the Census Bureau to give the army demographic data about the location of Japanese Americans—despite a law prohibiting such a transfer—is instructive. Just how much pressure would the chairman of the board and chief executive officer of TRW have to bring on the vice-president in charge of the company's information division for the CIA to gain access to credit reports stored in the division's computers?

Evidence of the deep involvement of certain divisions of TRW in the secret spy operations of the CIA emerged in 1977 during the trial in federal court of two young men who ultimately were convicted of espionage. One of the two men, Christopher Boyce, had worked for a TRW office that used computers to process and distribute information collected by surveillance satellites for the CIA. The two were convicted of informing agents of the Soviet Union in Mexico City about the orbiting satellites and the astonishingly detailed information they were able to collect from hundreds of miles in space.

The details of this TRW/CIA spy operation are of particular interest because of evidence that during the late 1960s and early 1970s the CIA used computer-enhanced photographs taken from satellites to determine the crowd sizes and activities of a number of antiwar demonstrations and urban riots in the United States. The aerial surveillance was discussed in cryptically censored documents released several years ago under the Freedom of Information Act to the Center for National Security Studies, a privately financed research organization frequently critical of American intelligence activities. The reference to satellite surveillance was contained in a document prepared by the CIA describing its activities as "possibly outside the CIA's legislative charter."

The CIA document said one of its offices had reviewed "satellite imagery from National Aeronautic and Space Administration programs to identify photography too 'sensitive' for public release" and that some of these photographs had involved "domestic coverage for special purposes such as natural catastrophes and civil disturbances."

It further appears that at least some satellite surveillance was undertaken for the CIA and other government agencies by an even more secret organization called the National Reconnaissance Office. The NRO is hidden within the Air Force and reportedly has a budget of more than $2 billion a year. Though the evidence is murky, it appears that the National Reconnaissance Office has provided the Environmental Protection Agency with satellite photos to help EPA enforce the nation's pollution laws. The photographs were passed from NRO to EPA through another little-known group called the Committee for Civil Applications of Classified Overhead Photography of the U.S.

The unannounced EPA surveillance prompted an angry response from one of America's largest corporations. In a suit brought in federal court in March of 1980, the Dow Chemical Company charged that "spy-like military surveillance tactics have been used by the Environmental Protection Agency for nine years to conduct illegal 'remote searches' of industrial facilities throughout the United States for EPA enforcement proceedings." The company said the surveillance was illegal and a violation of the constitutional amendments forbidding unreasonable searches and the taking of property without due process of law.

Many of the effects of surveillance, however, are more subtle than what happened to Dow Chemical, Bennie Bryant, Donald Segretti and Ray Okamura. Kent Greenwalt, a professor at Columbia University's Law School, discussed one such indirect but powerful effect of surveillance in a thoughtful report he did for the White House a few years ago. "If there is increased surveillance and disclosure and it is not offset by greater tolerance, the casualties of modern society are likely to increase as fewer misfits and past wrongdoers are able to find jobs and fruitful associations. The knowledge that one cannot discard one's past, that advancement in society depends heavily on a good record, will create considerable pressure for conformist actions. Many people will try harder than they do now to keep their records clean, avoid controversial or 'deviant' actions, whatever their private views and inclinations. Diversity and social vitality is almost certain to suffer, and in the long run independent private thoughts will be reduced."

The question looms before us. Can the United States continue to flourish and grow in an age when the physical movements, individual purchases, conversations and meetings of every citizen are constantly under surveillance by private companies and government agencies? Sometimes the surveillance is undertaken for innocent purposes, sometimes it is not. Does not surveillance, even the innocent sort, gradually poison the soul of a nation? Does not surveillance limit personal options for many individual citizens? Does not surveillance increase the powers of those who are in a position to enjoy the fruits of this activity?

Aleksandr Solzhenitsyn wrote about this process some years ago. "As every man goes through life he fills in a number of forms for the record, each containing a number of questions. . . . There are thus hundreds of little threads radiating from every man, millions of threads in all. If these threads were suddenly to become visible, the whole sky would look like a spider's web, and if they materialized like rubber bands, buses and trams and even people would lose the ability to move and the wind would be unable to carry torn-up newspapers or autumn leaves along the streets of the city."

Data
Bases

It is a truism that we live in a world radically different from that of our grandparents. One way to measure the great distance we have traveled during this microsecond of human history is to compare the records that documented the life of an American before the turn of the century with the records that document our individual lives today. One hundred years ago, the few records that existed could tell us when a child was born, when a couple were married, when a man or woman died and what the boundaries of the land purchased by a family were. In those days, of course, only a handful of the American people went to college. Social security, income taxes and life insurance did not exist. Three-quarters of the population was self-employed.

Today fewer than 5 percent of the American people work for themselves. And of the remaining 95 percent, almost half are employed by large corporations that collect detailed information about the education, health, family and work habits of their employees. Today two out of three Americans have life insurance and nine out of ten are covered by health insurance plans. Insurance companies usually collect large amounts of information about their customers —revealing information such as whether they are seeing a psychiatrist, what drugs they use and whether they have a drinking problem. Today 60 million students are enrolled in schools and colleges that generally collect detailed personal and financial histories about both the student and his or her parents.

The vast scale of information collected by government agencies, private corporations and institutions such as hospitals and universities would not be possible without large centralized computers or, alternatively, linked series of smaller computers. It is also true, however, that some of these organizations did in fact collect some of this information before the computer. With armies of meticulous clerks, there were a few industries and a few countries like Germany and Chile that did compile massive handwritten records about the lives of an amazing number of people.

The computer, however, has powers well beyond that possessed by human scribes, no matter how numerous, and thus has fundamentally altered the nature of society's records.

The first important change is that the computer mass-produces what has come to be called transactional information, a new category of information that automatically documents the daily lives of almost every person in the United States. Exactly when did you leave your home? Exactly when did she turn on the television? Exactly when did he deposit the check? Exactly when were the calls made from their telephone? How many times have you driven your automobile? In the centuries before the computer, transactional information answering these kinds of questions was almost never collected. And in those very few instances where it was collected, it was not easily available for later inspection.

With the computerized filing systems now available, the larger organizations of our society can easily collect and store this new kind of information. Equally important, they can combine it with automated dossiers containing the traditional kinds of information such as a person's age, place of birth and the material contained in school and work records.

There is one more important development made possible by the computer: the incredible maze of electronic highways that can move the new and old information about the country in a matter of seconds at an astoundingly low cost. The automatic exchange of information between different data bases was not seriously considered in the first years of the computer age. But as the technology has become more subtle and sophisticated, it gradually is reducing the barriers between these giant repositories, increasing their ability to "talk" with each other.

The contributions of these linked data bases to our daily lives are enormous. The swift granting of lines of credit to a substantial number of American people would not be possible without the computerized data bases maintained by credit reporting companies like TRW and Equifax. The hundreds of millions of checks written each year by tens of millions of Americans could not be processed and cleared without the computerized data bases maintained by the separate banks and the Federal Reserve System. Easy movement about the United States would be far harder without the computerized reservation systems of the airlines and car rental agencies. The collection each year of nearly $500 billion in federal taxes from almost 100 million individuals and corporations would be extraordinarily difficult without the computerized data bases of the Internal Revenue Service and the large corporations who each year employ more and more Americans.

There are a variety of reasons why understanding the true significance of all of these changes is very hard. First there is the fundamental difficulty of putting anecdotal flesh on the bones of the abstract truth that information is power and that organizations increase their power by learning how to swiftly collect and comprehend bits and pieces of information.

This difficulty is greatly multiplied by the sheer force of the tools of the new information age: the machines that can locate a single item in a file of millions in the blink of an eye or that can swiftly develop statistical trends by massing these single items and the communication links that can shuttle the collected information about the world at almost the speed of light.

When thinking about the impact of these technical achievements, allow your mind to wander beyond the traditionally narrow boundaries of the computer debate. Consider how the technology is altering the power of large organizations. Consider how the technology is affecting our social values such as the notion of checks and balances, the role of work and the importance of spontaneity. Consider the far-reaching changes it is bringing to the nation's economy.

What does it mean, for example, that the officials and clerks of the U.S. government, each year armed with more and more computers, have collected 4 billion separate records about the people of the United States, seventeen items for each man, woman and child in the country? What does it mean that an internal communications network serving just one multinational corporation now links more than five hundred computers in over a hundred cities in eighteen countries and has been growing at a rate of about one additional computer a week in recent years? What does it mean that ten thousand merchants all over the country are able to obtain a summary fact sheet about any one of 86 million individual Americans in a matter of three or four seconds from a single data base in southern California? What does it mean that a handful of federal agencies, not counting the Pentagon, have at least thirty-one separate telecommunication networks stretching all over the United States?

Two of the world's largest and most complicated systems of linked data bases are controlled by the American Telephone and Telegraph Company and the Federal Bureau of Investigation. AT&T's gigantic network was deliberately developed by the company's scientists, engineers and businessmen. The FBI system, which seeks to link the computerized data bases operated by a majority of the fifty states, has developed in a more haphazard fashion.

Because the information collecting and distributing systems of both the telephone company and the FBI began to function long before the birth of the computer, they illustrate the important point that the new tools of information processing usually are extensions of old bureaucracies, not shiny stand-alone machines that can be considered on their independent merit.

A second trait shared by these two very different systems is that neither has been subject to much outside scrutiny during much of their development. AT&T is a private company regulated by fifty state utility bodies of widely varying quality and a federal commission that never had the staff to adequately monitor the company's interstate operations. And very few congressional committees or state legislatures have taken the time or possess the perspective to consider the impact of the gradually growing network linking the FBI to the states.

First a little background about the two organizations that have developed computerized data bases and communication systems for their very different purposes.

For many years the American Telephone and Telegraph Company has been the largest and most powerful corporation in the history of the world. With more than 1,044,000 employees, 3.5 million stockholders and property and equipment worth $119 billion—that's more than the *combined* assets of General Motors, Ford, Chrysler, General Electric and IBM—AT&T has been a formidable force in the economic life of the United States.

But AT&T is much more than a commercial giant. Simply put, the telephone company has become the central nervous system of the American society, as essential to the functioning of the nation's political, cultural and social activities as the circuitry of neurons in the body are to our ability to move, eat and breathe.

As the result of an antitrust suit initially brought by the U.S. government in 1974, AT&T has agreed to reorganize itself. Under the proposal accepted by the Justice Department in 1982, the long-distance, research and manufacturing arms of AT&T will remain a single company, while the local operating companies that provide telephone service to different areas of the country will be spun off and reestablished as seven independent regional companies. Whatever the final outcome of these complex negotiations, however, the system's incredible network of computerized data bases and complex overlapping webs of fiber optic cable, microwave towers, coaxial cable and satellite hookups must remain connected. The system, as AT&T television advertisements proclaim, is the solution.

The Federal Bureau of Investigation is the primary law-enforcement agency of the federal government. The FBI has 19,421 agents and other employees and an annual budget of $739 million, not counting a separate secret account for money spent on counterintelligence. The bureau is responsible for investigating violations of federal law concerning such problems as espionage, official corruption, organized crime and some kinds of white-collar crime. During the mid-1970s the FBI encountered a strong wave of public criticism because of a variety of illegal activities it had engaged in under J. Edgar Hoover. The FBI, however, is not just one more law-enforcement agency. As the result of an intense public relations campaign and extensive educational and technical assistance programs for state and local police agencies, the FBI continues to enjoy a powerful mystique among both the public and many police officials.

The primary purpose of the many computerized data bases of

AT&T is to facilitate the operation of the national telephone network by such activities as automatically routing and switching calls, automatically identifying and correcting technical problems, and automatically compiling and mailing monthly bills to the system's 72 million customers. But AT&T does not just transmit telephone calls. More and more it is moving a much broader range of data, including business reports, production plans and television images.

The FBI's National Crime Information Center (NCIC) is a computerized network designed to directly or indirectly link the more-than-1,100,000 policemen, prosecutors, judges, probation officers and correctional officials who together work for about 57,000 different federal, state and local criminal justice agencies. The primary purpose of the NCIC, as defined by the FBI, is to improve the ability of all levels of government to combat crime by speeding the exchange of information about stolen property and criminal suspects. In many ways the NCIC is the single most complex communication system operated by the federal government. Because of its direct connection to computerized data bases operated by other federal agencies, many states and some foreign countries, the NCIC has an unusually broad reach.

Computers generate transactional information for many purposes and many organizations. Computers allow the construction of huge, speedy and low-cost communication networks to transmit many different kinds of information to thousands of different customers. But the very different information processing systems developed by AT&T and the FBI provide clear examples of how transactional information and mass networks have enhanced the impact of these two pre-computer bureaucracies on all of our lives. First consider AT&T. Through its millions of miles of cables, microwave highways and satellite hookups, the American people make 500 million calls a day—four calls, on the average, for each of the nation's 130 million telephones. Thanks to the computerized data bases that are tied into this massive electronic network at a steadily increasing number of junctures, AT&T has become the largest single holder of transactional information in the world. Buried in the computers of the system are records that can be helpful in drawing an amazingly detailed portrait of any single person, group or corporation who uses the telephone.

The astounding power of these records is not appreciated by the public, the courts or Congress. But for government and industry investigators, they have become an important tool. A few years ago, for example, the Senate created a special committee to investigate a very sensitive and delicate subject, the relationship between President Carter's brother Billy and the government of Libya. After many months of embarrassed maneuvering, the Democratic Senate committee issued a report on the antics of the brother of the Democratic president. Almost every other page of the committee's 109-page final report contains a footnote to the precise time and day of calls made by Billy Carter and his associates from at least ten different telephones operating in three different states.

In describing the somewhat tawdry history of how the Libyan government sought to increase its influence in Washington by giving money to the president's brother, the report said that on November 26, 1979, Billy Carter and an associate began driving to Washington from Georgia. Shortly after beginning the trip, the report said, the two men stopped to telephone the Libyan embassy and request a meeting with a high-ranking official. The assertion was supported by a footnote to telephone company records showing that "a five-minute call at 3:43 was charged to Billy Carter's telephone from [a pay telephone in] Jonesboro, an Atlanta suburb."

Another footnote to telephone records described Billy Carter's many conversations with Libyan officials after a meeting with them on March 4, 1980. The footnote said that calls were made from Carter's office telephone in Georgia to the Libyan embassy in Washington "on March 7, March 10, four times on March 11, twice on March 12, three times on March 13, three times on March 14, March 15 and March 17."

The investigations of the special Senate committee were publicly announced and the telephone records that document the report were obtained by a formal legal process. But this sometimes is not the case. One of the top officials in the Nixon White House, for example, claims that shortly after the automobile accident that claimed the life of Mary Jo Kopechne in Martha's Vineyard, the White House political operatives ordered the FBI to obtain the telephone credit card records of Senator Edward Kennedy. These records, which almost certainly would have revealed who and when Senator Kennedy called immediately after the accident, obviously would have been considered useful to those Nixon advisers who thought Kennedy was a likely opponent in the coming elections. Though reporters for the *New York Times* determined the records in question disappeared from the files of New England Bell shortly after the accident, they never found documentary evidence confirming the account of a top Nixon lieutenant that they were obtained by the White House.

Both the Billy Carter and Teddy Kennedy cases illustrate why investigators are so interested in transactional information. First, the information can be extraordinarily revealing. Only considering the data that can be collected from a telephone computer, investigators can learn what numbers an individual has called, what time of day and day of the week the calls were made, the length of each conversation and the number of times an incorrect number was dialed. Considered as a whole, such information can pinpoint the location of an individual at a particular moment, indicate his daily patterns of work and sleep, and even suggest his state of mind. The information also can indicate the friends, associates, business connections and political activities of the targeted individual.

But there is an even more fundamental consideration at stake. Almost by definition, transactional information is automatically collected and stored in the data bases of the telephone company, the electronic equipment of banks and the computers of two-way interactive television systems. This means that transactional information can be obtained months after the instance when the particular event that is documented by the records actually occurred.

This ability greatly enlarges the scope of any investigator. Before the computer age, it was extremely hard to develop concrete evidence about the activities and whereabouts of an individual unless someone had been assigned to follow him. In most cases, investigators were limited to pursuing the handful of individuals they believed might undertake a forbidden act in the future. Now they can move back in time, easily gathering concrete evidence about any person of interest long after the forbidden act occurred.

An example comes to mind. During the last few years, the FBI at any one time has assigned teams of agents to listen in on the telephone conversations of a few hundred people it thought were about to commit serious crimes. As a result of these taps, the FBI was able to collect substantive information about what was said by the handful of official suspects. But now the FBI can supplement this old kind of information with transactional information. After a suspicious event has occurred, after the initial investigation has been completed, after the bureau has drawn up a list of possible suspects, it now can obtain long-distance telephone records, computerized bank records and other documents to pinpoint the exact location in both geography and time of all of those on the FBI list.

The broad broom of transactional information, however, can sweep up much more than the highly revealing computer tracks of an individual citizen. In at least two instances, for example, evidence has recently come to light where this same kind of computerized information was used by AT&T to track the activities of several large corporations and even the ethnic and economic groups living in a single state.

As long as AT&T enjoyed a near monopoly in the provision of telephone services in the United States, the company was able to project the friendly, protective and faintly patronizing image of Ma Bell. But beginning in the mid-1960s a series of changes in the technology of communications led to a gradual shift in the philosophy of federal and state communication regulators. Because of this shift in perceptions, the regulators slowly began to encourage companies to compete with AT&T.

One company called MCI, for example, built its own network of microwave radio towers and offered businessmen and individual families a way of making long-distance calls at significantly less cost than through the long-lines division of AT&T. What the bargain hunter does is use the local AT&T service to dial the MCI terminal in his city. MCI transmits the call to the desired city via its own microwave networks. Then the call is switched back into the local AT&T network and relayed to the final destination.

AT&T was not amused by this innovation and decided to go on the offensive. For many, the old image of Ma Bell as the friendly, warmhearted and faithful helper underwent a rapid transformation. Washington lawyers and others familiar with the communication industry began sporting bumper stickers and T-shirts saying "Reach Out and Crush Someone," a takeoff of the company's faintly weepy television advertising slogan, "Reach Out and Touch Someone."

The U.S. Justice Department took notice of the changed mood of AT&T and began a lengthy investigation. After six years of shifting through company and industry records, the department formally charged the Bell System with monopolizing the telecommunication service and equipment markets of the United States in violation of the nation's antitrust suit. In response to the request in this suit that the federal courts order the breakup of AT&T, the company agreed to spin off the local telephone operating divisions before the case went to the jury.

About a year before AT&T's offer to settle the matter out of court, the Justice Department lawyers filed a pretrial brief summarizing the company's activities which they believed supported the formal antitrust charges.

One of the activities that AT&T was accused of by the Justice Department harked back to transactional information—specifically, to how AT&T had extracted the data in its computers about telephone usage to keep track of the companies who had decided to hook into the long-distance service offered by MCI.

"AT&T kept extremely close track of the market status of its competitors," the brief charged, "going so far as to create a centralized data base to organize its competitive information. Included were data culled by the operating companies from their customers' confidential billing records and forwarded to AT&T."

The lawyers explained that it was not illegal for one firm to keep abreast of what its competitors are doing by collecting and analyzing publicly available information. "However, the utilization by AT&T of confidential billing records and other information assembled at the local exchange level is an example of AT&T's making use of its monopoly in one market (local telephone service) to reinforce its monopoly position in another market (long-distance service)."

William Caming is a precise and elegant man. His silver hair is parted in the middle. A handkerchief is tucked in the left breast pocket of his suit. His office in the massive AT&T headquarters building in Basking Ridge, New Jersey, has white gauzy curtains, an antique desk, old prints and a thick beige carpet. William Caming is the senior AT&T lawyer responsible for developing and defending AT&T's policies, procedures and legal tactics on all matters relating to protecting the company's data from improper use.

As is appropriate for a company that prides itself on careful businesslike engineering, William Caming seems to hide his genuine concern about the importance of protecting the privacy and freedom of individual Americans behind a businesslike facade. "We feel that privacy of communication is imperative to our business," he said. "If people do not believe they can talk privately, they won't talk or they will talk less."

Given this philosophy, how did AT&T respond to the Justice Department allegations that the company had used its equipment to improperly monitor the activities of its customers?

Neither the AT&T lawyers handling the antitrust action of the Justice Department nor Mr. Caming deny that information was drawn from the operating companies and collated by a high-level company market analysis group. The transactional information in question, the Justice Department said, "included data such as the names of customers, types, usage and numbers of circuits, monthly charges and end links ordered from the operating companies."

But there is disagreement about why the information was collected and what was done with it. In the statement of fact agreed to by both sides in the early stages of the case, AT&T lawyers contended the collection program was undertaken in response to orders from the Federal Communications Commission. The Justice Department, however, rejected this explanation. "No regulatory body ever imposed an obligation on Bell or affirmed the propriety of Bell's decision to exploit its access to confidential customer records for use in planning and executing its responses to competition," the government lawyers said.

Mr. Caming offered this explanation: "When MCI won the right to compete with us, they told the Federal Communications Commission that they would offer new and innovative services. We contended that they were just skimming the cream, providing low-cost high-density services because they did not have to provide telephone links in rural areas. We decided to find out who was right, to determine what happened to the AT&T services when corporations decided to give some of their business to MCI and other carriers."

The lawyer also explained that steps were taken to protect the privacy of the individual corporations. Once the data on each company was collected, it was collated by types of industry, rather than single companies, and the last four digits of the numbers called were removed.

"The information was sent to a market research group at AT&T, not marketing," Mr. Caming said. "The resulting studies were made available to only the chairman of the board and a few top executives, and specific instructions were given that the information was not to be shown to marketing and sales people."

Even taking the company's precautions at face value, the AT&T decision to track the activities of the corporations who chose to leave the fold is a highly revealing example of the great power of transactional information.

The tracking also raises several difficult questions. Was the program a gigantic breach in the stated policies and ethical standards of AT&T? The Bell System has gone to great lengths to assure the American people that their telephone records will be protected. Every executive, scientist, secretary and worker coming to work for AT&T, for example, must sign a statement that he or she has read and fully understood a short booklet summarizing the ethical standards required of all employees. One provision of this booklet orders employees never "to engage in industrial espionage." Another provision states that "no transmission, either by voice, data or other non-voice communications, is to be tampered with or intruded upon" and that "communication arrangements with customers, and information about billing records, equipment or circuits, are not to be disclosed to any unauthorized person."

It is very easy, of course, for the chairman of the board and top executives of any organization to decide privately that they are authorized persons. In this particular case, the executives ran the telephone company. But they could just as easily have been the officials directing the Federal Reserve Board, the local bank, the company that won the two-way interactive cable television franchise in your city or any one of the growing number of computer-based businesses.

Private corporations, however, are not the only potential target of tracking by transactional information. A few years ago, for example, Southern New England Bell decided it would like to change the way it charged the people of Connecticut for their telephone service. Instead of a flat rate for local calls, the company wanted to bill customers according to how long they talked. Before acting on the request, the Connecticut Public Utility Control Authority asked the telephone company to use the unusually computerized telephone system in Connecticut to conduct a study determining how the proposed rate change would affect different segments of the state's population.

Without informing the people of Connecticut, scientists from Bell Laboratories helped Southern New England select on a random basis the telephones of 1,600 households. The computers at the necessary locations were then instructed to automatically record every local call made from the selected telephones. What time was each call made? How long was each call? How many calls on each telephone?

After the transactional information had been collected for one year, Southern New England sent each of the 1,600 households a questionnaire that did not explain that the telephones had been monitored. The questionnaires asked a number of detailed questions about the economic, ethnic and educational status of people living in each household. Two-thirds of the questionnaires were returned. Southern New England then combined the information about the financial and social position of the responding households with the information on how they used their telephones.

The study came up with some surprising findings. Poor black families used the phone a good deal more than poor white families. Poor blacks also used the phone more than middle- and upper-income families of both races. Black families earning less than $3,000 a year talked on the average 723 minutes a month. White families in the same income bracket only talked for 296 minutes. Black families earning $3,000 to $5,000 a year used the phone for 1,532 minutes a month, compared to 254 minutes for their white counterparts. The study found that the more intensive use of the telephone by black families continued up to the income level of $12,500 a year, when the pattern reversed itself. For families earning more than $20,000 a year, for example, blacks were on the phone for only 310 minutes a month, while whites used it for 417 minutes.

Fred Fagal, the now-retired sales executive who directed the research, said in an interview that the study was extremely useful in understanding exactly how the proposed change in billing would impact on the pocketbooks of the people of Connecticut. It is hard to fault Mr. Fagal's analysis. But along with a number of other similar AT&T marketing studies, it suggests how transactional information might some day be used to track the individual members of different groups.

David Watters is a Washington-based communications expert who once worked for the CIA. He is concerned that transactional information collected by the computers of such organizations as AT&T could be used to develop "signatures" of classes of people that would enable a subtle and hard-to-detect form of mass surveillance.

"Let's say one of our powerful federal agencies became worried about the activities of a group of people who share a common interest in stopping the country's involvement in some war or in halting the placement of some new missile system," the tall, slim computer engineer explained. "The organization conducts a detailed study of how the members of the group or organization use the telephone. Then the federal agency instructs the computers to raise a flag any time a series of phone calls are made from a telephone that fits the transactional signature already established as common for members of the group."

As fantastic as the scenario of David Watters sounds, it is worth noting that 30 to 40 percent of the local telephone switches in the United States are now equipped with the ESS computer equipment similar to that installed in Connecticut when Southern New England undertook its survey of the telephone use of 1,600 families. The amount of such equipment varies widely. In the Washington, D.C., area, for example, 70 percent of the equipment is now computerized, while in Massachusetts only 16 percent of the switches operate with the latest technology.

William Caming, the AT&T lawyer, explained the significance of the ESS computer: "We can get local message detail on the ESS for any specific number or small collection of numbers without adding any additional equipment, by just changing the program. To get such detail for every number attached to an ESS, the technicians tell me would require some additional equipment."

A significant characteristic of the transactional information collected by AT&T and other major computer systems is that its reach is universal. Transactional information is collected and stored about the telephone use and banking habits of everyone who lives in America, rich and poor, ethical and unethical, white and black, Republican and Democrat. Though the information ultimately may cast a revealing light on the activities of a single individual, it is collected about the activities of all.

The system of data bases that gradually are being linked by the computerized network of the FBI does not share this universal quality. Instead, it collects and distributes information about one segment of the population, the millions of Americans who are arrested each year in the United States.

The story of the FBI system begins almost a hundred years ago, long before the birth of either the modern computer or the FBI. The occasion was a meeting of reform-minded policemen who decided the time had come to ask Congress to finance an agency in the federal government to maintain a central record of all American criminals. The policemen, who called themselves the National Chiefs of Police Union, argued that the prompt exchange of information about "criminals and criminal classes" made possible by such an agency would improve the ability of their separate departments to control crime.

Nearly nine decades later, in the summer of 1981, a task force appointed by President Reagan's attorney general, William French Smith, acted to bring the original proposal in line with current technology: the panel endorsed a plan to have the FBI make a significant change in its existing communication system to speed up the exchange of the records of millions of people who are arrested each year all over the United States. As was suggested by the police chiefs in St. Louis, the Reagan administration's task force said the adoption of the proposal would help the government curb serious crime.

There is a good deal of plausibility in the belief of both the police chiefs at the turn of the century and the Reagan administration today that the swift exchange of summary information about an individual's past contacts with the criminal justice system will significantly improve the ability of the police, prosecutors and judges to catch and punish criminals. Careful examination of the sources of information that lead a policeman to make an arrest or a judge to decide an appropriate sentence, however, suggests that the nearly instantaneous retrieval of criminal history records may be considerably less useful than is generally thought to the business of crime-fighting.

Furthermore, the gradual computerization of criminal history records in most of the states and the development of a single computerized network to link all these state and local data bases raise questions that go to the heart of democratic institutions of the United States. So profound are these questions, in fact, that they have provided a handful of critical congressmen, working with communication experts of the Nixon, Ford and Carter administrations, with the necessary weapons to stall the construction of the federal network for the last decade.

But now, with the blessing of the attorney general's Task Force on Violent Crime, plans to have such a network constructed by the FBI appear to be nearing fruition. Should the FBI get its way, the single most powerful law-enforcement agency in the United States will control a computerized network linking a system of data bases of almost unimagined size and complexity.

The objections that prompted sober officials such as Attorney General Edward Levi and Attorney General Griffin Bell to order that the system not proceed were generated by three very different concerns.

The first concern focused on questions about the *communication network* itself. Should the control of the proposed network be placed in the hands of the FBI? Or would it be more appropriate to give the network to a separate federal agency not directly involved in law enforcement? Or perhaps it would be best if a consortium of the states took over the operation of the system? Will a network controlled by the federal government alter the relationships between it and the sovereign states? Will a computerized information system that is meant to serve the needs of the judicial branch of government but is controlled by a police agency in the executive branch undermine the system of checks and balances established by our Constitution?

The second concern focused on questions about the *records*. Because of the wide variation in state laws and local arrest policies and the frequently inaccurate or incomplete nature of arrest records, will their wide distribution reduce the chance for a fair trial that our Constitution guarantees every person? Might the increased flow of records to employers, state licensing boards and universities create a situation where individuals turn to crime because they are denied a legitimate opportunity to earn a living?

The third concern focused on questions about the *combined impact* of the proposed communication network and the huge mass of information contained in the frequently computerized criminal history data bases maintained by the states and many local jurisdictions. Could such a system be used to keep track of American citizens who are not criminals?

To comprehend the stakes involved in a decision to grant the FBI authority to build and control what is now called the Interstate Identification Index, it is necessary to learn something about the role of the FBI and the purposes and practices of the state and local institutions that would be linked by the bureau's new computer proposal. It also is necessary to understand the nature of the records that would circulate with increasing frequency and speed because of the creation of this network. How many Americans have records? What information do they contain? How accurate are they? Who has access to them? What are they used for? How effective are the rules intended to limit their improper use?

In almost all cases, a criminal-history record first comes into existence when a city or county law-enforcement officer makes an arrest. Depending upon widely varying law and custom, the officer usually will fingerprint the person who has been arrested because it is the only sure way to identify him. Again, depending upon widely varying law and custom, the record of each arrest may be stored at one or more levels of government. Sometimes the record remains in the shoebox filing drawer of a small-town police department; sometimes the record is stored in the files of the state identification agencies; sometimes it is dispatched to one or both of the two separate criminal file systems maintained by the FBI.

Virtually nothing is known about the number, size, contents and operating procedures of the local institutions holding criminal-history records. Thanks to some recent and very original studies by the research arm of Congress, however, considerably more is now known about the holders of arrest records at the state and federal level.

During the last three years, the Office of Technology Assessment (OTA) has hired researchers to answer a number of key questions about the organizations compiling and holding the records, the rules governing the distribution of the records, the information contained on the records themselves and the ways the records are actually used. A national survey conducted for OTA last year, for example, found that state repositories contain about 34 million criminal-history records, 8 million of which are computerized. Sliced another way, the same survey determined that thirty-four of the forty-nine responding states were then operating computerized criminal-history systems that could provide a policeman or district attorney with either an extensive summary of an individual record or instructions on where the record was located in a manual file.

At the federal level, there are two principal repositories where information is stored about people who have been arrested. Both are located in the FBI. One repository, first established in 1924, is called the Identification Division. The Identification Division contains 77 million fingerprint cards representing approximately 24 million people arrested for a variety of local, state and federal crimes ranging from public drunkenness to espionage. Attached to each fingerprint card is a rap sheet, a list of charges the police have brought against the person in question. There also is room on the rap sheet to record the individual's permanent FBI number, the agency making the arrest and the outcome of the case in the courts.

Upon the receipt of a set of prints from a law-enforcement agency or other authorized organization such as a bank or defense contractor, the FBI searches its records to determine if the person with those particular prints has been arrested before. If he has, the list of previous arrests is sent back to the agency that made the inquiry, usually through the mails. (The Identification Division has an additional 93 million cards representing 42 million people in its *civil* files. These cards contain the prints of all people who have sought to work for the federal government, all who have been in the armed forces and those who have voluntarily submitted their prints to the FBI.)

The second repository of criminal histories within the FBI is now tucked into the NCIC, the very large computerized communication system. The initial use of the data base and massive network of the NCIC was entirely different than the rap sheets of the Identification Division in that it was not established to transmit a list of an individual's past contacts with the law.

Instead, the first purpose of the NCIC was to give policemen a way of quickly determining if a particular person they had detained was wanted at that very moment for committing a crime in another jurisdiction or if a particular car had been reported stolen. To this day, about 90 percent of the millions of messages that move in and out of the NCIC's computers each year are concerned with outstanding arrest warrants and stolen property.

On December 10, 1970, however, a controversial attorney general named John Mitchell made a controversial decision when he authorized the FBI computer to begin providing the states and cities with an entirely new kind of service: almost instantaneous access to a summary of the past criminal records of those they were arresting.

From the very beginning, the new NCIC service ran into a storm of criticism. The service was called CCH, an acronym for "computerized criminal history." Because of the strenuous and repeated objections by some officials in the Justice Department, communication specialists under Presidents Nixon, Ford and Carter and a number of senators and House members, the CCH has yet to be fully implemented eleven years after it first was authorized by John Mitchell.

Partly in response to the stream of criticism, the FBI has substantially changed the design of the CCH. At first the FBI fought for a central repository in Washington that would have stored a summary notation about all arrests throughout the United States except for the most insignificant crimes. Now, with the endorsement of the Reagan administration's Task Force on Violent Crime, the FBI has proposed a "pointer system" to guide the policemen or other authorized investigators in one state to the records of interest held by other states. The current proposal, the Interstate Identification Index—sometimes called the Triple I—would work like this. A policeman in California wants to determine the past criminal record of a person he is investigating or has arrested. He types out an inquiry to the FBI. Within a few seconds the index reports that a person with the same name, age, sex and race as described by the policeman has arrest records in Florida and New York. At the same time the FBI system sends a message to the criminal-history repositories in Tallahassee and Albany asking them to send a summary of the records about the individual in question to the policeman in California.

The III pointer system design was tested by the FBI and Florida in 1981 and ten more states in 1983. The bureau hopes to offer it to all the states sometime in 1984.

It is the actual development of the computerized criminal-history segment of the NCIC, the forging of a direct electronic link between all the agencies of the crime-fighting system, that has served as the focus of the debate for the last decade. But the issues at stake are far broader. To understand the full dimensions of the controversy, it is necessary to consider the nature of the information that will move through the linked computers and the potential impact of this information on the workings of our government and society—not to mention the lives of millions of individual citizens.

In 1974, J. Edgar Hoover said the bureau's NCIC was the first government computer system that directly linked federal, state and local agencies. This use of the computer to unify three levels of government operating under the separate laws and customs of fifty separate states makes the NCIC significantly different from most of the other large government communication systems created by federal agencies in the last decade. The very large communication net of the Internal Revenue Service, for example, must speak only to a single group of uniformly trained bureaucrats engaged in administering a relatively narrow spectrum of federal law.

But in an uncharacteristic way, Mr. Hoover's 1974 description of the NCIC significantly understated its capabilities. The network does not just link the federal, state and local law-enforcement agencies of this enormous and highly diverse nation. In addition, this federally funded and federally controlled system will provide a new kind of bridge between the police, an arm of the executive branch, and the judiciary.

It was the potential ability of the complex new linkages to undermine and erode the important principle of checks and balances that triggered the outspoken opposition of conservative lawyers like Clay Whitehead, director of the White House Office of Telecommunications under President Nixon, and John Eger, the man who succeeded Mr. Whitehead under President Ford. Mr. Eger, for example, did not mince his words in a letter opposing the FBI plan that he sent the Justice Department in 1974. The computerized criminal-history project, he said, "could result in the absorption of state and local criminal data systems into a potentially abusive, centralized, federally controlled communication and computer information system."

A very similar kind of objection was raised one year later in a study of the FBI plan prepared by the Law Enforcement Assistance Administration. The LEAA, which is now defunct, was then the fund-granting arm of the Justice Department and also happened to be engaged in an intense power struggle with the FBI. The computerized criminal history project raised concerns over "(a) the development of a Big Brother system, (b) reduced state input and control over security, confidentiality and use of state-originated data and (c) dangers from using non-updated, and hence inaccurate, centrally maintained rap sheets."

The impact of the information that would be transmitted through the vast maze of telephone lines, data bases and computer terminals is, however, of even greater concern than the network itself. When FBI officials call for the development of a bureau-controlled network to speed the exchange of criminal-history records—rap sheets—most Americans assume the proposal is designed to reduce the chance that they or members of their family will be the victim of a hardened criminal, an experienced mugger or a drug-crazed rapist.

But the reality of trying to control crime in America is much more ambiguous and complex than is sometimes suggested by advocates of a greatly enlarged computer network for the FBI. For example, only a small portion of the millions of traumatic events logged yearly into the criminal-history records involve what are now called career criminals—professional murderers, robbers and burglars who repeatedly prey on their victims.

The sad truth is that many of the murderers and rapists who terrorize the American people are not marauding strangers. Instead, they are wives who have been driven to kill their husbands in the dark heat of the night. They are uncles who have been asked to babysit for their young nieces. They are old acquaintances who fell to fighting at the end of an all-night bout of drinking.

The question of whether this kind of criminal has a record in another state is not of urgent importance to the family who already knows his flaws. The suspect's record also is of little immediate importance to the police, who frequently "solve" such crimes when the murderer either turns himself in at the local precinct house or is immediately known to the family and neighbors. Contrary to popular belief and what the police sometimes contend, research indicates that very few arrests are the result of any kind of investigation at all. The vast majority of clearances come from a police capture at the scene of the crime or the complete identification of the criminal by victims or witnesses.

But there is another reason why the police do not find the existing massed criminal-history records of much assistance in their search for the relatively rare professional criminal. Despite their name, criminal-history records deal with a staggeringly large number of people who may have broken the law at some time in their lives but whom we usually do not consider truly criminal: men who have been arrested for public drunkenness, youngsters who have been arrested for stealing a neighbor's car, college kids who have been arrested for protesting against the construction of a nuclear power plant or the draft.

There is a second reason why many of the individuals whose records are contained in the state and federal criminal-history files cannot be considered criminals: they were never convicted of a crime. Police in the United States are now making more than 10.5 million arrests a year. According to studies done in jurisdictions all over the United States, however, 30 to 40 percent of these arrests are dismissed by the police or the district attorney before the question of guilt or innocence has been resolved.

In a fair number of these millions of cases, it can safely be assumed that the individual involved actually was guilty of the charge for which he was arrested. But common sense and the constitutional principle of innocent until proven guilty strongly argue that millions of those listed in the files because of an arrest did not commit the act of which they are accused.

An astoundingly large number of Americans have at one time or another been arrested. Because some individuals have records in more than one jurisdiction and because millions of those with arrest records have subsequently died, it is not easy to estimate how many people have actually been arrested during the course of their lives. A recent authoritative study done for the Labor Department by Neal Miller, however, concludes that about one out of five living Americans have an arrest record somewhere in the United States.

In the past few years, local, state and federal law-enforcement officials throughout the country have successfully argued that society should provide them with statewide and national computerized communication systems that can instantly inform a policeman on the street whether the individual he has just stopped is currently wanted on suspicion of committing a crime. These systems make sense from the standpoint of protecting both the patrolman who is making the stop and society at large from the possibility of further hurtful activities by the person who is being temporarily detained.

But the acknowledged value of a hot-line system to inform a patrolman that the person he has stopped *currently* is a suspect for another crime does not necessarily justify a parallel system informing the patrolman that his target was arrested for a crime in a distant city at some possibly *distant period of time.*

The computer panders to the natural human instinct to desire more information about everything. But there are some law-enforcement officials who question whether more arrest records are actually going to help them do their work. They contend that the value of the arrest record has been greatly diluted, partly because so many Americans have been arrested for so many insignificant causes that it is hard to separate the wheat from the chaff. They further believe the records are of questionable value because they frequently do not disclose whether the case was immediately dismissed, whether the defendant was found guilty or innocent, and what sentence, if any, was imposed. Beyond the pragmatic judgment about the utility of providing the patrolman instant access to arrest records, they see a larger ethical and constitutional question: Do the American people want their police making arrests for *current* activities partly on the basis of *past* behavior?

"The idea that a national rap sheet system would make an important contribution to our work here is just a bunch of baloney," the skeptical supervisor of a burglary section in a large California city told a congressional consultant recently. "Our problem is not to find out who the guy is. Our biggest problem is once we catch him coming out of a house with the goods, how do we keep him in jail and how do we make sure he stays in jail. If anything, we have over-information-oriented and over-computerized this department. The patrol officer learns to use the vast array of information resources at his command, which means you learn to sit in a car and punch in the numbers of people's license plates and the numbers of people's driver's licenses. What this does is inhibit the development of traditional police skills, of interviewing, interrogating and investigating. We need people to get out of their offices and get out of their cars and talk to people. Most of our leads come from citizens reporting a crime or having heard about a crime. Without these resources, which have nothing to do with computers and criminal histories, we would be dead."

These critical comments are drawn from a 1981 report to the Office of Technology Assessment as part of a congressional effort to determine the impact—positive and negative—of the FBI's proposed system. This particular report was prepared by Dr. Kenneth C. Laudon, a professor at New York's John Jay School of Criminal Justice. During its preparation, Dr. Laudon interviewed over 140 experienced criminal justice officials working in four states and six cities.

Dr. Laudon found that the prosecutors and judges he talked with were even more doubtful about the utility of the FBI plan than the police.

"We know our local people and we can compensate for the activities of our local law-enforcement agencies," a midwestern judge said. "We know the victims of crime, and in 80 to 90 percent of the cases we know the local criminals. But in a national system it would be virtually impossible to understand rapidly what that out-of-state information was all about."

An assistant district attorney made a somewhat similar point. "The fact that somebody has twenty arrests in Oakland may be understandable to a district attorney here. In any event I can call the arresting officers to check on the nature of these arrests. And I do that. But this would not be the case with a person who had twenty arrests in Bangor, Maine, or Poughkeepsie, New York. These kinds of arrests could not be checked out and they probably would be thought meaningless to a D.A."

Charles Silberman, one of this country's most perceptive social commentators, in his book *Criminal Violence, Criminal Justice* summarized the important aspects of a crime that inevitably must go unnoted in a computerized criminal history record.

"In the great majority of criminal cases 'the facts' are not in dispute," he wrote. "What is at issue . . . is the significance that should be attached to the facts. Decisions about the seriousness of the offense and the degree of the offender's culpability involve complex and often highly subjective judgments about such factors as premeditation, intent, force, credibility, negligence, threat, recklessness and harm."

But the complaints of the policemen, prosecutors and judges interviewed by Dr. Laudon went well beyond simply questioning the utility of a summary record that has been lifted out of its original legal and social context. Over and over again the users complained that the records being moved along the experimental criminal-history segment of the FBI's communication network were incomplete and inaccurate. The subjective judgments of the police officials, prosecutors and judges about the poor quality of the information was supported by a second investigation undertaken by Congress's Office of Technology Assessment.

For this second study, the OTA arranged for Dr. Laudon to obtain access to a random sample of the criminal history records that recently had been dispatched to law enforcement and other agencies from five official repositories maintained and operated by three separate states and the FBI. The information in the records from the repositories was then compared with the information in the original records in files of the county courthouses. Procedures were followed that permitted the comparative analysis without disclosing individual names.

The findings are surprising. In North Carolina, only 12.2 percent of the summaries were found to be complete, accurate and unambiguous. In California, 18.9 percent were complete, accurate and unambiguous. In Minnesota, the researchers found almost half the sample—49.5 percent—met the same standards.

The quality of the FBI files, which of course rests on the information submitted by the fifty states, was not noticeably better. Based on a random sample of 400 records dispatched by the Identification Division during a single week in August of 1978, Dr. Laudon found that 25.7 percent of the FBI rap sheets met the standards suggested by federal law. Assuming the one-week sample was valid for the entire year, the OTA study suggests that 1.75 million of the 2.35 million records sent by the FBI to criminal justice and other institutions all over the country had various failings.

The quality of the much smaller number of records disseminated by the Computerized Criminal History segment of the FBI's National Crime Information Center was somewhat better than that of the Identification Division rap sheets. In the computerized system, the comparison of the sample summary and the original records disclose that 45.9 percent were complete, accurate and unambiguous.

At the request of OTA, Dr. Laudon also checked a sample of 400 arrest warrants from the 127,000 contained in the FBI's "hot file" on a single day in August of 1979. Upon comparing the information on the FBI's warrant notices with the information in the local court records, he found that 10.9 percent of the sample already had been cleared or vacated, 4.1 percent showed no record of the warrant at the local agency and a small additional number of warrants had other problems. Again assuming the validity of the sample, it appears that on that single day in 1979, 17,340 Americans were subject to false arrest because the FBI computer incorrectly showed they were wanted when the warrants in question had been cleared or vacated.

Approximately the same number of FBI warrant notices involved cases so old that most district attorneys regarded them as not prosecutable because of the problem of missing or deceased witnesses.

The FBI strongly objected to the OTA research on a number of grounds. "The criteria chosen by OTA to judge the quality of records appear to have been set at levels which criminal-history record systems will never be able to completely achieve because of the limited types of information the systems contain, how the information is compiled, the limited resources available to compile the information," Conrad S. Banner wrote the OTA. Mr. Banner at that time was the FBI official in charge of the Identification Division.

David F. Nemecek, chief of the NCIC, said the OTA report on its research contained "many factual inaccuracies" and "undocumented conclusions which are the basis for ill-founded alternatives." At about the same time Mr. Nemecek addressed his complaints to the OTA, he was asked to testify about the system by the House Subcommittee on Civil and Constitutional Rights.

"We do have serious concerns regarding the draft report in terms of certain study methodologies, certain definitions that were used in terms of what is accurate, what is complete, etc.," he said.

In response to questions from Representative Don Edwards, the chairman of the subcommittee, however, the FBI manager acknowledged that the files have serious flaws and that correcting them raises serious constitutional problems. "It concerns me very much that we don't have disposition data," Mr. Nemecek said, listing several recent steps taken by the bureau to try to improve their quality. "As you are well aware, we are operating a voluntary system, and trying to balance states rights and federal rights."

Despite the documented shortcomings of criminal records, more and more employers around the country seem to be using them to screen new employees. "The most frightening thing about state and federal systems is that they are incredibly difficult to protect from non-criminal justice use," one California judge said.

"The situation in California, where so much of the rap sheet information is really used to keep people unemployed, and hence inherently prone to crime, is absolutely frightening and outrageous.

If they build a national system you can be sure that there will be more and more demands by employers, by state and local governments, to use the national resources along with the state and local resources."

The research director of a state legislative committee to revise the state's criminal code made a parallel point. "But the worst consequence would probably be to develop a national caste system of unemployables," he said. "We've already developed a racial caste system, and it would seem the national CCH system would create a parallel caste composed of racial minorities and poor people who would be unemployable in any state of the nation."

Official records, of course, were subject to improper use long before the computer became an important part of every major public and private bureaucracy in the United States. But an executive in a New York State agency explained how the computer has enlarged the opportunity to abuse.

"Technology may not be the only villain, but it is one villain," the official said. "Before high technology, you could actually control information better; at least it could not spread very far because it was impractical to transmit it. With the computer system, you can't control it any more, largely because of the automatic interfacing of the system, which makes it difficult for even us to know who's getting our information."

The Office of Technology Assessment asked a team at the Bureau of Governmental Research and Service at the University of South Carolina to try to determine exactly who was now receiving criminal-history information and to assess the social impacts of computerizing these histories. According to the South Carolina researchers—Lynne Eickholt Cooper, Mark E. Tompkins and Donald A. Marchand— the use of criminal records outside the traditional confines of the criminal justice system is enormous and growing.

All applicants for federal positions, all military recruits, many of the hundreds of thousands of citizens working for private contractors who are doing jobs for the federal government, and all new employees of federally chartered and insured banks are among the millions of persons who have long been subject to criminal-history record checks for many years, the researcher reported.

In addition, with the recent growth in the number of states and cities requiring licenses and permits for almost any kind of job, the population subject to criminal-record checks has further exploded. At last count, more than 7 million Americans must obtain licenses to earn their living. In California, for example, forty-seven separate licensing boards, fifty state agencies and thirty-two out-of-state agencies have access to the criminal-history records stored in the state's computerized record system. In New York, the use of criminal records by law-enforcement agencies has declined in recent years, while its use by private employers has gone up.

Many of the state and local licensing boards that may now rummage through the criminal-history repositories of the nation are not really government organizations. Instead, they are the enforcement arms of quasi-professional trade associations such as barbers, real estate dealers and morticians. Roughly parallel developments exist at the federal level. Just recently, for example, the FBI agreed to give the National Auto Theft Bureau direct access to records maintained by the FBI. The Auto Theft Bureau is a private organization established by the insurance industry to combat the stealing of cars. The FBI is also talking with the Wackenhut Corporation—a large private detective and security company with government and industry contacts all over the country—about what information in the NCIC files it may examine.

Some states have gone even further, throwing their computerized criminal-history records open to anyone who will pay the necessary search fee. Florida is one of these so-called open-record states. Peggy Horvath, the deputy director of Florida's Division of Criminal Justice Information Systems, said individual corporations such as Jack's Cookie Company and the Winn Dixie Stores are making about 90,000 requests a year for information in the state's computerized files. Ms. Horvath contended, however, that recent computerization of prosecutorial and court records in the state's major urban areas means that in Florida, at least, 80 to 90 percent of the current records now include dispositions.

In addition to giving any individual or private institution access to state criminal history records, Ms. Horvath said the legislature had approved laws granting twelve Florida licensing boards covering such individuals as bankers, mortgage brokers, real estate salesmen, security dealers and liquor dealers access to information kept in the FBI's files in Washington. She noted that requests to the FBI by the twelve licensing boards, which are processed through her agency, are now running about 80,000 a year.

Through a variety of federal and state laws, society has made the collective decision that individuals *convicted* of certain crimes may be properly denied certain privileges. Sometimes such individuals lose the right to vote. Sometimes they may not run for public office. Sometimes they are prohibited from bidding on government contracts.

The United States also pays a good deal of lip service to the principle that an arrest or investigation, *without a conviction*, should not be sufficient grounds to deny an individual an honorable place in the job market. In late 1981, President Reagan provided an eloquent testimonial to this principle when asked why he had not asked three officials in his administration to remove themselves from office after they were accused of illegal activities. The three men were Labor secretary Raymond Donovan, CIA director William Casey and National Security Council director Richard Allen.

"I believe in the fairness of the American people, and I believe that in recent years there has been a very dangerous tendency in this country for some to jump to the conclusion that accusation means guilt and conviction," Mr. Reagan told reporters. "And I think it is high time we recognize that any individual is innocent until proven guilty of a wrongdoing, and that's what we are going to do."

Mr. Reagan's eloquent statement has considerable backing in the laws and regulations of the United States. The Civil Service Reform Act of 1978 includes a provision limiting federal suitability checks to conviction records, and only for those crimes that are reasonably related to job performance. Three states have laws explicitly barring employer discrimination against ex-offenders. Many state and local human relations offices have issued rules barring private employers from requesting arrest information and limiting the use of conviction information.

Despite the various restrictions, however, there is considerable evidence that the president's policy for the high officials of his administration frequently does not obtain for the average job hunter.

According to one congressional survey, for example, the fifty states handed out a total of 10.1 million criminal-history records in 1978. Two million of the records—one out of five—went to private corporations and government agencies that were not part of the criminal-history system.

Because of the size of the United States, estimating the number of private employers who try to obtain arrest data about their employees is very hard. From the evidence suggested by several separate surveys and other data, however, Neal Miller concluded in his Labor Department analysis that "the majority of private employers and a preponderance of large employers seek criminal record information."

The Labor Department study that concluded that 40 million Americans have an arrest record also estimated that just under 26 million of them were in the job market. With so many people applying for so many different jobs it is nearly impossible to generalize about the impact of criminal records on their lives. Certainly the bank is on solid grounds when it decides not to hire a convicted bank robber. Certainly no one would argue about a hospital personnel director who decides not to hire a convicted narcotics dealer.

But there is good evidence that some employers assume that any kind of record, no matter what the offense, no matter what the outcome, is a powerful mark against the individual. More than a decade ago, two sociologists named Richard Schwartz and Jerome Skolnick attempted to measure this kind of bias in an experiment in which a number of employers were shown the employment folders submitted by a hundred men who were looking for a menial job in the Catskill area of New York. The applicants were broken down into four groups. The first group had no criminal records. The second group had been arrested for assault and acquitted of the charge with a letter from the judge explaining the presumption of innocence. The third had been arrested for assault and acquitted, but there was no letter from the judge. The fourth group had been convicted.

The employers were asked whether they would be willing to offer the individuals in each group a job. Thirty-six percent said they would hire the men with no record, 24 percent said they would hire the men who had been acquitted and had a letter from the judge, 12 percent said they would hire the men who had been acquitted but had no letter, and 4 percent said they would hire the men who had been convicted.

The findings of this simple study, replicated in a number of subsequent research projects, are a dramatic illustration of the powerful impact of a criminal record, even if the individual under consideration has been acquitted. The implications of these findings—when considered in terms of the number of Americans with records and the accuracy and completeness of these records—are staggering.

There are two broad strategies for reducing crime. One approach is to concentrate on apprehending and punishing the criminal at the time of his crime. The second is to try to eliminate those situations that encourage an individual to become a criminal. The sometimes conflicting goals of these two strategies are dramatically displayed by the computerized data bases and communication facilities that each day are increasing the availability of criminal-history information to both the police and employers. If the computerized records ultimately allow the police and courts to apprehend and punish more criminals, society benefits. If the computerized records work to create a permanent class of people who are unemployed and thus prone to crime, society loses. The complex balance between these two strategies is not clear.

But it does seem clear that the computerized records being rocketed around the country would be a greater help to the police and less damaging to the public if they were accurate and complete. In the pursuit of this worthy goal, after failing to reach a compromise on comprehensive legislation to govern the NCIC, Congress adopted a brief amendment to the Crime Control Act of 1973. The 139-word amendment, which all parties regarded as an interim measure, contained three very simple principles. First, to the maximum extent feasible, criminal-history information disseminated with the help of federal funds should contain disposition, as well as arrest data. Second, procedures would be adopted to require that the information is kept current. Third, the information would be used for law-enforcement, criminal justice and "other lawful purposes." As already noted, the exception for other lawful purposes has become something of a gusher.

The 1973 amendment also offered the citizen an apparent remedy. "An individual who believes that criminal information concerning him in an automated system is inaccurate, incomplete or maintained in violation of this title, shall, upon satisfactory verification of his identity, be entitled to review such information and to obtain a copy of it for the purpose of challenge or correction."

Almost three years later, the government followed up on the 1973 amendment by issuing a vaguely worded regulation that nominally required the states to develop policies and procedures to ensure the privacy and security of criminal-history records. Individual access and review was one of five specific areas the federal government said the states must cover in their regulations.

Ever since the computer became a major force in the administration of large government and business organizations in the mid-1960s, the individual's right to see and correct his own computerized record has been held up as a miracle cure for many of the potential abuses of the computer age. Alan F. Westin, in his pioneering 1967 book *Privacy and Freedom,* was among the first to find wonderful powers in the cure of public access. The principle was subsequently embraced by both the Privacy Act of 1973 and the 1977 report of the Privacy Protection Study Commission.

But the OTA report indicating that more than half of the millions of criminal-history records now circulating in the United States are incomplete, inaccurate or ambiguous is compelling evidence that the remedies prescribed by law and regulation are not very effective. And when the congressional researchers looked at the actual record-keeping practices of four states and six urban areas, they found strong evidence that the promises made in the 1973 Crime Control Act amendment are largely an illusion.

The California criminal justice system, for example, contains more than 3 million records, 1.1 million of which are in computers, the balance in manual files. In a recent year, authorized organizations made 5 million separate inquiries of the system. Despite the huge number of transactions, however, the researchers discovered that only three hundred to four hundred individuals each year ask to see their records, eighty find something they record as incorrect and forty are actually successful in forcing California to make a correction.

Approximately one out of four who check their California records discover what they claim to be discrepancies. Approximately one out of ten who check their records force the state to make a correction. No one believes that the same proportion of errors would be found if a thorough audit was made of all 3 million records held in California. At the same time, however, it seems certain that a very large absolute number of records used to make important decisions about people are flawed.

A second approach to assuring accurate records is to require that the record keepers periodically check their files and dump those that are inaccurate or incomplete. The government, at least in theory, adopted this alternative approach in 1976 when it required that all the states develop plans for regularly auditing and purging their criminal history files.

In 1980 the Office of Technology Assessment sent a questionnaire to the fifty states about how they managed their criminal-history records. One question was whether they checked the accuracy of the records in their files. Four out of five of the forty-nine states answering this question responded that they had never conducted record quality audits. So much for federal regulations.

The astounding finding that only one out of five of the states has ever sought to audit and purge the information in their criminal-history files may explain why so many of the records are inaccurate or incomplete. It also demonstrates how difficult it is for the federal government to force state and local agencies to meet a standard established by Congress.

But it is not only the states that have been unable to assure the accuracy of these records. Despite the 1981 testimony to the House Subcommittee on Constitutional Rights that the FBI is working to improve the records, the bureau has never conducted a systematic audit comparing the information sent to Washington against the information recorded in the nation's courthouses.

Kenneth Laudon, one of the researchers hired by OTA to consider the impact of the FBI plan to enlarge its computer capacity to speed the transmission of criminal-history records, is disturbed by their discoveries. "Systems can be thought of as politically accountable," he said recently, "when they operate under statutory authority and within statutory guidelines, when existing institutions are capable of effective oversight, audit and monitoring, and when such systems are open. By and large, the evidence we found shows that the criminal justice information systems at the local, state and federal levels simply do not meet these criteria."

Even with all the questions about the accuracy of the records, the impact of the records and the inability of Congress and most of the state legislatures to force the record holders to meet certain minimal standards, many policemen, probably a majority, support the FBI drive to enlarge its already dominant hold on an extensive communication system intended to forge the separate data bases into a single entity.

There are some law-enforcement officials and other experts, however, who flatly oppose the FBI's central role. "The bureau is a law-enforcement agency, not a communications agency, and I think it would be better if the federal end of the criminal-history repository was not under the control of the FBI," said Patrick V. Murphy, the former police chief of Washington, Detroit and New York City. Mr. Murphy now heads the Police Foundation, an independent research group.

Representative Don Edwards, chairman of the House Subcommittee on Constitutional Rights, was an FBI agent before he was elected to Congress. "It is bad public policy to locate this repository in the FBI," he said recently. "If the federal government should have any role at all, the repository should be placed outside the FBI, outside the Justice Department."

Kenneth Laudon articulated some of the concerns underlying the opposition of Mr. Murphy and Mr. Edwards to the FBI plan that has won the blessing of the Reagan administration's Task Force on Crime. "The very same technology which law-enforcement officials believe will increase the efficient administration of criminal justice records also creates an instrument of potential subjugation by a victorious foreign power, the internal subversion of the normal democratic process or, by the drift of bureaucratic growth, ever larger instruments of social control. There is no technical difference between instruments of subjugation and instruments of efficient administration. The possibility exists, however remote, that American society is building the tools of its own political demise."

Computer scientists and manufacturers purport to believe their machines are neutral. This is true, of course, as long as the technology remains in the showroom. The neutrality evaporates, however, when powerful officials running powerful bureaucracies harness the computers to achieve their collective goals. Often both the goals and methods of achieving them are in the public interest. History tells us, however, that the organizations of fallible men sometimes lose their way.

During the sixties and seventies the leadership of the FBI and a number of police departments throughout the country came to believe that their responsibilities went beyond arresting those who had committed criminal acts. Their job, some policemen thought, extended to trying to channel the political thoughts and lifestyles of the American people along certain narrow paths. Police departments in such cities as Chicago and Los Angeles enormously expanded their surveillance of individuals who did not share conventional police values. The U.S. Army ordered its intelligence agents to attend all sorts of political rallies. The FBI, with the explicit approval of J. Edgar Hoover, undertook a secret program in which it deliberately sought to have critics of the federal government fired from their jobs or otherwise discredited by mailing false and anonymous reports to their neighbors and colleagues.

The FBI's effort to expand its activities beyond the precise boundaries of criminal law did not stop with the anonymous smearing of thousands of Americans who did not happen to share Mr. Hoover's view of the universe. From 1971 to 1974 the FBI harnessed the computerized data bases of the National Crime Information Center to pick up the movements of persons who were not criminal suspects.

Under the public regulations establishing the NCIC and how it would operate, the FBI declared that only the names of persons who had been formally charged with a crime would be listed in the NCIC computer. In July of 1975, however, John Tunney, then chairman of the Senate Subcommittee on Constitutional Rights, announced the discovery that the bureau had violated its own regulations by using the NCIC "to keep track of individuals who might be of interest to the FBI for whatever purpose, including possible political reasons."

Three months later, the Justice Department confirmed that from 1971 to 1974 the FBI had instructed its NCIC's computers to sound an alarm any time a local law-enforcement agency sent a message to Washington indicating that any one of 4,700 individuals was arrested. When it is remembered what a large part of the population have arrest records and how many persons were being arrested during that particular period for taking part in civil rights and antiwar demonstrations, the automated flagging mechanism can be viewed as a potentially powerful surveillance device.

One indication of how embarrassed the Justice Department was about the FBI's secret operation of a surveillance system outside the limits set down in its own regulation was the way the project was abruptly halted on the precise day that the Senate subcommittee staff made its first inquiry. But seven years later, there are indications that the FBI and other law-enforcement agencies of the Reagan administration would like to resurrect the use of the NCIC computers to track persons who are not the subject of a formal arrest warrant.

The first hint of this possible shift in NCIC policy came at a meeting of the NCIC advisory board in June of 1981 in a talk by Kier T. Boyd, an FBI inspector and the deputy assistant director of that part of the bureau that controls the FBI's very large computerized telecommunication system. According to the minutes of the advisory board meeting, Mr. Boyd openly advocated the start-up of the same kind of surveillance that had been so suddenly halted in 1974.

The official began by acknowledging that the tracking of the early 1970s had run into a wave of adverse reaction because "of the political climate of that time" and that the policy under consideration in the spring of 1981 "smacks of the tracking system which in the past has not been very well received by certain quarters of Congress."

In an apparent reference to the growing power of conservatives in the Congress, however, Mr. Boyd said he now felt "that the climate is very definitely changing and now we have an opportunity to raise the system to a new level."

The FBI inspector told the policy board that if they examined "our past use of the system for tracking, that they would see these things were done pretty much unilaterally," without the approval of Congress. "I believe now is the time when things like this, which are controversial, if they are raised in the present climate and given a full airing, could have a good chance of succeeding and performing very material assistance to segments of the criminal justice community."

One of the major forces currently shaping the political climate of the United States is fear. People are afraid of communism. People are afraid of crime. People are afraid of terrorism. Whether these fears are entirely valid, whether these fears are greatly enhanced by television, whether other ages have had much more to fear are all irrelevant questions.

A powerful example of the violence many Americans believe has now become a world epidemic occurred on March 30, 1981, when a confused young man named John Hinckley tried to murder President Reagan. It is not entirely surprising, therefore, that the Secret Service, the agency responsible for protecting the president, has used the assassination attempt as an argument in favor of once again using the FBI computers to track individuals who have been determined "dangerous" but who are not subject to an arrest warrant. H. S. Knight, director of the Secret Service, made his argument in a letter to William Webster, the director of the FBI, on November 21, 1981.

The use of the NCIC computers to flag the names of persons of interest, Mr. Knight said, could be "a positive step in a more comprehensive coverage of individuals whom we have evaluated to be a continuing danger to the protectees of this service." It also could be used "as another resource to monitor or keep aware of the location of such individuals whose travels may not otherwise be known to us."

In the summer of 1982, the Justice Department approved the request of the Secret Service to use the FBI computer to keep track of persons it suspects may be a danger to officials. But Representative Edwards, the one-time FBI agent, asked the Justice Department not to implement the plan until a thorough public examination of the issues had been completed and possible legislation considered.

Without a law, Mr. Edwards said in a letter to Attorney General William French Smith, "what assurances do we have that this system will not evolve into the sort of system maintained by the Secret

Service in the 1970's when 'dangerousness' and 'threat' were interpreted to include political dissent? In 1972, the Secret Service had nearly 50,000 individuals on its lists, including such 'threats' as Jane Fonda, Tom Hayden, Ralph Abernathy, Cesar Chavez, Benjamin Spock and Walter Fauntroy. Among the organizations listed were the NAACP, the Southern Christian Leadership Conference and the John Birch Society."

It is very hard to challenge a Secret Service request for a tool that it declares will provide improved protection for the president. But it is easy to understand that the principle of restricting the FBI's computerized telecommunications network only to tracking criminal suspects is an important one. It also is easy to understand that changes in a powerful instrument of federal surveillance should not be made without public discussion, congressional hearings and legislative authorization. Once an exception has been made for one category of persons, each succeeding category will be that much easier.

Power

Power is the ability to persuade others by overt or covert means to do one's will.

There are many different ways that the computer enhances the power of organizations. With the computer, organizations can collect large amounts of information about the current and past activities of individuals and groups. With the computer, organizations can improve the way they file the information they collect and thus increase the speed and ease of reviewing it. With the computer, organizations can analyze information about the activities, opinions and social characteristics of individuals in ways that allow them to anticipate the future actions, desires and fears of the groups of people with whom these individuals associate.

The ability to make statistically reliable predictions about the future behavior of people is significant. Most computer experts, government officials and corporate pooh-bahs judge this ability benign, a tool to help them improve their communications with their customers and constituents and increase the efficiency of their organizations.

Something more malevolent, however, may be at stake. The ability may be used to allow the people in control to say only what they already have determined their listeners want to hear. The ability also may be used to develop a series of different, but not necessarily inconsistent, statements about a problem that raise complicated ethical questions about the nature of truth. The ability, in short, can be used for cynically manipulative purposes that tend to undermine the democratic process.

Because this particular application of the computer requires a large amount of sophisticated expertise and equipment, it usually is available only to the richest and most powerful institutions of our society. The isolated citizen sitting in front of his personal computer cannot be a player in this very special league.

To the presidents, corporate executives and often unknown bureaucrats who direct the great organizations of our day, the ability to anticipate the swings of mood of different segments of the population is clearly of great assistance when they seek to persuade others to buy their soup or vote for a particular candidate. It is not for nothing that Richard Wirthlin, the president of a company called Decision Making Information, did nearly $1 million worth of polling for the White House and the Republican National Committee during the first year Ronald Reagan was in the White House. According to Patrick Caddell, another pollster, this was about four times more than the Democratic National Committee paid him during the first year of Jimmy Carter's presidency.

But the computerized techniques of power involve much more than polling. Consider, for example, the state of Missouri in 1978. No major offices were up for grabs that year, but an issue had been placed on the ballot that stirred intense feelings among many voters. The leaders on one side of this particular battle were a group of businessmen who had decided the time was ripe to challenge a fundamental source of union power.

Ordinarily, when a new worker is hired by a unionized company, he is required to join the union, at least to the extent of paying monthly dues. This is required by federal law. But under this same federal law, state legislatures are permitted to modify the union-shop requirement. Twenty states so far have done this, passing right-to-work laws that eliminate mandatory union dues. The businessmen of Missouri hoped their state would become the twenty-first to take such action because the early polls showed that about two-thirds of the voters supported the right-to-work initiative.

The union leaders knew that if the initiative was approved their bargaining power would be significantly weakened. They convened a war council. To spearhead this difficult campaign they decided they needed the expert assistance of three highly skilled political tacticians from Washington, D.C.

The experts were Matt Reese, a long-time Democratic political

consultant; William Hamilton, one of the country's more sophisticated pollsters; and Jonathan Robbin, a sociologist who over the
past twenty years has developed a computer-powered marketing
technique that he calls "Geodemographics."

Together, during the summer and fall of 1978, these three men
joined forces with the labor unions of Missouri and waged a campaign that illustrates the unusual political power of the computer for
those who have the money and wit to hitch this powerful new tool
to the particular cause of their choice.

Jonathan Robbin is a short, intense, opinionated man who does
not hesitate to speak his mind. While usually polite, even likable, he
occasionally erupts with a furious burst of rhetoric condemning the
academics and government officials who do not fully appreciate the
elegance and strength of his marketing process. Despite his out-
bursts, Robbin somehow suggests a professional boxer who loves to
do battle but who seldom gets truly angry at his sparring partner.

"I am primarily a scientist, that is my calling," said Jonathan
Robbin as he sat in his fogbound office just across the Potomac from
Washington, D.C. "By scientist, I mean I am interested in the problems of measurement and interpretation and the concept of understanding how things work and using that information and knowledge
for the benefit of humanity."

Among the organizations willing to pay for Jonathan Robbin's
kind of humanistic science are Time, Inc., General Motors, Sears,
Reader's Digest and the U.S. Army. The 1978 campaign to persuade
the voters of Missouri to reject the right-to-work provision favored
by big business was the first time he had applied his science to selling
a complex political message.

Like almost all concepts that are effective, Geodemographics is
based on a few very simple perceptions. A key insight, Robbin explains with no sign of embarrassment about the hackneyed phrase he
chooses to illustrate it, is that "birds of a feather flock together."

Translated from the cliché to the real world, Robbin says, this
means that despite the penchant of the American people to move
from one area to another, the economic and social characteristics of
most American neighborhoods are remarkably stable.

Robbin's second and directly related insight is that because of this stability, the information collected every ten years by the Census Bureau can be used to define the social class and economic status of people living in most of the country's neighborhoods for the entire decade.

With these observations about the significant continuity of American neighborhoods and the nature of the decennial census, Robbin set to work. By using his computers to analyze thirty-four bits of information about the income, education and makeup of the approximately 900 anonymous people living in each of the 240,000 census units of the United States, the scientist-businessman was in a position to place each of these units on the rung of a gigantic social ladder.

But even in the computer age, comprehending a 240,000-rung social ladder is a challenge. So Robbin simplified his system in two ways. First, he reduced the number of districts by assigning the 240,000 census units to the 36,000 postal zip code areas in which they were located. Second, instead of ranking each district on a continuous scale, he shortened the ladder by devising a social hierarchy with forty specific rungs.

Robbin dreamed up catchy, easy-to-remember names for each of the rungs in his truncated ladder. He calls one rung Blue Blood Estates, another Furs and Station Wagons, a third Bohemian Mix. For the less elevated rungs, he has chosen names like Bunker's Neighbors, Urban Renewal, Tobacco Roads and Hard Scrabble.

About 0.5 percent of America's households, for example, live within the boundaries of the zip code areas that the sociologist has nicknamed Blue Blood Estates, the top rung of his ladder. He defines these zip codes as consisting of "America's wealthiest social economic neighborhoods, populated by super-upper established managers, and heirs to old money, accustomed to privilege and living in luxurious surroundings."

Bohemian Mix contains about 1 percent of the American households and includes the zip codes that cover such neighborhoods as Greenwich Village in New York, Dupont Circle in Washington, Hyde Park in Chicago and Russian Hill in San Francisco. The Bohemian Mix zip codes, Robbin explains, "have a high concentration of people in the entertainment field, and the graphic and communication arts, as well as students and educators. They are marked by well-educated young people with few children and frequently are adjacent to center city universities."

The zip code areas included in the cluster nicknamed Bunker's Neighbors is a mix of urban middle-class row- and apartment-house neighborhoods that contains 5 percent of all U.S. households, one of the largest groups in his taxonomy. Often bordering on urban fringe industrial parks, the residents tend to be second-echelon managers, technicians and skilled blue-collar workers.

"Humans group themselves into natural areas where the resources —physical, economic and social—are compatible with their needs," Robbin explained. "They create or choose established neighborhoods that conform to their lifestyle of the moment."

While neighborhoods thus tend to considerable stability in their overall makeup, the individuals living in them may be quite mobile. "As people's lives change, they may move on to more accommodating surroundings," the businessman-scientist said. "In their twenties, they typically marry and choose relatively transient rental housing. In their thirties, they buy housing suitable for raising small children. In their forties they are launching teenagers into society and in their fifties they are settling down to increased community participation —there are proportionately more registered voters in this age group than any other. During their sixties and beyond, they seek out domiciles suited to leisure and retirement."

The intricately detailed base of knowledge about exactly where different kinds of people live that has been developed from census information by Robbin and his staff is then meshed with a somewhat enlarged but conventional public opinion poll. The result: commercial and political salesmen no longer have to design their campaigns on the basis of polls that only measure the opinions of men or women, rich or poor, black and white.

"This means that a whole state can be polled with a sample of about 1,000 to 1,500 people and the results extrapolated through the cluster system so that the small component areas of the state will appear to have been completely polled," Robbin said. Because the computer has been instructed in which zip code area, ward, precinct, congressional district, township, county and city every census tract is located, accurate estimates of the proportion of those who are for or against or undecided about a given candidate or product can be presented at whatever level is desired by the customer.

"As a result, direct mail, phone or personal contact can be aimed at consumers or voters with a degree of selectivity hitherto unknown," Robbin said.

The 1978 right-to-work battle between big business and big labor in Missouri was the first time Robbin mobilized his Geodemographic data base for directly political purposes. "The early polls in July of 1978 showed the right-to-work initiative passing by a 60 percent to 40 percent margin," Robbin said. "After labor hired Matt Reese, Bill Hamilton and me—specifically the use of our marketing systems—the voters went to the polls and defeated the amendment by an overwhelming majority, 59 percent no to 41 percent yes."

What had Reese, Hamilton and Robbin done to help achieve this remarkable victory? First, a computerized list of 1,467,823 telephone households in Missouri were purchased from a commercial supplier. Then, by means of a computer, each household was labeled by social class according to the location of the household in any one of the state's 6,104 census units. In some areas the computerized lists of registered voters were matched with the list of clustered telephone households. A random sample telephone poll was conducted. The poll was large enough so that the views about the right-to-work issue of each of the state's social clusters could be predicted.

The team working for the United Labor Committee of Missouri then divided the state's voters into four primary groups. One group included the names and numbers of all the people living in zip code areas where the poll had shown that most voters favored labor's position. The second group includes the zip code areas where most of the voters indicated they might listen to labor's argument. The third group were the zip codes against labor. The final group contained the clusters where the polls showed a substantial number of people would not vote at all.

Because get-out-the-vote efforts were least likely to succeed in areas where the residents were opposed to labor or did not intend to vote, the political strategists discarded these people as a lost cause.

Again using the computer, the technicians obtained the telephone number and address of every household located in the clusters that the polls had shown contained the largest proportion of favorable or persuadable voters. The computers printed out phone-bank call sheets. The labor unions recruited the large number of volunteers necessary to operate the phone banks. The volunteers made 536,000 calls to identify precisely where each household in the target clusters stood, made an initial sale pitch and signed on block captains and new volunteers to the cause.

Based on the information collected during the original poll and the massive telephone survey, the team of Reese, Hamilton and Robbin again used the computer to print and mail eighteen different letters about why the right-to-work law should be defeated. One version of the letter, for example, was tailored to answer the questions of Missouri farmers, who the pulse finders had determined were willing to listen to labor's message. The other seventeen letters, while not providing any directly conflicting information, were carefully designed to appeal to the other specific economic and social groups that labor was attempting to influence.

The complex campaign mounted by the Missouri labor movement and its hired strategists—Matt Reese, William Hamilton and Jonathan Robbin—was extraordinarily effective. The right-to-work initiative was defeated by a two-to-one margin on election day of 1978. The abrupt turnaround shocked a lot of politicians and reporters.

Tom Eagleton, for example, is the Democratic senator from the state and a strong opponent of the right-to-work proposal. But he was sure that labor was going to lose. Just two weeks before the election he told a reporter—Dana L. Spitzer of the *St. Louis Post Dispatch*—that "we're going to get slaughtered."

Spitzer, in an interview, said the key to labor's victory was getting out a lot of people who were not normally labor supporters and thus not on the computerized mailing list developed from the membership rosters of the Missouri unions. A second important factor was timing. "Because labor restricted their campaigning to direct mail, telephone and door-to-door canvasing until the very end of the campaign, the business types didn't see what was coming at all. Neither did we in the press."

Not everyone agrees that labor's use of Geodemographics was the critical factor in its successful campaign. Sam Landfather, who was a spokesman for the Right to Work Committee, said the principal reason the provision was defeated was the decision of several large corporations not to become involved because of threats by labor. Frank W. Emig, the assistant director of the AFL-CIO's Department of Organization and Field Services, agrees with Landfather to the extent of playing down the importance of Geodemographics. "Labor had done an awful lot of organizing work before Matt Reese and Jonathan Robbin came to Missouri and those phone banks and neighborhood canvases could not have been done without our people," he said.

But the volunteers would not have known whom to call and where to canvas without the sophisticated use of computers, and Jonathan Robbin has gone to work in a number of other campaigns, including the 1980 drive to reelect Jay Rockefeller the governor of West Virginia.

Although Robbin is understandably enthusiastic about Geodemographics, even he acknowledges that it poses potential problems for the democratic process. "I am concerned about using knowledge and information for the benefit of humanity. That's not always true of scientists, those who have built weapons, bombs, all that. But it is absolutely true that an instrument for good can be turned around and used for evil. We, humanity, obviously have a sort of self-destructive tendency, and I appreciate the problem this entails."

But Robbin was unable to suggest an institutional safeguard to protect society from the potential abuses of the high-powered process he perfected and other entrepreneurs are now copying. "I have discretion about where Geodemographics is used and I exercise this discretion according to my conscience. As the proprietor of this company, I can always say no to any client. If the Nazi party came to me and said they wanted my help in persuading the American people to exterminate the Jews, I would report them to the FBI. I don't have to work for anyone I don't want to."

There are, however, more subtle problems than putting Geodemographics to work for the Nazi party. One such problem, common to all systematic targeting programs, is that they tend to encourage individual candidates or special interest groups such as the United Labor Committee of Missouri to systematically exclude voters who live in areas where the polls have determined there are a relatively large proportion of people who will not go to the polls. From the point of view of the individual candidate or group with a limited budget, of course, the process of concentrating all propaganda efforts on those who are favorably disposed or persuadable makes eminent sense.

"One of my biggest concerns is that we are playing into voter apathy," said Michael McAdams, a tall, likable political operative in the Matt Reese organization who is widely known by the nickname Goose. "With the exception of the occasional voter registration drives, most political campaigns now work on the assumption that you will throw out the nonvoters. You always concentrate your limited budget on the undecideds and the soft-pros. You don't bother trying to speak to the 50 percent of the population who aren't going to vote. I am afraid this polling technique, while completely sensible from the point of view of the individual candidate, may be hurting the United States by decreasing voter participation. We no longer try to package candidates, we package audiences."

A second problem related to targeting is that the hardware, data bases and expertise required to identify the clumps of people of greatest interest to a particular candidate or cause also can be used to communicate with these selected populations in a very special way. Consider, for example, how Jay Rockefeller used Geodemographics in his 1980 campaign to get reelected the governor of West Virginia.

"We went in with our extensive polling based on Jonathan's Census Bureau data and determined that coal was the overwhelming interest of the people of West Virginia," recalled Goose McAdams. "But the polls showed coal meant very different things to different people. If you were a working man, coal meant jobs. If you were the owner of a mom-and-pop store, coal meant workers with money to buy your groceries. If you were an academic type, coal could mean several things but the issue of energy independence usually was of interest to you. So everywhere that Governor Rockefeller campaigned during the fall of 1980, he talked about coal. But when he was talking in working-class neighborhoods, he talked jobs. When he was talking in middle-class areas, he talked about improving the economy, and when he was talking at the universities, he talked about coal helping the United States achieve energy independence."

Is there anything inherently wrong with this? In the democratic process of a small New England town, every candidate for office is known to all the voters in the village. Because the candidates and the voters know each other, work together and shop together, the candidates rarely are able to make conflicting or inconsistent promises. That is the ideal. In the larger state and national elections, reporters have come to serve as surrogate scorekeepers for the voters, scorekeepers who can write a story about the campaign speech in the South that conflicted with the campaign speech in the North.

But in an age when computerized direct-mail machines are spitting out scores of different but not necessarily inconsistent messages directly aimed at the mailboxes of millions of prescreened voters, the truth about a candidate and his promises may be obscured for both the individual voters and even the most aggressive reporters.

Politicians often make private promises to groups or organizations in order to win their backing. On October 20, 1980, for example, Ronald Reagan, then a presidential candidate, wrote a letter to the Professional Air Traffic Controllers Organization promising that if elected he would "take whatever steps are necessary to provide our air traffic controllers with the most modern equipment available and to adjust staff levels and work days so that they are commensurate with achieving a maximum degree of public safety." Neither candidate Reagan nor the controllers chose to make this important policy decision public. The controllers, however, did make public their decision to fully support Mr. Reagan's election, and then they learned that presidents do not always keep their promises.

Republicans are not the only ones to make private promises for public support. Candidate Jimmy Carter promised the national fire fighters union that he would back a change in the labor law reducing their working hours, and for the first time in its history the union endorsed a candidate. When he got in the White House, however, President Carter reneged on his promise and vetoed the bill giving the fire fighters their requested relief.

Despite Jonathan Robbin's admission that his technology could be abused, he contends that it does not encourage politicians to put on one mask for voting group A and another mask for voting group B. "I have found politicians remarkably honest in this sense," he said. "None of the politicians I have worked with—and I include the special interest groups—have ever suggested or even wanted to say one thing to one person and another thing to another person in a way that would conflict with their own feelings or point of view. None of them have ever suggested taking internally inconsistent positions for the sake of getting elected."

Dr. Walter Maner, a professor of philosophy and computer science at Old Dominion University in Norfolk, Virginia, does not share Robbin's positive views about the new techniques of computerized politics. "Selective disclosure threatens the foundation of autonomous action," he contends. "This is because filtered truth, though still the truth, reduces the quantity of information available, which in turn reduces our perception of the options. And since we can only make choices to the extent we are aware of the alternatives, it is easy to see how selected disclosure places limits on the exercise of choice."

He adds that if the *intent* of a candidate in making different statements to different segments of society is to misrepresent or conceal the truth, then the practice is the moral equivalent of lying.

Many politicians and political buffs dismiss the notion inherent in Dr. Maner's criticism that the direct mail targeting made possible by the computer may be inflicting serious wounds on the democratic process of the United States. "Politics is politics," they say. "We used to have ward heelers, now we have consultants, and I don't see any important difference."

David S. Broder, the highly respected national reporter for the *Washington Post*, disagrees. "There has been considerable change since 1960, real change," Mr. Broder said in an interview in the curious echoing glass cubicle that serves as his office in the middle of the *Post*'s newsroom. "The way national candidates and special interest groups are now using the tools of targeting tends to lessen accountability," he said. The reporter also said he agreed with the thesis of Goose McAdams and others that as used so far, modern computer techniques seem to be increasing the number of nonvoters. Mr. Broder believes that this trend might possibly be reversed with reawakening of the Republican and Democratic parties, who by definition have far broader goals than the election of a single candidate.

At least in theory, any political candidate or party or cause has equal access to the targeting machinery offered by the computers of Jonathan Robbin and his competitors. But as noted in an entirely different context by George Orwell, some are more equal than others.

One particular group that is uniquely more equal than almost anyone are the members of the United States Congress. During the last few years, for example, they have voted to spend millions of dollars of public tax money to build themselves a wondrous computer system that provides them with all sorts of handy services. House and Senate members can keep abreast of the exact status of any particular bit of legislation by tapping out a few inquiries on a computer terminal located in the office of each and every one of them. They can also locate relevant studies of controversial issues that may have been prepared by the Library of Congress, the General Accounting Office or other expert fact-finding organizations. The congressional computers thus can be used to increase the knowledge and power of individual members who are seeking to keep track of complex social issues, the legislative activities of special interest lobbying groups or the program of the lumbering bureaucracies of the executive branch. When used for these purposes, the congressional computers can be seen as tending to right the balance between the David of the legislative branch and the Goliath of the federal agencies.

But the elegant, tax-supported computers of Congress are used for another purpose: helping individual members of the House or Senate stay in office. When combined with a massive subsidy that allows each member of Congress to mail a steady flow of self-serving literature at the expense of the public, the congressional computers give incumbents a significant financial advantage over their challengers. The computers and the subsidized mass mailings made possible by a privilege called "the frank" thus undermine democracy by making it hard for individual citizens to challenge the beliefs and policies of those already holding office.

A few years ago, for example, Senator Jacob Javits placed a direct mail expert named Lee MacGregor on the payroll of his Senate office in Washington. It was primary time again, and like all senators, Mr. Javits was authorized by law to harness the Senate computers and the U.S. Postal Service to prepare and deliver to his constituents just about any letter he decided was appropriate.

It was Lee MacGregor's task to prepare a strategy by which the computer and Postal Service could be most effectively used to reelect his boss. In a preliminary memorandum to Senator Javits, MacGregor noted that among the lists of names "on our computer" were 22,000 Republican county and state officials, 40,000 federally licensed pilots, 400,000 persons with state licenses for such occupations as selling real estate and cutting hair, and an Agriculture Department list of 75,000 New York farmers.

Because of Senator Javits' image as a Wall Street lawyer who was primarily interested in urban problems, MacGregor recognized that the computerized Agriculture Department list was important to winning the primary. What was needed, he thought, was a gimmick that would demonstrate Javits' deep commitment to an issue of significance to the folks down on the farm.

After several months of searching, the direct mail expert found the gimmick he was looking for: a bill that had been introduced some months before by a midwestern senator to improve the safety of school buses. MacGregor persuaded Senator Javits to add his name as one of several co-sponsors to the legislation already proposed by his colleague.

In July of 1973, Mr. Javits sent a folksy two-page letter to most of the 75,000 New York State farmers on the Agriculture Department list. "I wish you could see some of the school bus accident statistics and reports I have spread out on my desk," he began. "For me, as for many parents, these figures are more than statistics, as my own daughter was once injured in a school bus accident. They prompted me to introduce legislation directing the Secretary of Transportation to establish strict school bus safety standards," he added, deftly inflating his role as co-sponsor to sponsor.

Senator Javits won the primary and subsequent general election, thanks in part to the strategic skills of his direct mail expert, the collating and printing power of the Senate computer and the massed muscle of the Postal Service.

Two questions are raised by the computerized campaign tactics of Senator Javits and of virtually all incumbent congressmen who seek reelection. First, should the taxpayer be required to provide his congressman with a substantial involuntary campaign contribution in the form of thousands of dollars worth of computer time and Postal Service deliveries? Second, does the ability of the computer to print 15,000 individually tailored letters in a single day encourage the members of the House and Senate to leap on issues merely because they possess a computerized mailing list and not because they have identified a genuine social problem?

One major obstacle to understanding the fundamental changes being wrought in our political lives is that the systematic targeting of voters by the AFL-CIO, most members of Congress and the special interest groups is in a narrow way as old as politics itself. It seems likely, for example, that a toga-wearing elder in ancient Greece sometime or other anticipated the noble words of Barry Goldwater and declaimed: "You only go duck hunting where the ducks are."

But the speed, size and versatility of today's computers have carried the up-to-date political operator a long way from the Republic of Athens. Consider, for example, Sacramento, California, in the year of 1980. Sacramento is the capital of California and at that time was the base camp of Governor Edmund G. Brown, Jr., a political mystic of some note. In December of that year, W. B. Rood and George Reasons, two excellent reporters with the *Los Angeles Times,* sent their paper a cracking good story. Governor Brown was using state funds to compile a massive list of political backers that was to be cranked into a sophisticated and highly computerized mailing system that also was being paid for by the state.

In their first story, the two reporters wrote that a cadre of seven persons already had gone through 750,000 letters sent to Governor Brown and compiled cards containing the names of and personal data and background information about 50,000 political activists. The name cards had been prepared for use in an advanced computer system that California had leased from the Xerox Corporation.

"Our new record processing system has 130 [storage category] fields," the *Los Angeles Times* quoted one official in the governor's office as saying. "The first three or four are for names and addresses, then all the rest are for things like antinuclear, environmentalist, or whatever. Then you can tell the machine, 'I want to write all the women that are for abortion or against abortion.' The machine will go through and pick out all the women that fit that description, even those just in a certain zip code. The machines also can store form letters for specific purposes such as answering people opposed to or supporting a particular piece of legislation.''

Two weeks after the printing of the story, at a news conference in Los Angeles, Governor Brown said the new system had not been developed for political purposes but that to insure its integrity the names of political supporters would be removed from the computer. "This was an attempt to create a two-way communication instead of an isolated entity that I thought my office had become," he told reporters. "It was done with the best of motives."

But back in Sacramento, Mr. Rood and Mr. Reasons discovered some rather convincing evidence suggesting that Brown's motives were not quite as he described them. The new evidence was a confidential memo showing that the seven-person task force and the computer system were part of a master plan that called for using the governor's "entire staff" to put together a national political organization for Mr. Brown.

The memorandum, which was written on November 14 in the state's office in Washington, D.C., called for the mobilization of the governor's staff "to develop a national constituency to assist in refining the governor's themes and thereby expand the base of his support."

This goal was to be achieved by putting together dossiers on people identified as "suspects," a term used in the memorandum to refer to people whose backgrounds and views were under study to determine their usefulness as political contributors and volunteers for Governor Brown. "To tap the larger pools of the universe it is essential that every member of the staff participate to the fullest extent in culling names from various sources."

The staff, the memorandum said, would be given cards to fill in the names of "suspects" and "will be responsible for doing preliminary research which will include tracking down the addresses, occu-

pations, employers/affiliations, sources and contacts on those people
we intend to put in our outreach program."

When asked about the memorandum, the governor's chief of staff
told the *Los Angeles Times* reporters that six employees had been
fired after Brown learned of the master plan and that steps had been
taken to make sure that "neither the letter nor the spirit of the memo
would be implemented in this office." The sincerity of this second
promise to avoid using a state computer to build a national constituency for Governor Brown was put into question a year and a half
later in a report by the California Fair Political Practices Commission.

Top campaign aides to Brown, the report said, had sought to block
the commission's investigation by destroying, concealing and altering important evidence. While Brown himself was not accused of
misconduct, the report said he too had failed to make evidence
available as he had promised when he testified under oath about the
matter.

Politicians like Jerry Brown use computers to enlarge their personal power. Corporations, government agencies and other bureaucracies use computers to enlarge their institutional powers.

The Internal Revenue Service is an example of one of the latter.
Before turning to how computers have been harnessed by the IRS
during the last few decades, consider its legal mandate. In the knowledge that collecting taxes is vital to the government, the United
States Congress and the courts gradually have granted the IRS an
extraordinary legal authority which in many ways exceeds that
handed to any other federal enforcement agency. The power begins,
of course, with laws that make it a serious crime for almost every
household, corporation and other kind of institution not to file an
annual report describing its yearly income, the sources of the income
and, to a somewhat lesser extent, where the income was spent. For
the individual or institution whose income is derived from a single
source, this annual report can be quite brief. But for those receiving
dividend checks, interest, commissions, rents and other forms of
income, the reporting requirements are incredibly broad.

The power of the IRS is enhanced by the authority of the agency
to make very broad inquiry of the taxpayer to verify tax returns.

Under the law and the interpretations of the Supreme Court, the IRS has the unique power to issue a summons to a taxpayer, employer, accountant or any other third party. The authority of the IRS to issue a summons on its own authority contrasts with other law-enforcement agencies such as the FBI, who must apply to a court when they wish to compel the presence of a person of interest.

The precise reach of an IRS summons is subject to some controversy. According to a report done for an independent federal study group a few years ago, a citizen must appear when served by an IRS summons, but does not actually have to produce the requested papers until compelled to by a judge. But as noted in the report prepared by a team of legal scholars headed by Charles Davenport, then at the Law School of the University of California at Davis, the IRS does not tell the taxpayer that only a judge can order him to produce his records. Instead, the report said, the IRS gives the taxpayer an "uninformative and misleading" statement that "wrongfully implies that the summoned party must appear and give testimony or produce documents or penalties will follow."

Over the years, the detailed personal information collected about millions of Americans by the IRS has made the agency's files an almost irresistible temptation to those who could gain access to it. The tape-recording system installed in the White House by President Nixon gave the world a unique indication of the pull of this particular magnet.

"Do you need any IRS (unintelligible) stuff?" Mr. Nixon asked his assistant, John Dean.

". . . We have a couple of sources over there I can go to," Dean replied. "I don't have to fool around with Johnnie Walters or anybody, we can get right in and get what we need."

This particular exchange has a unique place in American history because it was part of the evidence supporting one of the proposed articles of impeachment against Mr. Nixon. The president, the article said, "acting personally and through his subordinates and agents, endeavored to obtain from the Internal Revenue Service, in violation of the constitutional rights of citizens, confidential information contained in income tax returns for purposes not authorized by law."

The subsequent Senate testimony of John J. Caulfield and Clark

Mollenhoff, both White House assistants, and Roger V. Barth, an aide to the head of the IRS, indicates there were at least fourteen occasions when information was drawn from the IRS files at the request of someone in the Nixon White House. Individual subjects included George Wallace, his brother Gerald, the Reverend Billy Graham, the actor John Wayne and a candidate for a post in the campaign to reelect Mr. Nixon. While there are no records of such White House requests during either the Eisenhower or Johnson years, there is a record showing that Carmine S. Bellino, a consultant to President Kennedy, examined an unknown number of returns and associated documents in the spring of 1961.

But the abuse of the information that every American must file with the IRS under the penalty of law was not limited to the White House. In 1965, for example, FBI agents obtained the tax returns of several Ku Klux Klan leaders. The tax information, Senate investigators later learned, was used by the agents in what the FBI called COINTEL, a formal and secret counterintelligence effort to "disrupt" groups and "neutralize" individuals who had been judged a threat by bureau director J. Edgar Hoover. In this case, according to an FBI memorandum of May 10, 1965, the purpose was to "expose" the selected Klan leaders to the members of their organization and the public "by showing income beyond their means."

The investigative power of the IRS has focused on far less sinister targets than the Ku Klux Klan. In early 1967, for example, the Central Intelligence Agency heard rumors that a magazine called *Ramparts* was about to publish an article about the CIA's direct involvement in the funding of the National Student Association. On February 2, 1967, a CIA official met with the assistant commissioner of the IRS and several of his aides. "I suggested that the corporate tax returns of *Ramparts* be examined, and that any leads to possible financial supporters be followed up by an examination of their individual tax returns," the CIA man wrote in his action report.

The CIA request and the IRS response were an astounding example of how two established government agencies attempted to frighten a magazine in a way that appears to fly in the face of the First Amendment of the Constitution. Until 1969, however, the use of the IRS tax data for political purposes seemed somewhat limited and even erratic. That year, however, the IRS established the Special Service Staff (SSS) to systematically gather intelligence on a category of taxpayers mostly defined by their political activities.

According to a much later report by the Senate Select Committee on Intelligence Activities, the SSS was formed as a result of pressure from a group of senators concerned about organized crime and subversion and from President Nixon, acting in part through Dr. Arthur Burns, then the chairman of the Federal Reserve Board. According to a memorandum written on June 16, 1969, Dr. Burns informed the head of the IRS about the president's concern "over the fact that tax-exempt funds may be supporting activist groups engaged in stimulating riots both on the campus and within our inner cities."

The Senate report said its investigators had failed to uncover any evidence suggesting that either President Nixon or Dr. Burns had provided the IRS with evidence to support the assertion that such tax-exempt groups were violating tax laws.

Immediately after the IRS created the SSS, the Justice Department and the FBI provided it with shopping lists of 2,300 organizations categorized as "old left," "new left," and "right wing" and a computer printout of about 10,000 individuals who had been identified as being active in the civil rights and antiwar movements. The computer printout of the activists had been compiled a year or so earlier at the request of Ramsey Clark, the Johnson administration attorney general who later became an outspoken opponent to the Vietnam War and a strong advocate of many liberal causes.

"The SSS opened files on all these taxpayers, many of whom were later subjected to tax audits and some to tax fraud investigations," the committee found. There was no evidence, it continued, that the names on the Justice Department and FBI lists subjected to IRS investigations "were selected on the basis of probable noncompliance with the tax laws. Rather, these groups and individuals were targeted because of their political and ideological beliefs and activities."

Names on the SSS list included Nobel Prize winner Linus Pauling, senators Charles Goodell and Ernest Gruening, Representative Charles Diggs, journalists Joseph Alsop and Jimmy Breslin, and Washington attorney Mitchell Rogovin. Organizations included political groups ranging from the John Birch Society to Common

Cause, professional organizations such as the Legal Aid Society, publications including *Playboy* and *Commonweal,* and government institutions such as the United States Civil Rights Commission. No explanation has ever been provided why an agency that naturally pays no taxes would be of interest to the IRS.

By the time the SSS was abolished with the first breath of publicity in 1973, the unit had gone over about half of the 10,000 names on the Justice Department list, some of which were referred to IRS field units for formal investigation.

The IRS was not to be left naked before its enemies. During the same year that the agency was dismantling the SSS, it was establishing a central computer index—the Intelligence Gathering Retrieval System—for collecting general intelligence data, a good deal of which is not directly related to tax law enforcement. Within a few months, more than 465,000 Americans were indexed in the new system, including J. Edgar Hoover, the IRS commissioner and thousands of others not suspected of any tax violation. Under the system, intelligence gathering was begun on an individual before the IRS had received any specific allegation of wrongdoing. The sole criteria for deciding whether to add a name to the computerized file was possible "future value."

But the computers of an agency as large and powerful as the IRS do not have to be specifically dedicated to intelligence gathering before they become a matter of concern. In 1976, for example, the IRS proposed to Congress that it approve the Tax Administration System (TAS), a new computerized network that the House Appropriations Committee estimated might cost $1 billion.

Because of the great size and complexity of the TAS network, Representative Al Ullman, then chairman of the House Ways and Means Committee, and Representative Charles Vanik, chairman of the Oversight Subcommittee of the Ways and Means Committee, worried that the new IRS computer might grow into a "system of harassment, surveillance and political manipulation." The two men joined in requesting that the Office of Technology Assessment, an arm of Congress, undertake an independent analysis of the network.

After a lengthy investigation, the OTA concluded in its windy but thoughtful way that TAS would have an enormous impact. The system, the report said, would "determine or affect the collection, use, maintenance and dissemination of large amounts of information about citizens. It will play a pivotal role in governmental and private data banks and information systems which contain the details of the personal, organizational and business lives of Americans at home or abroad."

The OTA made a long list of the attributes of TAS that it thought Congress should consider. The system, the investigators said, would decentralize taxpayer files and make them instantly available to those who share and use federal tax information. It would create a national system for quickly transferring these histories anywhere in the United States. It would give the IRS an expandable data base with the capacity to acquire and store more detailed histories of individual taxpayers for longer periods of time. The system, by increasing the capacity of the IRS to associate the bits of information it collected, would enable the agency to create what in a sense can be considered new information.

Because of these various attributes, the OTA concluded, the proposed computer system "could be perceived as posing a threat to civil liberties, privacy and the due process rights of taxpayers. These effects might include a potential for surveillance, harassment or political manipulation of files, for which specific controls and safeguards are of concern to Congress."

Much to the annoyance of the IRS and many of the computer experts in government and industry, the Carter administration in January of 1978 decided too many questions had been raised about TAS and the project was scuttled. Instead, virtually all of the money the planners had estimated it would cost to build TAS was diverted to improving the IRS's existing computer system. This time the fresh memory of the Watergate years and how the Nixon administration had sought to use computerized dossiers to harass its ideological enemies had halted a system sold under the usually invincible banner of increasing government efficiency.

Meanwhile, however, the IRS has continued to develop and refine a very different kind of computerized information system called the Taxpayer Compliance Measurement Program (TCMP). Although it is largely accepted by critics both in and out of Congress on the grounds that it improves the ability of the agency to collect taxes, Paul M. Strassels and Robert Wool in their book *All You Need to Know About the IRS* said the TCMP was "the closest thing to 1984 market research that our country has."

Simply stated, the TCMP is a computer-assisted process to help the IRS predict the behavior of every American taxpayer. To the degree that it is successful, the TCMP enhances the power of the IRS in relation to the citizenry by allowing it to concentrate its small army of investigators and accountants on the targets most likely to have tried to cheat the government.

The program works like this: since 1962, a random sample of different kinds of taxpayers have been selected on a periodic basis. These are not individuals, corporations or other organizations who are suspected of any wrongdoing, just a cross section of taxpayers. Once identified, the individuals and institutions are subjected to an extremely intensive examination.

"Experienced revenue agents and tax auditors from the IRS Examination Division conduct in-depth audits of each of the sampled returns," reported Susan B. Long in a Justice Department–financed study on the government's response to tax evasion.

"Detailed check sheets are made out by the IRS examining officer on the amounts reported line by line on the return and the 'corrected' amounts after the audit," Mrs. Long continued. "Supplemental information concerning the taxpayer's financial affairs, who prepared the tax return and what procedures were used in carrying out the TCMP are also included."

In one recent survey, 200 separate items were collected about each of the 50,000 individuals who had been randomly selected to represent the entire population of 93 million American taxpayers. Once collected by the auditors, the 10 million bits of information collected by the survey were fed into a giant IRS computer for analysis. The result: a line-by-line, income-level-by-income-level, region-by-region list of probabilities that a taxpayer in any one of these categories incorrectly stated the amount of tax due the government.

In addition to providing an estimate of what kinds of taxpayers might give the IRS trouble concerning what aspects of their income, the survey also provides the government a statistical indication of how much would be recovered if any particular hole was closed. Who are the real cheaters? How do they cheat? How much might the government expect to recover if it concentrated on Line 33?

From the elaborate statistical tables developed from the periodic audits of selected taxpayers, the IRS develops its enforcement strategy for the entire nation, the marching orders for its 87,000 employees. But the TCMP is more than that: it is the basis for virtually all of the agency's basic policy decisions. The IRS uses the TCMP data to support its budget requests to Congress, to make proposals for changes in the tax law and to make decisions on such matters as staffing levels, training requirements, taxpayer education programs and the form of the tax returns.

Mrs. Long, who has a Ph.D. in sociology and is an assistant professor at the Department of Quantitative Methods at Syracuse University, has conducted research on the administration of the tax laws for many years. Because of this professional interest, she asked for the underlying data of the TCMP more than five years ago.

The Internal Revenue Service rejected her request, arguing that releasing the data would enable taxpayers to anticipate the service's enforcement strategies.

Because of the Freedom of Information Act, however, the IRS had a serious legal problem. This law establishes the principle that any document or report prepared at public expense by a government agency must be made public unless it concerns an important military secret, the trade secret of a private company or the personnel matters of an individual citizen. The data requested by Mrs. Long clearly did not fall into any of the accepted categories, and a Federal Court of Appeals upheld her right to receive it.

In arguing the matter before the courts, Mrs. Long and her lawyer, Stephen K. Strong of Seattle, contended that a fundamental principle of American government was at stake in the refusal of this powerful agency to publish the computerized data created by the publicly funded survey. This principle is that the government of the United States is supposed to operate with the consent of the governed. Analyses of TCMP data by congressional and independent researchers, they said, "could lead to the uncovering of problems in the tax laws, tax returns and instruction forms, and administrative practices and could provide suggestions as to how to deal with these problems."

Mrs. Long noted that the IRS often refers to TCMP data in making requests for appropriations to hire more IRS auditors. "Since the underlying data are not revealed, the public is forced to speculate on the validity of the service's conclusions, which may or may not be valid. Analysis of the data by outside researchers could enable the public and its representatives in Congress to better evaluate the IRS's strategy and the appropriation requests that are made to carry out its strategy."

Despite winning the battle against the IRS at the court of appeals, Mrs. Long and her lawyer lost the war when the IRS managed to persuade Congress to pass an amendment to the Freedom of Information Act exempting what the government claimed was sensitive data from the requirement that it be made public. By preventing a knowledgeable and independent expert from examining computer-generated information that would have enabled her to judge the effectiveness of the IRS in administering the nation's tax laws, one of the government's most powerful agencies became even more powerful.

Thus has the computer strengthened the hand of the IRS in relation to citizens who pay taxes and citizens who seek to monitor the performance of the tax collector. The computer, however, serves to enhance the power of the management of the IRS in a third way: to help the bosses keep track of the employees.

The computer program developed by the IRS managers for this purpose is called the Audit Information Management System (AIMS). The purpose of AIMS, in the indirect language of government, is to provide the IRS with an inventory control system, timely data to make sure that its 87,000 employees are doing their job. But in the impolite language of the workplace, AIMS is a de facto quota system that requires every agent in the IRS to meet certain standards, what is known as the "plan," to audit a sufficient number of tax returns, to identify a sufficient number of clinkers, to recommend bringing a sufficient number of criminal cases.

When General Motors imposes a quota requiring the workers in a factory to produce a certain number of cars each day, most Americans would agree that the GM managers are within their rights. But when a massive, highly computerized law-enforcement agency like the IRS imposes quotas, there can be trouble. What happens, for example, when an IRS agent knows his next promotion is dependent upon making ten cases and the luck of the draw brings him only seven? Might he be tempted to bring charges of some sort against three individuals who had not actually violated the law?

Top IRS officials have repeatedly denied that the IRS operates by quota systems. The IRS handbook for audit group managers stresses over and over again that statistics are an aid to good management, not a replacement for it. Nonetheless, an extensive investigation of the IRS for a small government watchdog agency called the Administrative Conference of the United States found that substantial numbers of IRS employees believe quotas are set and used to measure their performance.

"Group managers are well aware of the 'plan' and their group's part in accomplishing it," the report to the Administrative Conference said. "One manager, in fact, stated that he was well aware of management's expectations for his group and he saw his primary function as assisting his group in 'making the plan.' This view was shared, but not so bluntly stated, by most if not all managers. Numerous interviews with agents and management personnel indicate they believe that closing cases so as to 'make the audit plan' is the most important part of the job."

The first step in developing a quota system is to create a reliable mechanism to count the activities of whoever it is you want to control. For many years, for example, clerks in the offices of each of the 94 U.S. attorneys laboriously compiled lists of the investigations, prosecutions, convictions, hours in court, collections and many other activities that occupy the time of federal prosecutors. The monthly statistics were dispatched to the Justice Department in Washington, where a dreary report would be published a long time after it could assist the attorney general in directing his small army of federal prosecutors.

But the good government lobby of the federal establishment—the Office of Management and Budget, the General Accounting Office and sometimes even a Congressional committee—began to notice that the statistics did not always add up and regularly were printed many months after the events they described. Gradually the Justice Department managers decided it would help them better justify their appropriations requests if they had a way of collecting accurate and up-to-date information about the actions of the 94 U.S. attorneys and the 3,500 assistant attorneys, clerks and secretaries who work for them.

The experts decided on two converging approaches to meet the demand for better information. First, a great deal of effort was spent on deciding what data would be collected and how it would be recorded. Second, after experimenting with several approaches, a decentralized system was adopted in which the personnel in each office would file case information via terminals hooked into a small local computer.

Thomas Hagerty is a cheerful man with a broad Irish face and a small office on the sixth floor of the Federal Building in Newark, New Jersey. Three Miss Piggy posters decorate his wall and a computer terminal sits next to his gray steel desk. Thomas Hagerty is not an attorney or an FBI agent, someone you might normally find in a U.S. attorney's office. He is instead a systems manager, the man responsible for helping a cranky old legal office adapt itself to the computer age.

"Because the information we used to send to Washington was processed on a batch basis, every month or so, and often had coding errors, it just wasn't much help for managing the government's business here in Newark," Mr. Hagerty explained.

"Now, with our local on-line system, there is a tremendous immediacy of data. You can run reports by division or by attorney, you can determine how many cases so-and-so has, you can see if one attorney is overloaded or if another is not pulling his or her load. You can call up cases by opposing counsel, or defendant's name. You can ask the computer to give you a report on cases by statute of limitations or ask it to warn a particular attorney when a lab report should be back. It is a wonderful management tool."

The computer sits in a small locked room next to Mr. Hagerty's office. As such matters are measured these days, it has a rather small memory, one million bytes. With seventeen terminals in Newark and one each in satellite offices in Camden and Trenton, the computer serves the needs of the fifty-five attorneys and sixty-five clerical workers. The equipment was installed in July of 1981. The Justice Department hopes that similar equipment will be installed in twenty-five additional offices within the next two or three years.

The computer systems being installed in the separate U.S. attorneys' offices almost certainly will improve the management efficiency of the federal prosecutors. But because the tapes from these computers will be sent to the attorney general in Washington, something more subtle but perhaps more important is also happening. Without any discussion in Congress, without any change in law, the power of the attorney general to influence public policy is being enormously enhanced.

From the beginning of our government, U.S. attorneys have been somewhat independent from the attorney general. To this day, for example, no one is nominated to be a U.S. attorney without the approval of the senators in the state where the federal district is located even if the senators happen to be from a different party than the president.

The fact that U.S. attorneys are beholden to senators, as well as to the president and his attorney general, has meant that federal prosecutors could be a little bit independent from the dictates of the Justice Department. Federal law enforcement in Wyoming has not been a carbon copy of federal law enforcement in Massachusetts. Law enforcement in Oregon has had a different character than that in Florida.

Because this is a huge country, with widely varying climates, economic conditions, ethnic groups and religious backgrounds, there are some advantages in this modest flexibility. There also are some disadvantages. U.S. attorneys in some parts of the West, for example, may not have enforced environmental laws with the vigor mandated as national policy by the Congress and attorney general. U.S. attorneys in the South may not have brought an honest enthusiasm to enforcing the civil rights laws.

But with the installation of the computers in every office, the attorney general will be able to keep track of every investigation, every prosecution, every conviction and every acquittal. He will be able to do this on an individual basis—the name of a defendant, the name of a prosecutor, the name of a defense lawyer—or by broad categories of law-enforcement actions. How does the pattern of civil rights enforcement of the U.S. attorney in Louisiana compare with that of the U.S. attorney in Minnesota? Is the U.S. attorney in Missouri bringing as many official corruption cases as his counter-part in Illinois? Is the federal prosecutor in northern California paying the same attention to draft dodgers as the prosecutor in Houston?

Benjamin R. Civiletti, the attorney general in the last years of the Carter administration, believes the new computer system will be beneficial. "It was obvious that the system was going to increase the power of the attorney general—that was one of its main objectives," he said in an interview in his Washington office. "In part, the purpose of the system is to give life to what is really the legal responsibility of the attorney general which he cannot effectively exercise now because of the semi-autonomous nature of the U.S. attorneys and the lack of information to determine whether they are following the policies of the attorney general."

The former chief prosecutor of the United States, who now is in private practice, has an office that looks down Pennsylvania Avenue toward the Justice Department. "If the attorney general determines and publicly states that the investigative and prosecutive forces of the Justice Department are to be concentrated on certain goals, he wants to be able to determine these goals are being pursued. Let's say the priorities are white-collar crime, organized crime, drug trafficking and espionage. If a U.S. attorney in Chicago is concentrating on stolen-car cases, then he obviously is not following policy."

Mr. Civiletti, acknowledging that the computer system is strengthening the hand of an already powerful federal official, does not see any hazards. "Even with the computers," he said, "there is little practical risk of an attorney general forcing the wrongful disposition of a particular case."

Another experienced prosecutor, however, is less sanguine. Robert Morgenthau is a slim, elegant man with sharp blue eyes and carefully brushed white hair. He now is the district attorney of Manhattan. A few years ago, he was the U.S. attorney for the southern district of New York.

"The system, of course, will give the attorney general a better idea what his agents are doing and how well they are doing it," Mr. Morgenthau said. He was sitting behind a huge conference table in his large sunny office in lower Manhattan. "But if you are going to take away or reduce the discretion of a U.S. attorney, if you are going to make him a simple instrument of the attorney general, then you are going to give an awful lot of power to the attorney general to do both good and bad. If an attorney general wanted to abuse this power, the system would give him the wherewithal. He could suppress cases, he could give out confidential information about the status of cases, he could make the Justice Department a much more formidable national force."

The complex computer systems of the IRS nurture the growth of quotas that reduce the exercise of independent judgment of the individual agent and increase the power of Washington. The gradual development of a computerized reporting system within the Justice Department lessens the discretion of the U.S. attorneys and strengthens the hand of the attorney general.

Some contend the increased administrative controls are good, that they contribute to an evenhanded application of the law and are a way the attorney general may be held accountable. Others believe the systems are bad, that they lead to an inflexible application of the law and give Washington too much power over too many people. Jeffrey A. Meldman is a professor at the Sloan School of Management of the Massachusetts Institute of Technology. A short man with a neatly trimmed mustache and glasses, Professor Meldman has given a good deal of thought to how the new information technology is changing both business and government.

"In engineering," he explained, "there is a principle which holds that it frequently is best to have a loosely coupled system. The problem with tightly coupled systems is that should a bad vibration start at one end of the machine, it will radiate and may cause difficulties in all parts of the system. Loose coupling frequently is essential to keep a large structure from falling down. I think this principle of

mechanical engineering may be relevant to the way we use the computer in the United States."

Professor Meldman's analogy is an interesting one. As long as the
United States is served by well-meaning, intelligent attorney generals
who share the widespread American concerns about the importance
of the independent autonomy of every citizen, then a tightly coupled
system may best serve these goals. But should a president appoint an
attorney general who had a fundamental abhorrence to organized
crime figures or civil rights demonstrators or war protesters, a tightly
coupled system might create vibrations that could severely damage
the Justice Department, and possibly even the entire government.

The
National Security
Agency —
The Ultimate
Computer Bureaucracy

The true danger is, when liberty is nibbled away, for
expedience and by parts.

—Edmund Burke

The two diplomats met in total secrecy. One was the representative
of a great superpower. The other spoke for a political organization
regarded by many Americans as nothing but a terrorist gang. There
would be serious worldwide repercussions if the meeting between the
two men ever became known to anyone.

The date was July 26, 1979. The place was a Manhattan townhouse
at 33 Beekman Place, the elegant New York residence of the Kuwaiti
delegate to the United Nations. The participants were Andrew
Young, the outspoken civil rights activist whom President Carter
had appointed to head the U.S. delegation to the United Nations, and
Zehdi Labib Terzil, the diplomatic observer for the Palestine Libera-
tion Organization.

Two weeks after the clandestine meeting in New York, the National Security Agency, one of the most secretive organizations in the
U.S. government, provided the White House with an authoritative
account of the session. Partly because President Carter and his advisers thought it essential to protect the source of their information,

partly because of the difficult diplomatic and political problems that would be created if the unauthorized meeting became known to the world, the administration chose to take no action.

But the Israeli government had an entirely different perspective. Israel had received a bare hint of the meeting, perhaps from the National Security Agency, but more probably from a double agent buried within the diplomatic corps of an Arab nation, and it was deeply concerned about the policy implications. Israel passed the tip to a *Newsweek* magazine correspondent in Jerusalem, and within hours the magazine's Washington Bureau made an official inquiry at the State Department press office.

Five turbulent days later, Andrew Young resigned amid a blizzard of official statements that the meeting had not been authorized by either the State Department or President Carter and certainly did not reflect a change in U.S. policy toward Israel. Though the actual reason for the forced resignation was never disclosed, it lay in Carter's anger toward his ambassador. Because of the electronic eavesdropping of the National Security Agency, the president knew that Young's account of his meeting with the Arab diplomat was not the full truth.

Thus did the information supplied by the NSA prompt the president to request a resignation that served to confirm the doubts of a large number of Jewish voters about the reliability of Mr. Carter.

This is not an isolated example of the great power that can lie within the information secretly collected by the NSA. On April 10, 1980, a short, soft-spoken Texan named Bobby Ray Inman went to the paneled fifth-floor office of the attorney general of the United States. Inman, a navy admiral and director of the NSA, showed Benjamin Civiletti two highly secret documents about another serious political problem for the Carter administration.

One document indicated that the president's brother, Billy Carter, was about to receive a payment from Libya, a North African country that for the last few years had been a rabid enemy of Israel. The second document discussed Billy Carter's dealings with an American oil company that was attempting to obtain oil from Libya and the efforts of the Libyan government to exploit Billy's involvement for its own purposes. "Civiletti read the documents and returned them to the official who had delivered them; the whole meeting took three or four minutes," a special Senate investigating committee reported some months later.

Inman's secret briefing prompted the attorney general to order the Justice Department not to close its then-limping investigation of Billy Carter's highly embarrassing involvement with one of the U.S. Jewish community's least favored nations.

Both the Andy Young and the Billy Carter cases illustrate that information is power and that the organization that collects and distributes information is powerful. Thus the National Security Agency, which has been likened to a worldwide electronic vacuum cleaner, is among the least known and most influential organizations within the U.S. government.

The public makes up its mind about political candidates in many different ways. In the case of President Carter, the meeting between his bold ambassador to the United Nations and a representative of the PLO and the entanglement of his brother with Libya were two of a number of key events that may have contributed to the shift in public opinion that later led to the defeat of the Georgia peanut farmer turned politician, in his campaign for a second term in the White House.

The public controversy surrounding Andrew Young's secret meeting and his subsequent firing by President Carter certainly influenced the judgments of a substantial number of New York voters who in the spring of 1980 handed Senator Edward Kennedy a victory in the New York primary. Carter's defeat in New York was important because it signaled that the incumbent president was vulnerable. The news stories about Billy Carter's connection with Libya and the subsequent investigations by the Justice Department and the Senate were added embarrassments to a president already on the defensive because of the Iranian hostage crisis.

There is no evidence that either Admiral Inman or the NSA deliberately set out to undermine the political strength of President Carter. At the same time, there is no question that the information collected with the help of its computerized eavesdropping systems did influence an important segment of the voters.

The NSA's unique leverage on world events is based on its massive bank of what are believed to be the largest and most advanced computers now available to any bureaucracy on earth. Computers to break codes. Computers to direct spy satellites. Computers to intercept millions and millions of electronic messages transmitted by friends and enemies from every corner of the globe. Computers to recognize certain target words in spoken communications. Computers to store, organize and index all this information so it can be retrieved when needed.

It is hard to comprehend the vast reach of the NSA. But a stack of dusty documents in the Baltimore office of the Army Corps of Engineers provides one graphic, if indirect, yardstick. The NSA's headquarters is a large, heavily guarded complex located at Fort George C. Meade, an army base seventeen miles northeast of Washington. A little more than ten years ago, NSA officials decided that they needed a new way to destroy the classified waste created each day behind the chain-link fence, the six strands of electrified wire and the second chain-link fence that surround the agency's headquarters. On November 11, 1971, the Corps of Engineers signed a contract with a New York company to build a huge high-temperature incinerator to burn the classified computer printouts and other papers generated every day by the special breed of electronic spies that work for the NSA.

The planned capacity of the $2 million incinerator was amazing. "The unit shall be capable of destroying at least six tons an hour and not less than thirty-six tons within one eight-hour shift from the initial start-up to the final shutdown for the day," the specification declared. That amounts to 72,000 pounds of secret paper in a single day. Because of technical troubles, the incinerator never met this incredible goal, and the NSA ultimately turned to another method to dispose of its classified waste paper.

But the NSA is much more than a massive computerized funnel that collects, channels and sorts out information for the president, secretary of state and organizations such as the CIA and the FBI. Hidden behind the thick wall of secrecy required for its stated mission as an electronic spy, this virtually unknown government agency has also sought to influence the operation and development of all kinds of communication networks widely used by the public.

For the last three decades, for example, the NSA has been a frequent and secret participant in regulatory matters before the Federal Communications Commission, where important decisions are made that directly affect the structure of the telephone company, the use of radio airwaves and the operation of communication satellites. During the same time, the NSA probably was the single largest source of federal research dollars spent in the development of advanced computers and thus was a significant but silent force in the shape of an industry that reaches into every aspect of American life. In recent years the NSA was authorized to enlarge its already considerable presence in the design and development of equipment used by individuals and corporations to protect the secrecy of their communications.

The power of the NSA, which has an annual budget and staff exceeding those of either the Federal Bureau of Investigation or the Central Intelligence Agency, is enhanced by its unique legal status within the federal government. Congress has never hammered out a law defining the responsibilities and obligations of the NSA. Instead, the agency has operated under a series of White House directives since it was established by a secret seven-page order signed by Harry Truman on October 24, 1952.

So intense was the secrecy, in fact, that during the first few years of the NSA's life its mere existence as an arm of the Defense Department was not acknowledged in an official manual of the U.S. government.

The lack of a legal charter is not just a lawyer's quibble. Rather, it is a fundamental flaw that allows the NSA to avoid one of the central principles of responsible government as developed in the U.S. Constitution. That principle: all government agencies must be subject to checks and balances. Because of the failure of Congress to draft a law spelling out the obligations of the NSA, because of the tremendous secrecy surrounding its work, because of the highly technical character of the equipment the agency uses to carry out its various missions, the National Security Agency is uniquely free to pursue whatever goals its director decides are essential.

While there is no law stating the purpose of the NSA, the mission of the agency was discussed several years ago in a report of the awkwardly named Select Committee to Study Government Operations with Respect to Intelligence Activities. Various aspects of the agency's responsibilities have also been touched upon in a handful of depositions filed by the agency in federal courts, several recent executive orders and a few aging documents found in the towering stacks of the National Archives.

According to these sources, the National Security Agency has two broad goals, one offensive, one defensive. First, the NSA attacks the communication links of the world searching for the foreign intelligence that can be gained by intercepting telephone messages and other electronic messages and intercepting the signals generated by such events as the launching of a missile or the operation of a radar set. Second, the NSA defends the communication links that carry information bearing on the national security of the United States from penetration by the spies of other nations.

Just these two goals are formidable. Throughout history, the communication lines of diplomats and soldiers have been important, almost as essential to the life of the individual nation as the brain and central nervous system are to the human body. But we now live in a time when international oil cartels and powerful multinational corporations dominate global economics, when instant retaliation is believed to be the best defense against a nuclear holocaust, when more and more essential information is transmitted by massive computerized networks.

The NSA's extraordinary power—enhanced by the lack of a precise legal mandate, the absence of effective oversight and a world environment of mass communications—has been further enlarged by its incredible technical capacity. This capacity, built on billions of dollars of secret appropriations, includes a formidable electronic eavesdropping network of satellites, thousands of earthbound listening posts and what almost certainly is the world's largest single computer complex based at Fort George Meade, just outside of Washington, D.C.

Details about the equipment, organization and budget of the NSA are among the most closely held secrets of the U.S. government. A sense of the size of the agency, however, can be gained from the occasional document that has slipped through the rigid censorship screen that surrounds every aspect of the NSA. A few years ago, for example, a once-classified report prepared for the Joint Chiefs of Staff in 1956 was placed in the public files of the National Archives. The report was that as of November 1954 the National Security Agency had 3,699 "intercept positions" manned or operable on a twenty-four-hour basis. It added that an additional 421 positions could be made available, "for a total of 4,120 positions."

The report to the Joint Chiefs of Staff did not describe what an intercept position was or explain how many technicians were required to operate them. But an unpublished analysis by the House Government Operations Committee estimates that in 1976 the NSA may have employed 120,000 persons when the military personnel under the agency's direction were included in the count. The NSA's annual budget was thought to be as high as $15 billion. By way of comparison, if the congressional estimate is correct, the FBI had one agent or other employee for every six working for the NSA.

The most extensive independent examination ever made of the National Security Agency was initiated several years ago by the Senate Select Committee on Intelligence in the wake of Nixon's Watergate and the disclosure of other abuses by federal intelligence agencies.

In speeches and statements made during the course of this investigation, the committee's chairman, Senator Frank Church, repeatedly emphasized his belief that the NSA's intelligence-gathering activities were essential to the security of the United States. But he also emphasized that the NSA was a serious threat to freedom.

The equipment used to monitor the Russians, he once said, could just as easily "monitor the private communications of Americans" and creates "a tremendous potential for abuse." If ever turned against the communication system of the United States, "no American would have any privacy left. . . . There would be no place to hide."

The final report of the Senate Intelligence Committee, approved by a majority of its members, echoed the stark warning of the chairman. "If not properly controlled," the report said, the massed eavesdropping devices and computers of the NSA "could be turned against the American people at a great cost to liberty."

One reason for the concern of Senator Church and his committee was the attitude of the top officials of the NSA about the congressional investigation of their surveillance activities. This attitude was clearly expressed during an exchange at a committee hearing.

It was Senator Barry Goldwater's turn to ask the questions, and the conservative Arizona senator was upset. He had opposed holding the hearing, he had opposed questioning the witnesses who sat before him, he had opposed any public discussion about the activities of the NSA. The witness, a ferociously intelligent air force computer expert, was completely unknown to the American people. But because the general had headed the NSA, his name was certainly known to intelligence officials in nations throughout the world.

The appearance of Lieutenant General Lew Allen, Jr., before the Senate Intelligence Committee was a small but significant event in American history. It marked the first time in the twenty-three-year history of the NSA that one of its officials ever had testified in public.

In an earlier private session with the committee, Senator Goldwater reminded General Allen, "you stated that the law did not allow you to testify on any aspect of the National Security Agency."

Allen: "That is what I believe to be the case, yes, sir."

Goldwater: "Then theoretically you are violating the law in being here?"

Allen: "Yes, sir."

Despite his objections, the Senate committee ultimately forced General Allen to testify in a public hearing. But with the backing of the White House, he agreed to discuss only a few of the NSA's programs.

The head of a powerful government agency had informed a properly constituted Senate committee that in his view Congress was violating the law simply by asking him questions in a public forum. It was an astounding statement, a fascinating insight into how in the mind of this highly trained Air Force general the imperative of the cold war took precedence over the constitutional requirement that Congress and the American people be informed of the activities of their government.

What are these activities? What does the agency actually do? The seemingly contradictory ability of the NSA to act like an electronic microscope peering into the most intimate secrets of nature while at the same time serving as a gigantic telescope sweeping the vast reaches of outer space is nothing less than astounding.

It was the NSA, after all, that picked up the electronic order from Tripoli authorizing the Libyan diplomats in the United States to give money to the president's brother. It was an NSA spy satellite called Ferret that some years ago reportedly reached down from the edge of space and recorded the voice of Nikita Khrushchev giving orders on the mobile telephone in his speeding limousine. At the same time, the NSA is also equipped to acquire and automatically scan most or all of the written electronic messages that enter, leave or transit the United States. Not long ago, this amounted to 75 million telexes in a single year.

In addition to scanning written messages, the NSA has the equipment and manpower to monitor all the spoken conversations moving along a specific communication pathway or all the calls made from or to telephones that have been selected for surveillance.

One of the few specific examples of this capacity ever to be publicly documented occurred in the early 1970s when federal narcotics agents became convinced that illegal shipments of drugs were being arranged during conversations between some dealers speaking from public telephone booths in New York City's Grand Central Station to their colleagues in a single South American city.

After determining that the wiretap law barred the Bureau of Narcotics and Dangerous Drugs from installing a tap on the Grand Central pay phones, John Ingersoll, then head of the bureau, asked the NSA for help. Within a few months the spy agency was sorting through all the conversations it already was acquiring for general intelligence purposes, looking for the specific messages between the targeted public phones and the specific South American city.

To record the conversations of the drug dealers, of course, the technicians were required to acquire, monitor and discard a large number of calls made by people with no connection with the cocaine business. But so pleased was Mr. Ingersoll with the tips he was getting from the NSA that he ultimately persuaded the agency to look for narcotics intelligence from the conversations made over nineteen different communication links connecting New York and Miami with six large South American cities.

It is impossible to determine the number of innocuous conversations between separated lovers, lonely tourists and traveling salesmen that the NSA scrutinized in the government's search for the occasional narcotics dealer. During just one year of the three-year period that the program continued, however, records of the American Telephone and Telegraph Company show a total of 2,477,881 calls between the United States and all of South America.

Was the program worth it? Did the millions of dollars required for the salaries of the agents who monitored the nineteen communication links to South America on an around-the-clock, 365-day-a-year basis result in a real decline in the flow of marijuana, heroin and cocaine into the United States? Certainly no big claims of success were made by General Allen when the Senate Intelligence Committee asked him for an assessment of the surveillance. "Some large drug shipments were prevented from entering the United States because of our activities on international narcotics trafficking," he said. "Nonetheless, in my own judgment, the controls . . . placed on the handling of the intelligence were so restrictive that the value [of the program] was significantly diminished."

The controls referred to by General Allen prevented the Federal Bureau of Narcotics and Dangerous Drugs from using the intelligence to arrest a specific suspect because the NSA was worried its activities would be subsequently disclosed during the public trial of the suspect. Thus, under the ground rules imposed by the NSA, the BNDD could use the information obtained by the surveillance only for the purpose of general intelligence. It is probable that because of the NSA's increasing fear that its secret surveillance might become known that the program was halted three years after it was launched.

The Senate Intelligence Committee did not attempt to judge the ultimate value of the NSA's eavesdropping for the BNDD, only noting that the spy agency prepared 1,900 reports as a result of its telephone surveillance of 450 Americans.

The collaboration between the NSA and the Bureau of Narcotics and Dangerous Drugs was aimed at drug dealers engaged in serious street crimes. But over the years, some other NSA surveillance activities have focused on individuals who were merely stating their political opposition to the racial situation in the United States or the war in Vietnam.

The NSA first became involved in this more questionable kind of surveillance in the early 1960s when either Robert F. Kennedy, then the attorney general, or the FBI asked the agency to monitor all telephone calls between the United States and Cuba. The list of those individuals whose international calls should be monitored was significantly enlarged during the Johnson administration as federal authorities became concerned that foreign governments might try to influence civil rights leaders in the United States. As the years went by, the NSA developed "watch lists" of those American citizens whose international conversations various federal agencies nominated for surveillance. In addition to becoming more formal, the watch list was broadened to include those who had voiced their opposition to the United States war in Vietnam.

According to the subsequent investigation by the Senate Intelligence Committee, a total of 1,200 Americans were targeted by the NSA between 1967 and 1973 because of their political activities. The individuals had been selected by the Federal Bureau of Investigation, the Secret Service, the Central Intelligence Agency and the Defense Intelligence Agency. The subjects included members of radical political groups, celebrities and ordinary citizens. The organizations placed under surveillance included some communist front groups and some peaceful and nonviolent ones.

The surveillance was illegal and was instantly stopped when it appeared that Congress might learn about the eavesdropping. But the NSA put on a brave front when forced to testify about the program.

"Now let me address the question of the watch-list activities as the NSA saw it at the time," General Allen said in a carefully worded statement. "This activity was reviewed by proper authority within the NSA and by competent external authority. This included two former attorneys general and a former secretary of the defense. The requirement for information had been approved by officials of the using agencies and subsequently validated by the United States Intelligence Board."

Very impressive. Also very misleading. Consider, for a moment, the chain of events leading to the surveillance of the telephone calls of the civil rights activists and the Vietnam War protesters. The first link in the chain was forged in mid-1967 when the Army, in response to pressures from President Johnson and Attorney General Ramsey Clark, established a civil disturbance intelligence unit.

A few months later, on October 20, 1967, General William Yarborough, the commander of the special army unit, sent a message to the NSA requesting assistance. General Yarborough said he desired "any information on a continuing basis" that indicated "that foreign governments are controlling or attempting to control or influence the activities of U.S. 'peace' groups or black power organizations."

Twenty-four hours later, without referring the matter to any civilian authority, the NSA agreed to undertake the secret electronic surveillance requested by the Army. Contrary to the implication in General Allen's statement to the Senate Intelligence Committee that the watch-list program was activated after careful consideration by the highest political authorities, it was not until three years after it began operating that a memorandum including a very general statement about the NSA's "contribution to domestic intelligence" passed over the desks of Defense Secretary Laird and Attorney General Mitchell.

A second example of the slippery quality of General Allen's testimony concerns his statement of how individual targets were selected for surveillance. "The NSA produces signals intelligence in response to the objectives, requirements and priorities expressed by the director of Central Intelligence with the advice of the U.S. Intelligence Board," he testified. "The NSA does have operational discretion in responding to requirements, but we do not generate our own requirements for foreign intelligence."

The late Senator Philip Hart was not satisfied with Allen's statement. "But it is your testimony that out of the NSA itself there was no generation of new names or organizations?" he asked.

"That is correct," General Allen replied.

It was not, however. A footnote to this exchange in the printed Senate hearings states without comment that upon reviewing the transcript the NSA advised it had been responsible for adding fifty to seventy-five persons to the watch list.

In addition to misinforming the committee about a number of small but nevertheless important details concerning the NSA's watch-list activities, General Allen simply refused to testify about a second totally illegal surveillance program under which most of the international telegrams entering or leaving the United States between 1945 and 1975 were examined by the NSA.

Under the program, the Radio Corporation of America and the International Telephone and Telegraph Company turned over every message that had been entrusted to them, while Western Union cooperated on a somewhat more limited basis. The program was abruptly halted in May of 1975, a date that happens to coincide with the Senate committee's first expression of interest in it.

The records obtained by the committee indicate that from the earliest stages of the project, both the government officials and the corporate executives understood the surveillance of the messages flatly violated a federal law making it a crime for any person not authorized by the sender to intercept or divulge the contents of the telegrams. The officials and executives also may have been aware that the criminal prohibition was based on the Fourth Amendment to the Constitution, the one that guarantees to the American people the right to be secure in their papers against "unreasonable searches and seizures." The same amendment holds that a court order authorizing such a search can only be issued when there is probable cause to believe a crime has been committed.

Using the information obtained by its surveillance, the NSA's security office between 1952 and 1974 developed files on approximately 75,000 Americans, some of whom undoubtedly threatened the security of the United States. As General Allen acknowledged, however, the NSA also collected intelligence and developed files on civil rights leaders, antiwar activists, members of Congress and ordinary citizens who questioned the policies of the government in a lawful fashion.

For thirteen of the twenty-two years the NSA was building its intelligence files, Central Intelligence Agency employees also had access to them. Senate investigators determined that some of the information collected by the illegal surveillance of the NSA ultimately found its way into the files of Operation Chaos, another computerized and illegal tracking system set up by the CIA during the Vietnam War. At its peak, the Chaos files had references to more than 300,000 Americans.

In addition to misleading the committee about important details concerning one NSA program and refusing to testify about others, General Allen deftly declined to speculate on the potential impact of these surveillance activities on the democratic process in the United States. His answers to the questions posed by Walter Mondale, then a senator from Minnesota, echo the "good soldier" response of all powerful bureaucrats when called upon to defend an improper or illegal program: I was just following my orders.

Senator Mondale reminded General Allen of one unnamed person subjected to NSA surveillance, "a moderate, peaceful person, as a matter of fact someone who quit the antiwar movement even though he was desperately against the war because he so much opposed some of the militancy and violent rhetoric." The senator then asked the general whether the surveillance of this kind of person did not "undermine and discourage political criticism and dissent in this country?"

"I am afraid, sir, I have to dodge the basic philosophical nature of your question because the facts are that as a technical collection agency the NSA was asked a much more simple question," the general replied. "The requirement to us, the request for information, was very specific and very constrained and addressed to a very narrow point. The broader aspects of your question, I think, I am not really qualified to answer."

But because the NSA's mandate is not defined in public law, because the agency's performance is seldom examined by outside authority, because the record suggests that it repeatedly has sought to enlarge its power without consulting the civilian officials who theoretically direct the government, who else is there to answer Senator Mondale's question but the military men who direct the NSA?

The chairman of the committee, Senator Church, then explored the same critical ground from a different perspective. "Suppose we had a president one day who said to you: 'I have determined with my advisers, who are my appointees, that foreign intelligence is a seamless web and it is quite impossible to differentiate between domestic and foreign intelligence because we need to know it all and some of it can only be gathered from domestic sources,' " the senator hypothesized. " 'And so, in the overriding interest of obtaining the maximum amount of foreign intelligence, you are instructed to intercept messages that are purely domestic, and various agencies will provide you with lists of people whose messages you are to intercept —all without warrants, all without judicial process, all without any sanction of law.' Would you say we refuse to do this because it is illegal?"

Despite the evidence of extensive illegal surveillance by the NSA under President Truman, President Eisenhower, President Kennedy, President Johnson and President Nixon, General Allen did not hesitate a moment. Because of the NSA's abiding concern about the constitutional provision banning illegal searches, he said, the senator could be assured that the agency would never secretly eavesdrop on the domestic telephone calls of American citizens.

Several months after the hearing, the Senate's select committee on intelligence issued a report that expressed great concern about both the activities of the NSA and the failure of Congress and the federal courts to comprehend them. "The watch-list activities and sophisticated capabilities that they highlight present some of the most crucial privacy issues now facing this nation," the committee warned. "Space-age technology has outpaced the law. The secrecy that has surrounded much of the NSA's activities and the lack of congressional oversight has prevented, in the past, bringing statutes in line with the NSA's capabilities. Neither the courts nor Congress have dealt with the interception of communications using NSA's highly sensitive and complex technology." The committee recommended that Congress approve specific legislation spelling out the precise obligations and limitations of the NSA.

Despite the bluntly worded warning, however, neither the Congress nor the courts have made much progress in comprehending the fantastic technical capability of the NSA and then developing a legislative or judicial framework to control its activities. More than three decades after its birth, the responsibilities of the NSA still are defined only in a series of largely secret executive orders.

An example of the federal courts' failure to understand the great power of the NSA occurred in the fall of 1982 when the United States Court of Appeals for the Sixth Circuit ruled that the agency may lawfully intercept messages between U.S. citizens and people overseas, even if there is no reason to believe the Americans are foreign agents and even if summaries of these messages are then provided the FBI.

The decision involved the government's surveillance of a Michigan-born lawyer named Abdeen Jabara who for many years has represented Arab-American citizens and aliens in federal court. In earlier court proceedings, the FBI acknowledged that it had received summaries of Jabara's conversations from the NSA and disseminated them to seventeen other law-enforcement or intelligence agencies and three foreign governments.

Jabara's lawyer, John Shattuck of the American Civil Liberties Union, said in his response that it was "difficult to imagine a more sweeping judicial approval of a governmental action in violation of constitutional rights than the decision of the panel in this case."

The establishment of the NSA was first formally recommended in a report dated June 13, 1952, by a special presidential committee headed by George Brownell. The committee concluded a unified effort was essential because electronic surveillance of international radio traffic "ranks as our most important single source of intelligence today."

The report said the importance of communication intelligence had been firmly established during World War II. Its cost cannot be accurately computed, but an informed guess would be perhaps a half billion dollars annually at the outside. Admiral Nimitz rated its value in the Pacific as equivalent to another whole fleet; General Handy is reported to have said it shortened the war in Europe "by at least a year."

But with the coming of the cold war between the Soviet Union and the United States shortly after the ending of the hot one in 1945, the value of effective intelligence remained high. Partly because of the recognition of this undeclared war, the committee recommended the replacement of the four separate surveillance agencies within the Defense Department with a single highly professional organization.

With the creation of this new agency came an expanded definition of the intelligence required by the president and his national security policy planners. Intelligence, the cold war logic dictated, was no longer just the secret blueprints for the latest machine gun or the planting of a spy in the ranks of your opponent's diplomats. Intelligence must now include early signs that a blight has hit China's rice crop, indications that a productive new oil field has been located in a remote corner of Russia, orders placed by a non-nuclear nation for a special kind of piping that could be used to make an atomic bomb or analysis of radio traffic at an important Iron Curtain airport.

The already expansive appetite of U.S. intelligence analysts was further sharpened by technical advances that were occurring, not entirely by chance, during the same period the cold war was developing from a squalling infant to a scowling giant. The technology in question was the digital computer, the wondrous tool developed with great diligence by American scientists working for such companies as AT&T and IBM, supported in a major way by secret research dollars from the NSA. The computers' ability to acquire, organize, store and retrieve huge amounts of data was an essential factor leading to the broad definition of intelligence that was fostered by the National Security Agency and its godfather, the National Security Council.

The importance of the broadest possible intelligence gathering became even more critical when the computer know-how began to spread beyond a technological elite—primarily in the United States —to scientists working in many nations. Simply stated, the spread of advanced computer skills and the related mathematical concepts meant that governments could reduce the chances that their top secret messages would be intercepted and decoded while at the same time increasing the ability of these nations to undertake programs to collect the broadest kinds of economic and technical intelligence.

As a result of these changes, according to several U.S. officials, the intelligence apparatus of the Soviet Union began eavesdropping on millions of telephone conversations between Washington and New York and several other major cities in the early seventies. Because of the unusual sensitivity of the subject, however, the United States did not exactly trumpet the news of the Soviet surveillance to the American people. One of the first to discuss the possibility of such surveillance in public was Thomas C. Reed, at the time the director of the Pentagon's Telecommunications, Command and Control System.

In a speech to a business organization in California in 1975, Mr. Reed noted that at one time a "distinctly illegal tap or 'bug' " had been required to eavesdrop on a telephone conversation. "But technology has changed all that," Mr. Reed went on, explaining how through-the-air microwave radio links had replaced most of the under-the-ground intercity telephone cables. "At the present time, these microwave radio trunks are completely unencrypted [uncoded]. The interception of these trunks is a simple and straightforward matter for any underworld organization, blackmailer, terrorist or foreign power. Modern computer techniques make it possible to sort through that traffic and find target conversations fairly easily."

Mr. Reed, however, knew a great deal more about Russian telephone surveillance than he let on to the California businessmen. For more than a year, in fact, he had been a member of a highly secret National Security Council study panel that had held a series of unannounced Saturday meetings in Washington to discuss the evidence of the Soviet eavesdropping and decide what the government should do about it. The panel, named after its chairman, a former top Bell Laboratories scientist named Edward David, included General Lew Allen, the head of the NSA, and several of his agency colleagues. Fragmentary evidence suggests, in fact, that by the time Mr. Reed gave his California speech the David Panel was well on its way to recommending a remedy that would have cost the taxpayers billions of dollars.

The evidence suggesting the apparent direction of the David Panel's thinking is a brief memorandum prepared for President Ford on June 30, 1975, about what steps the government should take to control "telephone espionage." Written by John Eger, the acting director of the White House Office of Telecommunications Policy, the memorandum said the final decision in the matter could have an important impact on the structure of the communications industry, the use of the radio spectrum and the cost of telephone services. Mr. Eger recommended that his office and the Domestic Council Committee on the Right to Privacy should be consulted before President Ford made his decision on the appropriate "policy for dealing with the telephone interception threat."

But time was running out on the lengthy and totally secret proceedings of the David Panel. When the voters went to the polls in November 1976, Mr. Ford lost his mandate to Jimmy Carter. Because of the far-reaching impact of whatever action the United States took to counter the Russian surveillance, the Ford administration decided to pass the problem to the incoming president, who immediately ordered a whole new study. This one was headed by Dr. Frank Press, President Carter's science adviser, and David Aaron, deputy director of the National Security Council.

On a cold February afternoon two years after Mr. Carter entered the White House and at least four years after the Russian surveillance became known to the U.S. government, a few Washington reporters were summoned to the Old Executive Office Building for a briefing. The officials doing the talking were Press and Aaron.

The two men were brief and vague. Their conclusions had to be accepted as a matter of faith because security restrictions prevented them from offering any supporting evidence. The intense involvement of the NSA was not acknowledged. The Russians, they said, were conducting wholesale telephone eavesdropping from at least four locations in three different cities. The cities were New York, Washington and San Francisco. The targets of real concern were the government, defense contractors and other large companies whose activities would contribute to the Soviet's collection of economic intelligence. The two men added that to the best of their knowledge individual citizens had not been placed under surveillance by the Soviet government.

The Carter administration's countermeasures at first blush seemed far more modest than some of the grandiose options that had been considered by President Ford's advisers.

First, classified information relating to national defense and foreign relations henceforth would be transmitted only by secure means. In essence, the administration proposed the immediate purchase of an additional hundred "voice scramblers" for what is called the Executive Secure Voice Network. Though Dr. Press did not mention it during the briefing, the central switching point for the network later was determined to be the National Security Agency.

Second, and far more important, the executive order signed that cold February afternoon created an entirely new category of information requiring the scrutiny of the government. Until that moment, the government sought to control and protect only those military and diplomatic secrets that had been declared confidential, secret or top secret under a long-established and formally prescribed classification procedure. But now, the briefers said, the president had decided to create a vast new category of material worthy of government protection: information that "would be useful to an adversary."

Information that fell into this category, whether moving between a government contractor and an agency or between two private parties, should not fall into the hands of the Russians or any other nation. Telephone links in the specific areas where Soviet spies were known to be eavesdropping were being rearranged so that calls were transmitted via underground cable rather than through the air by a chain of radio microwave towers. To further reduce the leakage of the new category of information, the National Security Agency was authorized to approach large corporations and other institutions, collect information about their communication networks and assist them in making changes aimed at better safeguarding "information that would be useful to an adversary."

President Carter's decision to create by executive order a broad category of information requiring government scrutiny and authorizing the NSA to play a major role in its protection was a major extension of the agency's power, an open-ended hunting license. No unclassified document, for example, defines what kinds of information would be useful to an adversary. Certainly a timetable of the trains running between Washington and New York could be useful to an enemy spy. Surely the articles published in the *Washington Post* and the *New York Times* serve as source material for intelligence operatives all over the world. Farfetched, you say? Unlikely that a dedicated organization like the National Security Agency would ever attempt to prevent the free press of the United States from publishing a story? Then perhaps you have forgotten that the NSA was the lead agency in the Nixon administration's desperate attempt to stop the *Times* and the *Post* from printing the Pentagon Papers, the bureaucratic history of the war in Vietnam. After blocking publication for fourteen days, the Supreme Court ruled that the government had failed to show why the material should not be published and that *without compelling reasons* prior restraint would be an unreasonable infringement of the freedom of the press.

But the directive authorizing the National Security Agency to become involved in the planning, organization and development of the communications systems of private organizations not handling classified secrets was only one of several ways in which the power of the NSA grew during the period immediately after the Senate Intelligence Committee warning that the agency could become a threat to freedom.

Within the last few years, for example, the NSA has forcefully moved to control the development and dissemination of inventive approaches intended to help the individual citizen, corporation or political organization maintain its privacy. On April 28, 1978, for example, George Davida, a professor at the University of Wisconsin, received an order to keep secret all details of a computer security device he had invented. The NSA informed Davida that under a little-known provision of the patent law, a violation of the order could subject him to up to two years in jail and a $10,000 fine. The only problem was that Dr. Davida, a professor of electrical engineering and computer science, already had violated it by sending details of his invention to the National Science Foundation, one of the sponsors of his research, and a number of his academic colleagues. On the same day Davida received his secrecy order, the NSA also obtained one on a patent for a voice scrambler that would let radio and telephone users talk without being overheard. The inventors— Carl R. Nicolai, William M. Raike and David L. Miller—charged that the order against them "appears part of a general plan by the NSA to limit the privacy of the American people. They've been bugging people's phones for years and now someone comes along with a device that makes this a little harder to do and they oppose this under the guise of national security."

After the NSA orders were publicized by several newspapers and magazines, the NSA decided to pull in its horns. Admiral Bobby R. Inman, then director of the NSA, told a House committee that the two orders exemplified "not a faulty law but inadequate government attention to its application." He characterized the agency's handling of the voice-scrambling equipment as a "well-meaning attempt to hold a line that had clearly already been passed by." When the umpire, in this case the House Subcommittee on Information and Individual Rights, blew the whistle, Admiral Inman was willing to admit a violation of the rules. But he was not about to concede the game.

More than three years before the two incidents, in fact, the NSA appears to have initiated an ultimately successful campaign to increase its voice in determining which cryptographic research projects were supported by the National Science Foundation and thus in turn with much of the research conducted in this sensitive area by U.S. scientists. The first sign of this concern came in June of 1975 when a computer expert working for the NSA informed Fred W. Weingarten, an official in the Division of Computer Research of the National Science Foundation, that the National Security Agency "has sole statutory authority to fund research in cryptography; and in fact, that other agencies are specifically enjoined from supporting that kind of work."

Weingarten was surprised by the assertion of the NSA official and asked the foundation's general counsel to determine whether such a law existed. The answer was negative. But the campaign was only beginning. In April of 1977, two top NSA officials—Cecil Corry and David Boak—visited Weingarten to discuss the foundation's plans for granting money in the area of cryptography. "Early in the meeting," Weingarten wrote in a memorandum, "they suggested that a presidential directive gave them 'control' over all cryptographic work and we were operating outside that directive." Once again, subsequent research discovered no such presidential order.

The foundation official then outlined his "strictly personal view" of the goal the NSA officials were trying to achieve by attempting to persuade the foundation to stop funding research in the development of procedures and technologies designed to encipher and decipher messages. "First, NSA is in a bureaucratic bind. In the past the only communications with heavy security demands were military and diplomatic. Now, with the marriage of computer applications with telecommunications in electronic funds transfer, electronic mail and other large distributive processing applications, the need for highly secure digital processing has hit the civilian sector. NSA is worried, of course, that public domain security research will compromise some of their work."

In his memorandum of May 2, 1977, Weingarten did not explain why he thought the NSA was afraid of such research or what NSA work might be compromised by it. But the foundation official warned that this fear had generated a desire within the NSA to maintain their control of computer security research and to corner the bureaucratic expertise in the area.

He saw the development, however, as a policy issue of great consequence. "It seems clear that turning such a huge domestic responsibility, potentially involving such activities as banking, the U.S. mails and cable television, over to an organization such as the NSA should be done only after the most serious debate at higher levels."

Shortly after Weingarten's suggestion, though apparently not because of it, the director of the National Science Foundation, Richard C. Atkinson, and the director of the NSA, Admiral Inman, began privately discussing whether the role of the spy agency in supervising cryptographic research should be expanded. The precise outcome of these discussions remains murky, but it appears the NSA won the debate. On August 14, 1980, for example, the National Science Foundation informed a computer scientist associated with the Massachusetts Institute of Technology and the University of California at Los Angeles that the foundation would not support part of his research but that NSA would. With the funding of such research, of course, comes control over what is published. The scientist, Leonard Adleman, was concerned and reluctant to take the NSA research dollars. "It is a very frightening collusion between agencies," he said.

The long-term arrangements that have developed between the NSA and academic researchers working on cryptography, however, go beyond the Adleman affair. First, the lengthy negotiations have led to the establishment of a system in which the foundation routinely allows the NSA to review any request for the funding of cryptographic research. Second, the NSA has begun providing financial support for unclassified civilian research in the area. Interestingly enough, the first recipient of such support was Martin E. Hellman, a Stanford University code expert who for many years has been sharply critical of the NSA.

"Five years ago I was very much on the opposite side of the fence from NSA," said Dr. Hellman, a slim, bearded man who was wearing blue jeans when I interviewed him in his small campus office. "I wouldn't say I have been co-opted. But on the other hand, I am a lot more friendly. As a result of them being more friendly and coming partway, I felt I should be more friendly. I guess I am now the first guinea pig."

Hellman, who describes himself as an escapee from the Bronx, said he was not sure why NSA was interested in funding nonclassified research. "I think from their point of view it seems like a good thing to do because it becomes an automatic way for them to have contact with the researchers in the area."

But he acknowledges the potential problems. "One of the fears is that they are trying to buy people. If they support you then they own you, and you really are going against them if they ask you not to publish something and you do."

Hellman doubts this will happen to him. It is worth noting, however, that Norbert Wiener, the MIT professor who is generally credited with being one of the principal minds behind the development of the computer, refused to take money from the Pentagon because he was convinced it would corrupt his research and undermine his independence.

There are, of course, other ways to influence men. And the NSA is actively pursuing them. In early 1979, Admiral Inman spoke to the Armed Forces Communications and Electronics Association. It was the first public speech ever given by a top agency official. Admiral Inman, speaking in the guarded language of his profession, noted that the agency's mission could "no longer remain entirely in the shadows." One reason for this change, he explained, was that the protection of communications was no longer of interest just to the government; it had also become a major concern to private institutions. Because of this new interest, tensions, which he did not define, have developed between "the national security interests of the government and the telecommunication interests of both the public and private sector." The time had come to open up a dialogue between the NSA and the academic and industrial worlds.

The result of this dialogue so far has been the recommendation by a special committee of the American Council on Education that all researchers submit their work to the NSA before publishing it. Only one of the nine members of the special committee opposed the "voluntary" system of prior restraint when it was published in early 1981. The critic was George Davida. Dr. Davida believes the system is unconstitutional, but his reasoning is at least as interesting as his conclusion.

"The increase in the computerization of society has led to the construction of a large number of data bases that are *electronic windows* into the most intimate details of people's lives. What is even more disturbing is that it is usually impossible to know who is looking in. Thus these data bases are like one-way mirrors. Encryption," he continued, referring to the coding of material placed in computers, "can serve as a curtain. Therefore, the need for civilian (or nongovernmental) effort in cryptography is a strong one."

Davida noted that the data bases used right now for statistical purposes, employment records, credit card operations and many other operations essential to American life are all subject to compromise. "The only effective method for maintaining separation of such data involves encryption," he declared.

The special committee of the American Council on Education ignored Davida's warning. The members of this prestigious group of academics, many of whom are engaged in research on a subject that directly relates to the freedom of every American, agreed to allow a powerful government agency to review their work before it is published.

Shortly after Admiral Inman persuaded the academic community to accept his system of prior restraint for cryptology, he was named deputy director of the Central Intelligence Agency by President Reagan. It was from this position that he called for even broader restrictions on American science. In a speech in January 1982, Inman warned that a broad range of researchers would face mandatory government censorship of their papers unless a system of review was established to limit the access of the Soviet Union to the benefits of American technology.

If scientists do not cooperate in keeping some of their papers secret on a mandatory basis, Inman said, they will encounter a "tidal wave" of public outrage that will prompt Congress to establish a mandatory system of censorship. The admiral delivered his stern warning during the annual meeting of the American Association for the Advancement of Science.

The admiral said there were many areas in addition to cryptography where restrictions were required because publication of certain "technical information could affect the national security in a harmful way. Examples include computer hardware and software, other electronic gear and techniques, lasers, crop projections and manufacturing procedures." The admiral's proposed shopping list was extraordinarily broad.

Though the Congress has yet to be heard from, Admiral Inman's suggestion ran into immediate objections from many scientists. "If you want to win the Indianapolis 500, you build the fastest car, you don't throw nails on the track," commented Peter J. Denning, the head of Purdue University's Department of Computer Sciences and president of the Association for Computing Machinery.

On the same day that Admiral Inman spoke, the Association for the Advancement of Science passed a brief resolution. "Whereas freedom and national security are best preserved by adherence to the principles of openness that are a fundamental tenet of both American society and the scientific process, be it resolved that the AAAS opposes governmental restrictions on the dissemination, exchange or availability of unclassified knowledge."

A few months before Inman's speech, Dr. Edward Teller, the physicist credited with being a major proponent of and contributor to the construction of the hydrogen bomb, wrote a general essay attacking government attempts to restrict scientists.

"Secrecy is not compatible with science, but it is even less compatible with democratic procedure. Two hundred years ago, James Madison said, 'A popular government without popular information, or the means of acquiring it, is but a prologue to a farce or tragedy or perhaps both,' " Dr. Teller wrote.

The benefits and losses of the security system developed to protect nuclear research seem clear, he noted. "Decisions made with inadequate preparation, self-deception and diplomatic failure prompted deterioration in the free world. In addition, by tainting science with secrecy, an unfortunate public attitude is perpetuated: science is nobody's business but the scientists'."

The effort of the federal government and the U.S. intelligence community to restrict the work of a broad range of American scientists is worrisome. The successful NSA drive to cork the unclassified research of cryptologists is ominous.

No laws define the limits of the NSA's power. No congressional committee subjects the agency's budget to a systematic, informed and skeptical review. With billions of federal dollars—the exact amount kept secret from most congressmen and all of the public— the NSA is able to purchase the most advanced communications and computer equipment in the world.

But to truly comprehend the growing reach of this formidable organization, it is necessary to recall once again how the computers that power the NSA are also gradually changing our individual lives: the way we bank, the way we obtain benefits from the government, the way we communicate with family and friends. Every day, in almost every area of culture and commerce, systems and procedures are being adopted that make it easier and easier for the NSA to dominate our society should it ever decide such action is necessary.

Values

Where is the wisdom we have lost in knowledge?
Where is the knowledge we have lost in information?

—T.S. Eliot

In March 1969, the U.S. Air Force initiated a series of bombing raids against the people and jungles of Cambodia. Partly because Richard Nixon correctly perceived that the Cambodian raids would reinforce the already bitter opposition to the Vietnam War, he decided the bombing should be kept secret. On the basis of Nixon's decision, Defense Secretary Melvin Laird and General Earle Wheeler, then the chairman of the Joint Chiefs of Staff, signed a top-secret memorandum directing the air force to falsify its records about the B-52 raids.

"All sorties against targets in Cambodia will be programmed against preplanned alternate targets in the Republic of Vietnam and strike messages will so indicate," the Laird-Wheeler order commanded. A short time later, an unknown Defense Department programmer adjusted the instructions of the Pentagon computer that processed the bombing reports coming from Southeast Asia so that the raids against the targets in Cambodia would appear to be raids on targets in Vietnam. Computer summaries that included the false information subsequently were submitted to the Senate Armed Services Committee.

The Nixon administration's effort to keep the raids secret collapsed a few months later when William Beecher wrote a story about them in the *New York Times*. It was not until four years later, however, that Congress learned about the Laird-Wheeler cover-up memorandum ordering the air force to deliberately lie about this significant extension of the Vietnam War.

In 1973, Admiral Thomas H. Morer, the new chairman of the Joint Chiefs of Staff, was called to testify to the same Senate committee that had been handed the false reports in 1969. The admiral attempted to persuade the incredulous senators that contrary to the unequivocal language of the Laird-Wheeler order, "no one authorized the falsification of reports."

What had happened, he explained, was not the fault of any individual officer, but simply a perverse technical requirement of the Defense Department's naughty computer system. The raids against the Cambodian targets, he said, carried such a high classification that information about them could not be recorded in the Pentagon's computer, which was authorized to store only lesser categories of military secrets. But it was absolutely essential that the flying time consumed by these most secret raids somehow be noted in the central computer so that the fuel, bombs and other supplies actually used in sending the B-52s over Cambodia were accounted for and therefore replaced in the supply line. This was the only reason, he explained, why the program in the Pentagon computer had been adjusted so that the geographic coordinates of the actual targets in Cambodia appeared in the printouts as the coordinates of targets in Vietnam.

"It's unfortunate that we have become slaves to these damned things," Admiral Morer told the committee. National leaders have of course sought to deceive their citizens as long as there have been nations. But the lie about the bombing in Cambodia demonstrates how in certain circumstances the computer helps leaders deceive.

In the heavily computerized environment of big government, the incident first shows how easy it is to make a small change in a computer program that will then create a continuing stream of false information. In the unquestioning acceptance of the Pentagon data by the Senate Armed Services Committee, the incident also demonstrates the great credibility granted any information displayed on a computer printout. Finally, in Admiral Moyer's twisted explanation, the incident shows how hard it is to hold the large computerized institutions of our age accountable for any single act.

The story of the computer's role in the deception of the American people about the bombing of Cambodia is just one example of the way that computers are now affecting our morality, our ethics and our appreciation of the truth. More fundamentally, it shows how computers are changing our values—what we think is important—and the very process of thought.

While absolutely essential to the consideration of the place of the computer in modern life, discussion of the influence of this particular machine on the values of the American people is difficult. History tells us, for example, that anticipating the effects of technical developments is always hard. How many planners, for example, foresaw that the horseless carriage ultimately would lead to the growth of the suburbs and the decline of many cities? How many scientists of the seventeenth century understood that the invention of the telescope would lead to profound changes in man's view of life and of the power of God? Like the automobile and the telescope, however, it can be safely predicted that the direct and indirect effects of the computer will be far greater than the rather limited consequences claimed for this tool by its boosters.

When attempting to understand these conflicting currents, we must distinguish between the tasks computers theoretically can take on and the tasks computers are actually given by the large organizations that generally control them.

Finally, defining the effects of computerization on ethical and human values is difficult because the subject has received very little attention. In the rush to enlarge the capabilities of Charles Babbage's analytical engine, few engineers, business executives, government officials or academics in the computer field have looked beyond the challenge of completing their immediate assignments. It seems unlikely, for example, that the computer whiz kids who began the Pentagon's rush for the machines during the Kennedy administration ever contemplated how the political and military leaders of a later administration would use the systems to obscure a war in Cambodia.

Ross Snyder is a senior public relations executive at Hewlitt

Packard, one of the country's largest and most aggressive computer companies. Perhaps because he is involved in trying to explain the computer to the public, Snyder is more aware than most of those in his industry how it has largely failed to consider the social impact of the computer.

"Hewlitt Packard, IBM and most of the rest of the industry are in the business of selling computers, not musing on their implications," he said during a leisurely lunch at a club located in the hills looking down on California's Silicon Valley, the corporate computer center of the world. "We have no resident philosopher. Very few of our executives give much thought to problems like the invasion of privacy or the concentration of power in the hands of fewer and fewer organizations."

But there are exceptions to Snyder's generalization. One such exception, in fact, is a senior scientist at Hewlitt Packard itself. Dr. Egon Loebner is the manager of the company's advanced computer languages laboratory and a short, heavyset man with dark quizzical eyebrows, long gray sideburns and a thick European accent. The scientist is also a survivor of five German concentration camps during World War II. From 1974 to 1976, he served as the United States counsel for scientific and technological affairs in the American embassy in Moscow.

"I think the major social problem of our time is understanding bureaucracy," he said during a long conversation in his house in Palo Alto, California. "Since I am one of the survivors of the Holocaust, I have kept asking myself that question because it was the bureaucracy that allowed these events to take place, just as Hannah Arendt and the Eichmann trial showed us. Was there—is there—something malfunctioning in bureaucracy, and what role will technology play in its future development?"

Dr. Loebner spoke with great intensity, leaning forward in his low chair, elbows resting on his knees, hands folded under his chin. The physicist, at sixty years old, pulsed with physical and intellectual energy.

"Do we throw away all the benefits that come with the large organizations of our society because they are potentially dangerous, or can technology offer some means to counteract the undesirable effects? Can technology provide a helpless individual with a way to escape from under the wheels of bureaucracy?" he asked, a quizzical smile lighting up his face.

"I am very impressed by the idea in the *Federalist Papers* that there is a proper size for a representative district. If the district is too small, you have a cabal. If the district is too large, the elected representative can't digest the information he needs to know about his constituents. Technology has made it very easy for one man to be heard by the many. But technology so far has done very little to help the many express their views to their representatives. We have a crude mechanism in opinion polls, but they only give you the answers to the questions you already know how to phrase. If you want new information about something you don't know about, opinion polls can't help."

Dr. Loebner turned from the everyday problem of governing to the more abstract question of the nature of information in the computer age. "There is a widely accepted theory that information can either be organized or disorganized. This theory, in my opinion, is incomplete. In this world there is order, disorder and anti-order. Sometimes life is organized and purposeful. Sometimes it is mixed up and confused. But there are times when some aspects of life are perverted and actually become destructive. We recognize this last possibility in people. But for some reason we don't want to even consider that machines, too, can be destructive."

Dr. Loebner illustrated his statement of principle with an example. "Let's say we have a self-organizing thing that is a truck, a very good truck that stays on the right side of the road and stops for stoplights. Now if the truck becomes disorganized, it drives off the road and smashes into the wall."

Fascinated with the analogy, I interrupted Dr. Loebner's train of thought with a question. "If the truck is properly organized, it delivers the goods. If the truck is disorganized, it drives off the road. If it is 'anti-organized' the truck starts aiming for people?"

"No," Dr. Loebner replied, "it's not that crude. If the wires are crossed so that the truck confuses left from right, it will do everything it is supposed to do but the truck is now driving on the wrong side of the road and can destroy anything that gets in the way. The more intelligent the truck, the more information it has, the more powerful it can be in both a helpful and a harmful way."

Another one of the nation's genuine computer geniuses who worries about where the computer is leading us is Dr. Joseph Weizenbaum, a professor of computer science at the Massachusetts Institute of Technology. His intense concern dates back to the mid-1960s when the scientist developed a language analysis program that enabled one to apparently converse with a computer. He called the program ELIZA because, just like the character in George Bernard Shaw's play *Pygmalion,* and in the later musical *My Fair Lady,* the program appeared to allow one to teach the computer to "speak" with increasing fluency.

For his first experiment, Weizenbaum gave ELIZA a script designed to allow it to parody a psychotherapist. "I am not happy today," the "patient" might type into the computer terminal. "Why are you not happy today?" the machine would reply. Or perhaps the patient would make a comment about his mother and father. This would trigger the machine to reply with the vague, but acceptable, response, "Tell me more about your family."

The reaction to ELIZA was astounding. A number of working psychiatrists, for example, suggested the program be fully developed so that all Americans could have access to low-cost automated psychotherapy. At a more personal level, Weizenbaum later reported, he entered his office one day and found his secretary engaged in a "conversation" with the machine even though she "surely knew it to be merely a computer program. After only a few exchanges with it, she asked me to leave the room."

Weizenbaum was deeply disturbed by these reactions. To him, they suggested that many in society were unable to make the appropriate distinction between a machine and a human being. One of the first products of his concern was a book with the title *Computer Power and Human Reason: From Judgment to Calculation.* As he acknowledged in the introduction to this passionate appeal for caution in the swift and pervasive spread of the computer, the second part of his title was drawn from some comments by Hannah Arendt. She was speaking about Vietnam, the Pentagon and the computerized decision-making technique brought to Washington by Robert S.

McNamara. "They were eager to find formulas, preferably expressed in a pseudo-mathematical language, that would unify the most disparate phenomena with which reality presented them; that is, they were eager to discover laws by which to explain and predict political and historical facts as though they were as necessary, and thus reliable, as the physicist once believed natural phenomena to be. . . . [They] did not judge, they calculated. . . . An utterly irrational confidence in the calculability of reality [became] the leitmotif of decision-making."

Weizenbaum's criticism, articulated in his book and in a large number of subsequent research papers and articles, is complex. First, he argues, even highly educated people are prepared to grant the computer far more power than it actually possesses. The technology, he contends, is inherently limited in its ability to decide the important issues of humanity. Society requires more than calculation, it requires intuition and wisdom. The task of assuring that computers are not used for the wrong purposes, however, is extremely difficult because so few people understand the limitations. "The real contest is between those who think it can do everything and those who think there should be limits on what it ought to do," Weizenbaum writes. In his view, the use of computers to undertake psychotherapy or to engage in any interaction requiring respect, understanding or love is immoral.

While arguing that computers are in many ways less powerful than most people think, Weizenbaum nevertheless contends they exert a powerful influence on the direction and form of our civilization. Tools, for example, shape man's imagination. "A computing system that permits the asking of only certain kinds of questions, that accepts only certain kinds of 'data,' that cannot even in principle be understood by those who rely on it, such a computing system has effectively closed many doors that were open before it was installed," Weizenbaum said. Abraham Maslow made the same point: "When the only tool you have is a hammer, everything begins to look like a nail."

At a private conference of computer experts in the desert of southern Colorado in the summer of 1981, Weizenbaum restated his profound concern. "One of the great dangers of the computer is its impact on the metaphoric way we think about ourselves. Just a few minutes ago in this room I heard someone talk about people being programmed. This shows the pervasiveness and perversity of the computer as a metaphor. It suggests that society is beginning to think of human beings as merely another species of the genus information processing system. Which is in fact what many of my colleagues at MIT believe," he said.

"The technological elite at Stanford and Carnegie Mellon and MIT are deadly serious about this metaphor. But remember well that what happened in Nazi Germany was preceded by a period when the Germans talked about people as insects. It's going to take something like us thinking about ourselves as nothing but computers, it's going to take something like that, to make the nuclear holocaust possible."

Weizenbaum's words are apocalyptic. But his vision of a world in which the arbitrary rules of large computer systems diminish the significance of the individual is hardly surprising to anyone who has done battle with an automated credit card company or mail-order house or city tax agency over an improperly recorded item.

Often these battles with computerized bureaucracies are merely demeaning. Sometimes, however, they are genuinely abusive. Leonard Smith, for example, was a retired postal inspector. One May night in 1977 he was picked up outside his home on charges of public drunkenness. Two days later he pleaded not guilty and the judge ordered his release on his own recognizance.

But the jailers did not let Leonard Smith go. The computerized wants and warrant system had come up with another Leonard Smith who was wanted for violating his probation twenty-seven years earlier, in 1950. The retired postal inspector insisted he was not the same man. He was six feet tall, had hazel eyes and weighed 205 pounds. The man they were looking for was five feet nine inches tall, had blue eyes and weighed 137 pounds.

The warrant was so old, in fact, that the judge who had signed it was dead and the courthouse where he sat had been demolished. Six days after Leonard Smith had been ordered freed on the original charge of public drunkenness, the confusion over his identity was cleared up and he finally was released. One footnote: the warrant for which he had been incorrectly held was for a Leonard Smith who was on probation for bouncing a ten-dollar check.

The reason Leonard Smith was held is not hard to understand once the rules of the computerized wants and warrant system are explained. Under these rules, each item of identification like a person's name, social security number or color is given a different numerical value. If the authorities have about 60 percent of possible points of the various identifiers, they are authorized to detain a person.

Mr. Smith's case is not unusual. In fact, he was one of the thousands of Los Angeles citizens who were mistakenly taken into custody each year because of a faulty computerized warrant system by thirty separate law-enforcement agencies in Los Angeles. Because the Automated Wants and Warrants System was allowed to continue operating under the same identification rules for the last decade, the Los Angeles Center for Law in the Public Interest estimates that tens of thousands of wholly innocent persons have been improperly detained for various lengths of time since the computerized system was established.

The arrest of Mr. Smith is a graphic example supporting the contention that the industrial nations of the world have become enmeshed in a complicated political and technical process that is transforming them into increasingly powerful but relatively benign police states. One of the first to advance this theory was Jacques Ellul, a French sociologist and World War II resistance leader who was mentioned briefly in the first chapter. Ellul believed that the driving force behind the transformation of the modern world is a process he called technique. He defined technique as the continuous search for greater efficiency and increased productivity. Technique, he said in his book *The Technological Society,* initially was a force limited to the use of machines. But as machines deepened their hold on all aspects of our lives during the last 200 years, so did technique. "Modern men are so enthusiastic about technique, so assured of its superiority, so immersed in the technical milieu, that without exception they are oriented toward technical progress," he wrote.

"There is an automatic growth—that is, growth which is not calculated, desired or chosen—of everything which concerns technique. This applies even to men. Statistically, the number of scientists and technicians has doubled every decade for a century and a half.

Apparently this is a self-generating process; technique engenders itself."

Ellul believes that technique has become an overwhelming force in all industrial societies, regardless of political orientation, and has come to influence such professional disciplines as economic planning, medicine and teaching and the operation of all private and public organizations, including the police. Some analysts, Ellul notes, argue that the police will only utilize the processes of technique against the criminal classes.

> But there is an error of perspective here. The instrument tends to be applied anywhere it can be applied. It functions without discrimination because it exists without discrimination.
>
> The techniques of the police, which are developing at an extremely rapid tempo, have as their necessary end the transformation of the whole nation into a concentration camp. This is no perverse decision on the part of some party or government. To be sure of apprehending the criminal, it is necessary that everyone be supervised. This does not imply a reign of terror or of arbitrary arrests. The best technique is one which makes itself felt the least and which represents the least burden. But every citizen must be thoroughly known to the police and must live under conditions of discreet surveillance. All this results from the perfection of technical methods.

Ellul made his predictions more than a quarter of a century ago, just before the industrial world began its incredibly dizzying leap into computerization. The distance covered by the new technology and its use by government and industry since Ellul wrote his book is almost impossible to comprehend. Christopher Evans, a British psychologist and computer scientist, offered one dramatic analogy, a metaphorical yardstick, in a book he completed just before his death in 1979. Assume for a moment, he wrote in *The Micro Millennium,* that during that thirty years from 1945 to 1975 the automobile had developed as fast as the computer. How much would the 1975 automobile cost, how much power would it have and how many miles per gallon would be listed on the Environmental Protection Agency sticker? Evans' answer: the local Rolls-Royce dealer would be selling one of the world's most luxurious cars for $2.75, it would develop enough power to push the *Queen Elizabeth II* across the Atlantic, and it would get three million miles for every gallon of gas.

The enormous increase in the efficiency of computers illustrated by Evans' analogy has been an important factor in the decision of public and private organizations in every walk of American life to harness the power of the computer to achieve their separate goals.

Other forces also were shaping the organizational view of the world. John Kennedy traveled to Dallas. Martin Luther King, Jr., was shot and the black urban poor of Newark and Watts and Washington, D.C., vented their rage in a wave of looting and arson. College students and some of their parents, opponents of the war in Vietnam, marched across the Kent State campus and the approaches to the Pentagon. Year after year the police recorded more and more Americans murdered in the bedrooms of their homes and the streets of their cities. Terrorists killed Olympic athletes in Munich and businessmen in Italy and seized airplanes all over the world. Within a period of just a few months, President Reagan and Pope John Paul II were shot and seriously wounded and Anwar Sadat of Egypt was assassinated.

We now live in a world in which the twin forces of chaos and uncertainty strike our psyches with increasing persistence, an age in which the possibility of nuclear devastation has become deeply embedded in our souls, a time when the traditional pillars of religion have ceased to offer meaningful support to many Americans. Confronted by formidable challenges, struck by a loss of faith in the spiritual and ethical signposts that guided our fathers, we cast about for new pathways and new pathfinders.

For the first half of the twentieth century, the prophets we turned to as best expressing the high hopes of our civilization frequently were scientists seeking to understand the most profound secrets of the human body, the universe and life itself: Pierre and Marie Curie, Sigmund Freud, Thomas Edison, Albert Einstein and Albert Schweitzer. Since the end of World War II and the beginning of the space age, however, we appear to have turned in a different direction and the character of our prophets has undergone a subtle metamorphosis. A pioneer such as Einstein, whom the public perceived as a lonely voyager single-handedly tacking through the high abstractions of time and space, no longer catches the public fancy.

Instead, we have begun to look to multidisciplinary teams of experts, with names like the Rand Corporation, Mitre and the General Planning Corporation, for our answers. Citing the supposedly rigorous catechisms of "cost benefit analysis," "games theory," "planning-programming-budgeting systems" and "modeling," these latest prophets use the computer as a space-age divining rod to advise our leaders on when to make war, how to operate the public schools and whom to drop from the welfare rolls.

The words, the thought processes and the social perspectives of these prophets have permeated almost every aspect of American life. Rashi Fein, a professor of economics at the Harvard Medical School, for example, has written about their pernicious impact on the delicate relationship between the physician and the patient.

"Some years ago a physician friend told me that he had a James Barrie concept of what was causing the loss of humaneness or humanity in medicine. In his view, whenever a physician or nurse was called a 'provider' and whenever a patient was called a 'consumer,' one more angel died. When all the angels were dead, we would be left with a totally dehumanized medical-care system," Fein wrote in *The New England Journal of Medicine.*

"In speaking the new language, doctors have adopted the attitudes and methodology of economics—a narrow economics that emphasizes efficiency more than equity. Thus, because of the manner in which we finance health care in the United States, an increasing number of hospitals have formed 'marketing committees.' An unfilled bed, after all, translates into a loss of revenue, and we all know what that would do to the 'bottom line.' Today, 'marketing committees' and 'bottom lines'; tomorrow 'sales' and 'customers.' The angels are dying and fewer and fewer of us notice or care."

One of those who does care is Ida Hoos, a research sociologist at the University of California at Berkeley and the widow of Sidney Hoos, who before his death was the dean of academic personnel at Berkeley. In August of 1979, Sidney Hoos entered a large, widely admired hospital near San Francisco. Hoos had developed an extremely high temperature which his doctors could not explain. Mrs. Hoos was worried about the condition of her husband. She also was concerned about the care he was receiving from the nursing staff.

"After my husband had been in the hospital for a few days," she said, "I realized to my horror that he was being cared for by a new set of nurses every day. That's strange, I thought, where are those nice people we saw yesterday? I then made an inquiry and discovered the administrators had done a computerized cost-benefit study which concluded it was not 'cost effective' for the hospital to maintain a permanent nursing staff. Instead, they had a skeleton force of supervisors and then, depending upon what they called the 'current inventory of patients,' they would order in the required numbers of nurses from the registry. So there were new nurses every day who would spend half the morning tracking down the ladies' room and the other half locating the coffee machine. The nursing care that my husband received because of this decision was definitely inferior."

Several weeks later the doctors in the hospital determined that Sidney Hoos had bacterial pneumonia, antibiotics were prescribed that finally brought down his fever, and he was sent home. Shortly thereafter, on September 20, 1979, he died of a massive stroke.

"I know his death was not directly related to his stay in that hospital," Mrs. Hoos said a year later. "But he did get poor care there. The administrator said that calling the nurses of the registry was 'cost effective' because it saved the hospital money. But is the hospital there to save money or serve the patients? And when the hospital did the cost-benefit study, what value did they place on human life?"

Despite many years in California, her voice rang with the rich New England twang of her hometown, Skowhegan, Maine. Curiously enough, the questions raised by the poor care received by her husband are the questions she has been thinking and writing about during much of her academic career.

"Systems analysis is really the marriage of engineering and economics, two very highly favored disciplines in our world," Mrs. Hoos said as we sat in her living room in Berkeley. "But anyone who knows anything about these fields knows that economics is not a hard science. And as I have said about engineers before, they are often wrong but seldom in doubt!

"There is something procrustean about the systems engineers. They deny history, they deny reality, they deny many of the dimensions of any given problem because the only dimensions they can handle are those they can place a numerical value on. A perfect example of their failure is what happened during the revolution in Iran and what has gone on after. We could go in there with our fine machines, we could give the Shah all those modern tools, the airplanes, the computers, but history was waiting in the wings. The computers were smashed, the airplanes were burned."

In the United States, Mrs. Hoos said, the systems engineers have a special place because our society is surrounded by so many machines it cannot comprehend. "The experts, a wise man said a few years ago, have great power because in an uncertain world we all yearn for the 'grown-ups who know.' Just as primitive man turned to shamans, soothsayers, and sibyls, we have our own brand of wizards, the methodological Merlins who can conjure up certainty out of ever-growing uncertainty."

Is the computer the engine of systems analysis? "Yes," Mrs. Hoos replied. "The computer has encouraged us to think like machines instead of like people. As in Iran, you lop off history and all the other things you cannot count. It's the things you lop off that fester and lie in the dust and ultimately cause the problems. The way we handle crime, education and welfare in this country all offer terrifying examples."

In her book *Systems Analysis in Public Policy: A Critique,* Mrs. Hoos explores how the methodology was fostered within the military, faltered in its promise to take politics out of the Pentagon and then was applied to welfare programs, schools, public health questions and other social issues. "What must be questioned now, as in the earlier discussion of systems analysis in the military, are the particular methods, the assumptions on which they are based, the aura of precision surrounding them and the consequences of reliance on them," she wrote.

Despite all claims to the contrary, Mrs. Hoos contends that discriminatory political judgments are hidden within all systems analysis procedures. But because of the scientific mumbo jumbo, identifying these camouflaged assumptions frequently is difficult. "Experience may teach us that social planning needs to be recognized openly as a primitive, experimental art, its resources too limited to be dissipated or squandered in pursuit of mechanistic devices that add weight but shed little light."

On the basis of her studies and her experience, Ida Hoos aims her barbs at how the systems analysts, armed with the theoretically neutral numbers generated by the theoretically neutral computerized information systems, have made highly political decisions about the management of major social programs. Who gets what kind of education? Who is eligible for what kinds of government welfare and how will it be dispensed? What kind of nursing care will be provided a seriously ill patient by a hospital? The information-collection procedures made possible by the computer, however, have influenced more than the administrative decisions of these various powerful social institutions; they have also substantially undermined an important part of the personal code of ethics sworn to by all physicians.

Hippocrates devised the physician's oath almost 2,500 years ago. In it, the young healer makes a number of promises. "The regimen I adopt will be for the benefits of my patients according to my ability and judgment and not for their hurt or wrong." Computerized tools like the CAT scan and the data-processing techniques of the modern epidemiologists have helped physicians uphold this part of their oath.

In a second part of the oath, however, the doctor vows that "whatever things I see or hear concerning the life of men, in my attendance on the sick or even apart therefrom, which ought not be noised abroad, I will keep silence thereon, counting such things to be as sacred secrets." Here the computerized record-keeping that characterizes modern medicine has led physicians, willingly or unwillingly, to break their ancient vow of confidentiality. Indeed, the growing public recognition that doctors keep some treatments secret may lead patients to withhold information essential to treating their individual ills or to protecting society against epidemics.

Robert M. Gellman is a member of the staff of the House Subcommittee on Government Information and Individual Rights and an expert on the practices and ethics of the use of medical records. In an unpublished analysis of the conflicting pressures of practicing medicine in the information age, he discussed the tension that has developed between the tradition that a doctor will not disclose the secrets of his patients and the demands of computerized health institutions that are heavily subsidized by tax dollars.

Even before the mass collection of information by government agencies, insurance companies, schools, social workers and the police, the ethical questions confronting physicians could be troublesome.

"Does the physician," Gellman asked, "have an obligation to inform a patient suspected of suffering from a venereal disease that the patient's identity and diagnosis will be disclosed to a public health agency? A consequence of so informing a patient is that the patient may not seek treatment, may refuse treatment, or may accept treatment only on the condition that the physician agree to violate the law and not report the disease. All of these results could have undesirable effects on the patient, the physician and society at large."

Gellman added that "it always has been true that a patient could be embarrassed by the disclosure of information about his medical condition. However, society's increasing interest in information and its ever-expanding ability to manipulate data can magnify the consequences of disclosure."

Dr. Marcia Goin, speaking for the American Psychiatric Association, outlined the particular effects when information about an individual's mental state gets passed around among government agencies and private health organizations. "It can lead to social embarrassment, strained or broken ties with family, friends or coworkers, career and economic damage or refusal of admission to graduate school," she told a House Ways and Means subcommittee.

But the consequences of the slow erosion of the individual citizen's belief that personal information will be protected by the physicians do not end there. Because of the widespread fear of such leakage, for example, the National Institute of Mental Health believes that about 15 percent of all Americans who have medical insurance and are undergoing therapy pay for the therapy out of their own pocket.

The institute cannot even estimate the number of people who forgo therapy completely because they are unable to afford it and are afraid to apply for insurance benefits that might lead to the disclosure of their most private secrets to the insurance company, their employer or others.

Some argue the worry about confidentiality is absurd. Mark Siegler, a physician associated with the Pritzker School of Medicine, the University of Chicago, recently did an analysis of the persons who had access to one of his patient's records. Not even considering the insurance and government officials who ultimately might be able to examine documents concerning the patient, Dr. Siegler said he was amazed to discover that at least twenty-five and perhaps as many as a hundred health professionals and administrative officials "at our university hospital had access to the patient's record and that all of them had a legitimate need, indeed, a professional responsibility, to open and use the chart."

Also writing in *The New England Journal of Medicine,* Dr. Siegler said that the "principle of medical confidentiality described in medical codes of ethics and still believed in by patients no longer exists. In this respect, it is a decrepit concept. Rather than perpetuate the myth of confidentiality and invest energy vainly to preserve it, the public and the profession would be better served if they devoted their attention to determining which aspects of the original principle of confidentiality are worth retaining."

Has the computer given modern medicine more than it has taken away? It may be impossible to answer this question. But during the last two decades, computers have assisted the medical profession in many significant ways. Epidemiology, for example, could hardly exist today without the computer's ability to handle huge amounts of information. Epidemiology is the discipline of charting the frequency and distribution of diseases and other effects in hopes of discovering their causes. It is responsible for such achievements as identifying cigarettes as a principal cause of the worldwide epidemic of lung cancer and several other diseases.

There are other fields, of course, where computers ultimately may prove to be a mixed blessing. My profession, journalism, is one of them. Daily newspapers are imperfect instruments. Even the best of them are biased transmitters of usually incomplete and often inaccurate information. Despite their acknowledged flaws, however, many papers offer their separate communities an important service. With widely ranging levels of success, the editors and reporters attempt to give their readers a daily summary of events that somehow may affect their individual lives. What happened in El Salvador or China or Israel? What happened in Washington? What happened at City Hall? What happened in Hollywood or on Wall Street or Broadway?

The daily newspaper has been a significant mechanism in the operation of American society for at least two hundred years. With all its flaws, the newspaper attempts to present a unified collection of information about a variety of events that an informed citizen should consider as she or he votes, works, argues with friends, brings up children, demonstrates for and against various public policies and goes about all the other chores of life.

The two-way interactive television systems that currently are being installed in cities all over the United States may mean the end of the daily newspaper as we know it. Several of the large news companies, such as the Los Angeles Times, Knight-Ridder and the Washington Post, currently are experimenting with electronic "newspapers" where the individual subscriber uses a computer terminal to select from a vast menu the "articles" he wishes to have transmitted to his home.

Because the subscriber most likely will pay a small fee for each article he orders, the sports buff will be tempted to request only articles from the sports pages, the businessman only stories from the business section and the elderly only the obituaries of their friends. The print newspaper, characterized by its variety—the sports nut may accidentally get interested in a foreign story, the businessman might start reading about the development of a cultural center—could become obsolete and disappear. In this way the computerized newspaper gradually may come to narrow rather than broaden the knowledge and interests of the American people.

A second aspect of the electronic newspaper is worth noting. Because readers probably will pay for each article they order from the computer, a central record may be kept of precisely which articles are being sent to each subscriber. Thus an aggressive investigator may someday be able to determine both who is getting the news and precisely which articles, columns and editorials are being read.

Thus could the electronic newspaper gradually undermine representative government by reducing the information shared by literate Americans and increasing the ability of an investigator to determine the reading habits of the target. William Fulbright, the thoughtful former chairman of the Senate Foreign Relations Committee, is worried about another computer-based development he fears is already weakening the democratic process.

In a long interview published in the *Washington Post* in 1982, Mr. Fulbright expressed admiration for two senators who had lost their bid for reelection because they had taken positions that the opinion polls indicated were not supported by a majority of voters. "In other words," the seventy-seven-year-old former senator said, "they didn't follow the polls completely. One of the most discouraging things in the news—little things—I saw recently was that the White House had taken on a third pollster. If there's anything inimical to the exercise of good judgment, it's a pollster. That means you might as well have a computer as your leader. It means they're not even thinking about what ought to be done. They're only trying to find out what a majority says. And this popularity of poll-taking strikes me as inimical to good government."

But there are some who believe the computer is striking at an even more fundamental target than the process of representative government, that it is damaging the development of the individual human psyche. W. Lambert Gardiner is a large, ruddy-faced Scotsman, a Cornell University-trained psychologist who now lives and works in Montreal. Gardiner contends that the real threat from the proliferation of personal data banks is not so much the invasion of privacy but the gradual loss of personal autonomy, which Webster defines as "a quality of self-directing freedom, especially relating to moral independence."

"Privacy" is a relative term that varies from individual to individual and from society to society. But autonomy, Gardiner said during a Washington conference, is a universal phenomenon essential for growth. Studies of the development of animal life and the growth of humans from infants to adults suggest that these processes can be viewed as "the progressive emancipation from the tyranny of the environment, or, alternately, the acquisition of autonomy. The realization of human potential can therefore be well described as the acquisition of autonomy."

The psychologist further argued that the most important aspect of autonomy is controlling one's concept of oneself, and that the personal data banks of the modern computerized society are gradually undermining this ability. "Personal data banks make us all famous. That is, anyone who wishes to do so and has access to the personal data bank can know us even though we do not know them."

The key issue then, Gardiner continued, "is not privacy, since that is a personal choice, but autonomy, the extent to which personal choice is possible."

It is a long way from Admiral Morer's attempt to justify the lies about the U.S. bombing of Cambodia to Gardiner's speculation about the erosion of personal autonomy. Both, however, were talking about a new form of slavery that the computer can impose upon man. While some people may dismiss these concerns as extreme, others worry that Morer and Gardiner may be speaking a general truth. "In America and other advanced cultures, belief in technology has become a religious faith," Professor Mary Ellen Clark of San Diego State University contends. "We have come to think of ourselves as so technologically clever that we will be flexible enough to get through any crisis. But in many ways we have become so dependent on technology that we have lost our adaptability."

Charles Zracket, the executive vice-president of the Mitre Corporation, a private nonprofit organization that does analytic studies for the government, is sufficiently concerned about the growing role of machines that he seriously evoked the analogy of slavery during a long evening's conversation about computers at a kitchen table in Georgetown.

"The metabolic functions of society are being taken over by machines," he said. "There just doesn't seem to be any way the computerization of society will be stopped. But there are choices in how we respond to this apparently inevitable tide. We can build a society like that of classical Greece, where the slaves—in our case the computers —allow us to focus our thinking on philosophy, art and literature. Or we can build an Orwellian state, where we become dependent upon technology and the people who run it. A great deal is at stake in this choice, and we have to be very careful."

The
Rule of Law

Law may be defined as the ethical control applied
to communication.

—Norbert Wiener

During the last decade, under the mandate of a state law, physicians
and dentists in New York have submitted copies of more than seven
million separate drug prescriptions to the Bureau of Controlled Substances Licensing in Albany. The prescriptions of course include the
names of both the doctors and the patients.

Once the forms have been received by the bureau, the information
on them is typed into a computer and, with some restrictions, made
available to federal, state and local law-enforcement agencies responsible for preventing the illegal use of what are called Category II
drugs.

Shortly after the New York legislature approved the law authorizing the state to collect all the prescriptions written for a class of drugs
given to persons suffering from postoperative pain, migraine head-
aches, cancer and schizophrenia but also subject to considerable
abuse, a group of patients and doctors challenged the statute in
federal court. The program, they said in suits filed in 1973 and 1974,
violated the privacy of the individual patient. The challengers further
noted that in the first twenty months of the operation of the law, the
computerized files of hundreds of thousands of drug prescriptions
had proven useful in the investigation of only one case. The danger
of improper disclosures and the indirect pressures on patients and

doctors not to undertake the drug therapies that had to be reported to the state under the new law had not been balanced by the potential benefits to law enforcement.

The three-judge federal panel hearing the case agreed. "The diminution of constitutionally guaranteed freedom is too great a price to pay for such a small government yield," they ruled, enjoining the state from continuing that part of the overall program involving the collection of the names of individual patients.

As later argued by the lawyers for the patients and doctors, the ruling of the special panel was quite limited. It did not reject the right of the state to license the manufacture and distribution of the Category II drugs. It did not throw out the state's classification of these drugs. It did not question the requirement that physicians and pharmacists prescribing these drugs keep copies of their records for five years.

"The opinion leaves the state free to have the most thorough and intense regulation of drugs imaginable, including the use of codes, numbers, doctor reporting and so forth, as long as the state refrains from collecting and computerizing the names of all patients receiving Category II drugs," the lawyers contended.

On an appeal by New York State, however, the U.S. Supreme Court rejected the ruling restricting the state's right to collect individual names. "We hold that neither the immediate nor threatened impact of the patient identification requirements in the New York State Controlled Substances Act of 1972 on either the reputation or independence of patients for whom Category II drugs are medically indicated is sufficient to constitute any invasion of any right or liberty protected by the Fourteenth Amendment," a unanimous Supreme Court found. The Fourteenth Amendment provides that states cannot enforce laws that conflict with the privileges guaranteed by the Constitution and its Bill of Rights.

The Supreme Court's decision in the New York case is one tiny part of a broad and vastly intricate web of corporate policy, institutional rules, government regulations, laws, judicial findings and constitutional principles that together govern the flow of information in the United States. These thousands of regulations and laws and findings determine who is authorized to collect information, under what conditions the information may be collected, who may disseminate information and under what situations it can be disseminated.

Because information is one of the essential wellsprings of power, the shape of these rules and laws and judicial findings is a major factor in determining who controls society. The question that demands examination is whether—despite the protections embodied in the Constitution—the Congress, the courts, the federal government and the corporations are gradually adopting new rules and reinterpreting old ones in ways that enhance the power of large institutions by enlarging their authority to control information.

The collective force of these apparent shifts in the rules of information appears to be multiplied by economic factors. For it is the large organizations who are steadily gaining greater authority to collect, control and disseminate information that already have the capital and expertise necessary to purchase the computers and communication networks they need to put the information to use.

The combined effect of these two developments, one legal and the other economic, is the creation of organizations with unprecedented power. The Supreme Court's 1977 opinion endorsing the right of New York State to put the names of millions of persons receiving properly prescribed drugs in a large government computer is an example of the direct marriage of these two developments: the state legislature and the Supreme Court authorizing a massive data collection program, the computer enabling the program to be carried out. But almost any decision or law or regulation that widens the authority of the established organizations of our society to collect and distribute information has the same effect because data-hungry bureaucracies like the CIA, AT&T, the IRS, TRW and the FBI are so heavily computerized.

A legal analysis of the New York case by the U.S. Privacy Protection Study Commission noted that the Supreme Court has shown little sympathy to the arguments that some government reporting requirements raise the same kinds of constitutional questions that lawyers have posed when the government was discovered to have improperly searched a house, seized papers or tapped a telephone in its pursuit of information.

In the constitutional sense, the commission report argued, the

Supreme Court has limited the compelled reporting to the government by the citizens of the United States "only to the extent that the reporting violates a narrow interpretation of Fifth Amendment protections against self-incrimination or the information sought is patently irrelevant to the proper activities of government."

The Court's decisions, the commission said, reflect "its unwillingness to recognize the legal interest of an individual in records about himself held by a third party and its inaccurate understanding of how reported information may be used by the government."

Another important case that reveals the Supreme Court's thinking about an individual's right to control a personal record held by a third party is *United States* vs. *Miller*. In this case, which was decided in 1976, a U.S. attorney had subpoenaed from a bank the financial records of one of its customers who was a suspect in a criminal investigation. The subpoena was challenged by the customer on the grounds that the bank records belonged to him and had been improperly seized.

The Supreme Court ruled that the customer's bank records were not owned by the customer but by the bank. The customer was therefore not entitled to a notice of the subpoena or an opportunity to challenge the subpoena in court. The Supreme Court reached this conclusion despite the highly personal nature of information disclosed by a checking account and despite the expectation of most Americans that information they provide a bank will not be disclosed to anyone.

A third Supreme Court decision affecting the authority of large organizations to collect information concerns a briefcase-sized device, now computerized, that is known as the pen register. For many years law-enforcement officials have secretly attached a pen register to the line leading to a telephone of special interest when they wanted to record the numbers dialed from it, the time each call was made and the number of minutes required for each call. In recent years, the telephone company has begun to install computerized equipment at local switchboards all over the United States that can accomplish the same task without the bother of attaching the pen register to a specific telephone.

Some of the social implications of the transactional information collected by such equipment are discussed in the chapter on data bases. Information about the numbers dialed from a particular phone, for example, can reveal a good deal about the friends, associates and living habits of the telephone's owner. What is discussed here, however, are the legal rules that have developed to govern the use of the equipment by law-enforcement agencies.

The particular situation that led to the Supreme Court's consideration of the pen register began in the spring of 1976 when the Federal Bureau of Investigation made a routine request to the New York Telephone Company to attach pen registers to the two telephones of a gambler named T. Hamilton who allegedly was conducting his business from an office at 220 East 14th Street in Manhattan. The bureau agents also wanted to run a telephone line from the pen register attached to the gambler's telephone to their office so they could record the numbers dialed without having to travel to the Lower East Side.

Although AT&T claims it has never kept track of how many times it has agreed to install a pen register for local, state and federal law-enforcement officials, it seems certain that over the years the number of such installations is enormous. In 1976, however, AT&T apparently became concerned about the growing use of this investigative technique that would be possible when the new computerized switchboards were in place all over the country. The company decided the time had come to try to reduce the occasions when law enforcement sought such information. AT&T's strategy was to attempt to persuade the federal courts to increase the hurdles the police would have to overcome before they could legally obtain information about the day-to-day telephone use of its customers.

On March 30, 1976, telephone company lawyers filed papers asking the federal court in Manhattan to vacate or modify the warrant the FBI had obtained authorizing the company to install the pen registers on T. Hamilton's phones.

The dispute centered on whether the FBI—when it places a pen register on the telephone of a suspect—should be required to meet the very substantial restrictions required for wiretaps and bugs under the Omnibus Crime Control and Safe Streets Act of 1968. The telephone company, worried about the potential for abuse in its new computers, said it should. The Justice Department and the FBI contended that law enforcement should go on hooking up pen registers on the basis of the far looser restrictions required for a simple search warrant.

Under the Safe Streets Act, for example, an FBI wiretap must be approved in writing by the attorney general, authorized by a federal judge, and eventually reported in summary form to the public and in specific form to the person who is the target of the wiretap. The Safe Streets Act also authorizes wiretaps against people suspected of committing certain specific serious crimes.

To get a warrant for a pen register, however, the FBI need not get the approval of the attorney general. Nor is it limited to using the device just on those suspected of committing serious crimes.

The dispute between the telephone company and the Justice Department went to the Court of Appeals for the Second Circuit. There the order requiring the company to install the pen register for the FBI was reversed.

"We were told by counsel for the Telephone Company on the oral argument that a principal basis for opposition of the telephone company to an order compelling it to give technical aid and assistance is the danger of indiscriminate invasions of privacy," the appeals court said. "In this best of all possible worlds it is a law of nature that one thing leads to another. It is better not to take the first step."

But the Supreme Court rejected these concerns. By a 5-to-4 vote, the Court ruled that local federal judges could continue to require the telephone company to install pen registers under the relatively relaxed standards required for a search warrant. The serious questions raised by the case were underlined by the unusually sharp dissent of the minority. The ruling, they said, represented the first step toward the accretion of arbitrary police powers and was no less dangerous and unprecedented "because the first step appears minimally intrusive."

Thus did AT&T fail in its efforts to increase the legal obstacles blocking the use of pen registers. More ominous, however, have been several recent appeals court decisions finding that it was not even necessary for law-enforcement officers to obtain a search warrant when they desired the telephone company to install a pen register.

At this time, however, the company-wide policy of AT&T is to require a warrant before it will install the surveillance equipment even though such warrants are not required by the courts.

Given the growth of records containing all kinds of personal information, the Supreme Court's decisions increasing or upholding the authority of the government to collect drug prescriptions, bank records and telephone data have great significance. So do some of its decisions concerning the official dissemination of information. Consider the case of *Paul* vs. *Davis.*

On June 14, 1971, Edward Charles Davis III was arrested for shoplifting in Louisville, Kentucky. He pleaded not guilty. Seven months later, the police distributed a five-page flyer to approximately four hundred merchants identifying Davis and a number of other individuals as "known shoplifters." Shortly thereafter, the case against Davis was dismissed.

Davis sued the police in federal court for violating his right to due process by publicly branding him a criminal without a trial. In an opinion written by Justice William Rehnquist, a divided Supreme Court held that the "weight of our decisions establishes no constitutional doctrine converting every defamation by a public official into a deprivation of liberty within the meaning of the Due Process clauses of the Fifth and Fourteenth Amendments."

Justice William Brennan disagreed. "The court holds today that police officials, acting in their official capacities as law enforcers, may on their own initiative and without trial constitutionally condemn innocent individuals as criminals and thereby brand them with one of the most stigmatizing and debilitating labels of our society. If there are no constitutional restraints on such oppressive behavior, the safeguards constitutionally accorded an accused in criminal trial are rendered a sham, and no individual can feel secure that he will not be singled out for similar ex parte punishment by those primarily charged with fair enforcement of the law."

In the Davis decision, the Supreme Court enhanced the power of the police by endorsing their authority to disseminate information: to inform the public at large about an individual who had been accused but had never been tried on charges of shoplifting. In a second case, involving a former CIA official named Frank Snepp, the

Supreme Court enhanced the power of the federal government by increasing its authority to curb the dissemination of information: in this case the right of government employees to speak and write about the government.

The Court's decision in the Snepp case focused on his book *Decent Interval,* which described the last days of the U.S. presence in Vietnam, Snepp's role in this bitter moment and his criticisms of the government's efforts to protect its Vietnamese allies.

The six-member majority held that Snepp had violated his fiduciary and contractual obligations to the government when he gave Random House, a New York publisher, the manuscript of his book before it had been passed on by the CIA's publication review board. The acknowledgment by the CIA that the book published without review contained no classified secrets was deemed irrelevant.

In the harsh language of the majority of the Supreme Court, Snepp "deliberately and surreptitiously violated his obligation to submit all material for prepublication review" and must now "disgorge the benefits of his faithlessness."

For Snepp, the decision was a serious financial blow. The $140,000 of royalties earned by his book at the time of the Court's decision was denied him. Instead, the royalties past and future were assigned to the U.S. government.

More important than Snepp's immediate financial problems, however, was the general impact of the decision. "The rule of law the Court announces today is not supported by statute, by the contract or by common law," the three-judge minority argued. "The Court seems unaware of the fact that its drastic new remedy has been fashioned to enforce a species of prior restraint on a citizen's right to criticize his government."

For the first time in the history of the United States, the Supreme Court had upheld censorship rules that required an author to submit for government review all writing, scripts or outlines of speeches— even works of fiction—that mentioned "any intelligence data or activities or contained information that might be based on classified information." No steps will be taken toward publication, defined as communicating information to one or more persons, "until written permission to do so is received from the publications review board," declares the CIA regulation that now has the formal blessing of the Supreme Court.

The CIA contends that the unique sensitivity of its activities makes the censorship rule essential to protect the United States against the hostile powers of the world. The Supreme Court's sweeping decision, however, appears to extend the restrictive force of the CIA regulation far beyond the works of Frank Snepp or even beyond the thousands of intelligence experts and operatives who are now or who have ever been employed by the CIA. The rule could be applied to anyone working in government.

The apparently broad reach of the Supreme Court decision stems from two factors. First, the Court seemed to hold that any government agency has the right to review the writing of an employee or former employee even in cases where there was no specific written agreement because of the relationship of trust that binds the person to his agency. Second, the Court's decision upholds the validity of parallel regulations of dozens of different agencies within the Justice Department, the Treasury Department and the Energy Department imposing various restrictions on the right of officials or former officials to speak their minds.

Employees of the Federal Bureau of Investigation, for example, sign a statement agreeing that "I will never divulge, publish, or reveal either by word or by conduct or by other means disclose to any unauthorized recipient without official written authorization by the Director of the FBI or his delegate, any information from an investigatory file of the FBI or any information or material acquired as part of my official duties or because of my official status." No objections can be raised to restricting the right of an individual FBI agent to divulge information from the FBI's investigatory files. But the bureau policy of prohibiting an agent from divulging "any information" acquired while working as an agent is a gag rule that could have been written by Orwell's Big Brother.

It can be argued that there may be occasions when the government must ignore the rules of the Constitution to handle a particular domestic or foreign threat. But the compelling need for government action evaporates once the crisis has passed. Consider the wisdom of Justice Robert Jackson expressed in his dissent to the Supreme Court decision upholding the government's decision to incarcerate the Japanese Americans living on the West Coast. "When a government official violates the Constitution," Justice Jackson wrote, "it is an incident." But when a court approves such an action, "that passing incident becomes the doctrine of the Constitution. There it has a generative power of its own, and all that it creates will be in its own image."

The original constitutional doctrine concerning the collection and dissemination of information was drafted by James Madison in 1779. The doctrine was stated in three of the first ten amendments to the Constitution, known as the Bill of Rights. From the very beginning, the Bill of Rights was a subject of controversy, dividing the federalists, who sought to establish a powerful central government, from the anti-federalists, who worried that such a government would limit the freedom of the individual citizen. The ten amendments, in fact, were something of an afterthought, winning the belated support of the federalists partly as a maneuver to head off demands by more radical politicians of the day for another constitutional convention.

Madison began the task of writing the amendments as a member of the House of Representatives of the First Congress. On June 8, 1779, he introduced the proposed amendments in the House. By late September of that year, Congress had completed action on the legislation and it was sent to President Washington for his signature and transmission to the states. A bit more than two years later, fifteen years after the colonies had adopted the Declaration of Independence and three years after they had approved the Constitution, the Bill of Rights was ratified by three quarters of the states and became this nation's fundamental pillar of individual freedom.

The three articles of the Bill of Rights that to this day are basic to communication law and regulation are the First, Fourth and Fifth Amendments. It is hard to imagine how James Madison, writing at the end of the eighteenth century and drawing on even earlier precedents of English law, was able to devise three principles that remain so essential on the edge of the twenty-first century. The question posed today is whether the pen, in this case a sharpened quill, is mightier than the high-speed typewriters, laser-powered distribution systems, gigantic data bases and electronic surveillance devices of our age.

Congress, the First Amendment declares, shall make no law respecting the establishment of religion, or abridging freedom of speech or freedom of the press or the right of people to assemble peaceably and petition the government for the redress of their grievances. With some very limited qualifications, one has the right to speak one's mind, to argue unpopular causes, to publish anything.

The Constitution's Fourth Amendment holds that the people's right to be secure in their persons, houses and papers against unreasonable search shall not be violated. Judges shall grant the police a search warrant only when the police state the reasons they believe a crime probably was or is about to be committed and describing the place to be searched, the persons to be seized or the things to be taken. One's house is a private place and may be invaded by the state only after the state has persuaded an independent third party—the judge—that the invasion is essential.

The Constitution's Fifth Amendment, the final article of the Bill of Rights directly related to information control, establishes several major principles of American law. All citizens are entitled to the range of procedural protections that reside within the simple phrase "due process." No person in a criminal case shall be compelled to "be a witness against himself."

Taken together, these three amendments to the Constitution have been a central force molding the shape of the information rules of the American society. A second major force has been the Congress. Sometimes this force is expressed by legislation that wins congressional approval. Sometimes the force is a negative one that is expressed by the vacuum created when Congress fails to confront a problem. Here are examples of both.

In the summer of 1982, Congress approved a bill making it a crime to identify American intelligence agents if the person disclosing the information had "reason to believe" that such an action would hurt the gathering of intelligence by the United States. As the law is written, reporters and others could be prosecuted even if the information about the intelligence agencies came from public records and even if the agent was breaking the law or violating a presidential directive. Those found guilty could be sentenced to up to three years in prison and a fine of $15,000. The law, actively supported by President Reagan, was overwhelmingly approved by Congress despite the First Amendment prohibition that Congress "shall make no law abridging the freedom of speech or of the press."

The new law also makes it a crime for anyone who currently or in the past had authorized access to the identities of U.S. agents to disclose them to anyone who was not authorized to know them.

But the federal government has also used old laws to increase its control of information. In 1875, Congress passed a statute making it a crime to steal government property. For almost a hundred years, this law, now Section 641 of the U.S. Criminal Code, was used to prosecute individuals who stole or received *tangible* government property, such as horses belonging to the cavalry or typewriters belonging to the Treasury Department or buckets of paint belonging to the General Services Administration. But in 1971 the Nixon administration dreamed up the idea of using the old law to prosecute someone on charges of stealing intangible property—in this case, information.

The first target was Daniel Ellsberg and the charge was that he had stolen the Pentagon Papers—the embarrassing Pentagon study of the failure of the Vietnam War—and made them available to the *New York Times*. The charges against Ellsberg, however, were dismissed before the jury had time to render its verdict. The dismissal was required after the Justice Department acknowledged that part of its case was based on an illegal search of the office of Ellsberg's psychiatrist by agents of the Nixon White House.

On January 31, 1978, the born-again property law was once more unleashed, this time by the administration of President Jimmy Carter. The targets were Ronald Humphrey and David Truong. Humphrey was a thin, balding, mid-level employee of the U.S. Information Agency. David Truong was a part-time graduate student, the son of a once-powerful South Vietnamese politician. The two men were charged with conspiring with each other to pass documents to representatives of the Communist government of Vietnam.

As is the Justice Department's custom, Humphrey and Truong

were not indicted on a single criminal charge, but with violating a long laundry list of different crimes. They were charged with espionage. They were charged with acting as agents of a foreign power without informing the secretary of state. They were charged with delivering material related to the national defense to unauthorized persons. Finally, and most significantly for our story, the two men were indicted under the hundred-year-old law originally passed by Congress to deal with horse thieves.

During a long trial in the white-paneled second-floor courtroom of District Judge Albert V. Bryan, Jr., in Alexandria, Virginia, the prosecutors showed that Humphrey had given Truong copies of several hundred State Department messages. Most of the documents were unclassified. A few were not. When experts from the State Department and the Central Intelligence Agency first examined the purloined material, they said it was inconsequential. When the government decided to prosecute, however, the experts changed their testimony and said the material was significant.

In his summation at the end of the trial, Judge Bryan explained the legal definitions of each of the separate charges that had been brought against the two men. The judge further said that he agreed with the legal theory of the prosecutors that the defendants should be convicted of stealing *property* if the jury determined that *information* had been taken from the government. It did not have to be tangible documents, he explained, or even Xerox copies of documents. It did not have to involve classified government secrets affecting the security of the nation—just simple information.

The jury found Humphrey and Truong guilty and Judge Bryan sentenced the two men to fifteen years each in federal prison. This conviction, including the use of the property theft law to control the distribution of information, was upheld by the U.S. Court of Appeals sitting in Richmond, Virginia. One member of the three-judge court, however, recognized the dangers of the decision of the Nixon and Carter administrations to apply the old law to the intangible concept of information.

The ambiguity of the law, he wrote, "is particularly disturbing because government information forms the basis of much of the discussion of public issues and, as a result, the unclear language of the statute threatens to impinge upon the rights protected by the First Amendment." This new application of the law, he added, "could pose a serious threat to public debate of national issues."

Judges tend to choose their words with care. Certainly in this case the judicial commentary was unusually temperate. This is because the Humphrey-Truong conviction has given the federal government a powerful new weapon to control information, the equivalent of Great Britain's Official Secrets Act. Under both the modern interpretation of the old U.S. law and the Official Secrets Act, the government can prosecute government officials who give any kind of information to an outsider. Just as significantly, however, both laws also allow the respective governments to prosecute the recipient of the information. In the case of Britain, this was an explicit decision of parliament. In the case of the United States, the authority lies in the old law's language that permits the prosecution of the receiver of stolen government property as well as the person who steals it.

Even though it was the Carter administration that won the convictions in which Section 641 was broadened to include information, Attorney General Griffin Bell was sufficiently concerned about the potential for abuse that he issued a statement advising federal prosecutors across the United States that they should not use the law to indict "whistle blowers" who disclose information obtained from an agency in a lawful manner or reporters who publish it. As we shall see, however, advisory memos from one administration can be easily rescinded by another.

The cases where Congress passed laws that increased the powers of organization to control information in potentially harmful ways or where laws have been bent to achieve the same dubious goal are easy to spot. The occasions when national information policy has been shaped by the failure to act are less obvious.

On April 4, 1979, the House Subcommittee on Government Information and Individual Rights began a lengthy series of hearings on a proposed bill to protect the privacy of medical records held by such institutions as hospitals and nursing homes. The legislation was the outgrowth of recommendations by the Privacy Protection Commission and more than a year of study by the Carter administration. The supporters of the bill argued that a number of changes in American medical practice and general law made it essential for Congress to act.

Because of the major expansion in the government role in medicine, the relationships between patients, physicians, hospitals and other institutions had undergone a profound restructuring. In 1982, for example, federal government expenditures for health care were estimated to be $95 billion, or almost 30 percent of all the money spent for such purposes in the United States. The amount of medical information routinely recorded by practitioners had vastly increased, making these files of interest to more and more people. At the same time, the Supreme Court had ruled in its *Miller* decision that individual citizens had no legal hold over their bank records and by implication, at least, all those records held by other third-party organizations such as hospitals.

The administration's proposed remedy to these problems was modest. Patients would be allowed to see and correct their own records. Disclosure of information about a patient would be prohibited without the patient's consent except in the routine operations of the hospital or in situations where the individual identity would be protected or on certain special occasions when the information was required by law enforcement.

Although the legislation was approved by committee, it was overwhelmingly defeated when brought before the House of Representatives. Despite the limited extent of protection afforded the individual patient, the various organized groups with an interest in unregulated health records such as the FBI and the CIA were easily able to mobilize the votes necessary to defeat the proposal.

The principles laid down by the Constitution are always subject to reinterpretation, but the specific language of its provisions is hard to change. A resolution has to win the approval of a two-thirds majority of both the House and the Senate and be ratified by the legislatures of three-quarters of the states before the words of the Constitution and its amendments may be modified. The strictures of law are also subject to interpretation, but they become a permanent part of the federal code. Each law, or formal amendment, requires the approval of a majority of Congress and the signature of the president.

But government regulations, the rules published by the separate agencies of the federal government, are more flexible because they are subject to change at the whim of a single administrator or administration. Of course an executive order signed by the president can have the broadest possible reach of any regulation because it may affect the operation of the entire government.

President Reagan signed Executive Order 12356 in April 1982. It significantly altered the flow of information in the United States by enlarging the power of government officials to keep many of the documents about defense and national security matters from the public. The order reversed the policy begun during the Eisenhower years of making available to citizens, scholars and reporters more and more information from the government's archives.

The Carter administration's executive order required officials to prove that "identifiable damage" would be caused to the nation's security if the information in question was made public. The Carter order further required government censors to consider the public interest before they placed a secrecy stamp on a particular document. And in most cases the order set a six-year limit on how long information could be kept classified and therefore denied the public.

President Reagan, with a stroke of his pen, has reversed many of these policies. Instead of "identifiable damage," censors can classify upon a finding of "damage." The new order says the censors no longer must consider the public interest. Just as significantly, the Reagan order abolished the mandatory declassification of information after the passage of specific periods of time, mandating instead the suppression of information "as long as required by national security conditions."

A second important Reagan order governing the control of information sets out the guidelines for the agencies responsible for collecting intelligence and thwarting foreign spies. In this order, issued in December 1981, President Reagan broadened the authority of the intelligence agencies to collect information both at home and abroad. For the first time, the Central Intelligence Agency was explicitly authorized to conduct covert operations within the borders of the United States.

Under the new order, which replaced an executive order of President Carter, the CIA is authorized to collect "significant" foreign intelligence within the United States if that effort is not specifically aimed at the domestic activities of American citizens and corporations. In addition, the order permits the CIA to conduct secret "special activities" that have been approved by the president as long as they are not intended to influence the U.S. political process or public opinion. Mr. Carter's order prohibited such activities by the CIA within the United States.

In a suit brought several months after President Reagan signed the executive order, a coalition of several major religious organizations, a number of smaller groups and some individuals charged that the new marching orders for the intelligence organizations represented a serious violation of constitutional rights and of the federal law establishing the Central Intelligence Agency.

The organizations bringing the suit included the United Presbyterian Church in the U.S.A., the National Council of the Churches of Christ in the U.S.A. and the Trustees of the General Program Council of the Reformed Church in America, which together claimed an aggregate membership of over 40 million Americans.

"The order provides the ostensible legal authorization for a massive foreign intelligence gathering and surveillance operation which includes the extensive use of warrantless searches and surveillance infiltration and manipulation of groups and organizations deemed agents of a foreign power or sources of foreign intelligence and counterintelligence information; covert operations of the Central Intelligence Agency against organizations and persons associated with those organizations; and the dissemination to governmental and military authorities of information files on individuals who have done no more than exercise their constitutionally protected rights of freedom of religion, speech, press, association, travel and privacy," the suit charged.

John Shattuck has been the director of the Washington office of the American Civil Liberties Union since 1976. During this period he has watched three separate administrations struggle with the complex issues of information control and been actively involved in trying to resolve them. In the spring of 1982, in a lecture in New York City, he summarized his conclusions about the drift of law and regulation in the United States since the end of World War II.

The postwar growth of the executive branch that went with the American policy of communist containment and foreign intervention, he argued, has had "a fundamentally distorting effect on the Constitution. The premise of the founders that Congress makes the laws and the executive branch carries them out was a major obstacle to presidents seeking to shape world events to conform to their view of American security interests."

The national security powers that gradually have been assumed by our presidents during this period, he noted, "are powers to act in peacetime as if the country were at war. Orwell's maxim that 'war is peace' has governed American presidents for more than thirty years, all of whom have claimed that in order to keep the peace abroad, it is necessary for them to do things at home which can be done, if they can be done at all under our Constitution, only in a state of war.

"The rules of classifying information, protecting intelligence agents, preventing dissident government officials from speaking their minds have gradually evolved from raw presidential assertions of power to an extensive authority ratified by judicial decisions and congressional enactments," he said.

"National security," Shattuck said, "is what protects us from our adversaries, but the Constitution and the Bill of Rights are what distinguish us from them. In the end, the question of how to protect our liberty is not a question of law; it is a question of politics and a question of political leadership."

But because national security has become an "ubiquitous label which presidents have used for the last three decades to insulate their actions from review," he argued, the power of the executive branch has steadily grown.

"The result is that today we have greater secrecy, more censorship, a CIA with more domestic authority, an FBI with fewer restraints and a National Security Agency with broader power than we ever had in our history," Shattuck concluded.

As we have seen, however, in the age of the computer, the concentration of the control of information in fewer and fewer hands is not limited to matters of national security. In June 1982, the Social

Security Administration announced plans to require more than 4 million aged, blind or disabled poor people to disclose tax return information as a condition for receiving benefits.

The agency said it would terminate benefits under the Supplemental Security Income program to anyone who refused to allow the Social Security Administration to examine Internal Revenue Service records showing whether the welfare recipient also had received dividend or interest payments from corporations and banks.

The Social Security Administration emphasized it was not proposing to examine the tax returns filed by the individuals, but the statements submitted to the government by the corporations and banks. Because of the instantaneous matching ability of computers, however, this distinction is essentially meaningless.

Cono R. Namorato, a former official in the Tax Division of the Justice Department, also questioned the validity of the plan asking the recipients to agree to the Social Security Administration's gaining access to the IRS records. "Generally," he said, "a waiver has to be freely and voluntarily given to be effective. It doesn't sound voluntary to me if the government is conditioning future receipt of benefits on such a waiver."

How do the people of the United States think out such a complex question of equity? Who tells a government agency that it has gone too far? More than ten years ago, President Nixon became persuaded of the importance of developing a coherent government approach toward questions of the proper government role in the control of information. In an attempt to achieve this goal, he created a White House Office of Telecommunications Policy.

Though the OTP became involved in some highly political actions of dubious merit—it led an intricately orchestrated campaign to undermine the independence of public television—the office also examined a number of important policy issues. President Ford continued the office. President Carter, also concerned about information policy issues, especially what he called privacy questions, felt the office should be outside the White House. He received Congress's permission to abolish OTP and establish the National Telecommunications and Information Administration in the Commerce Department. NTIA continued research in a number of areas and developed and sent to Congress Carter administration legislation intended to curb the federal government's appetite for some kinds of personal information. Few of these proposals were approved.

In February 1982, President Reagan's NTIA sent Congress its budget estimates and justifications for the coming fiscal year. Because of considerable progress in the area guarding individual rights, the statement said, NTIA will "substantially reduce efforts in the protection of personal privacy. In FY 1983 NTIA will limit its efforts to commenting on the privacy implications of the legislative proposals of others and is not undertaking analyses of the future effects on privacy protection of new technologies."

Aristotle, a bit more than two thousand years ago, commented on the grave importance of contemplating the laws of a nation and their impact on the individual citizen. "For there is one rule exercised over subjects who are by nature free," he said, "and another over subjects who are by nature slaves." We have seen how law may be slowly moving us away from freedom. Now let us consider how it can be used to keep us free.

Can Anything
Be Done?

The death of democracy is not likely to be assassination from ambush. It will be a slow extinction from apathy, indifference and undernourishment.
　　　　　　　　　—Robert Maynard Hutchins

Alan F. Westin is a professor of public law and government at Columbia University. For the last fifteen years he has been one of the most influential figures in the United States studying and writing about the use of computers by government, business and other institutions. Like most lawyers, Westin invests the law with great authority. In much of his early work, for example, he viewed computerization as largely beneficial and contended that those problems that were created by the computer could be resolved by simple legal expedients such as a law giving individual citizens the right to see and correct their records.

But in congressional testimony four years after the publication of his first and most famous book, *Privacy and Freedom,* the New York scholar took a different tack. Much had been said, he told the senators, about the need to allow computers to work in the public interest as well as for the parochial goals of large organizations such as banks and government. Why, then, was the public interest so frequently ignored?

"We have an imbalance of power because computer technology is frightfully expensive," he said, answering his own question. "It requires high technology to bring computer systems into being. As long as the only people to build computerized record systems are those who use them to increase their own effectiveness, power and influence, then we have increasingly a consolidation of power in society."

Given the continued investment by government and industry in more and more computerized telecommunication systems and data bases, many Americans contend that nothing can be done to curb the abuses of the computer. Some of these cynics are technocrats who view technology as a powerful force that, in the inevitable march toward some predestined nirvana, may do accidental damage to the old-fashioned and ephemeral concept of individual freedom. Strangely enough, this mechanical and somewhat despairing view of the world is echoed by a significant number of civil libertarians who, overwhelmed by the complexity of the computer and its use, throw up their hands in defeat before the battle has begun.

The history of the last few decades, however, suggests that cynics of both persuasions are wrong; that with the application of intelligence and political will, effective remedies are possible. More precisely, history tells us that from time to time the American people have risen up and demanded a halt to some particular computer threat that the cynics had told us was inevitable.

Not that making sure the bureaucracies use computers in a publicly beneficial way is an easy task. First there is the difficult challenge of deciding what to worry about. The public is usually not asked to participate in the management decisions of large agencies and corporations, and if it is asked, rarely has the necessary skills to answer.

Many computer systems are so complex that even the executives who have been persuaded to install them do not understand their operation or their impact. Instead, they rely on the experts. But the judgments of the experts must be viewed with great caution. This is partly because the problems presented by a large system require the resolution of questions of ethics, law and equity that the experts are seldom trained to handle. There is also an inherent conflict of interest because the pay and professional status of the experts is directly related to the size and sophistication of the systems they are buying, selling, designing or managing.

Even assuming the good intentions of the executives and experts, the questions are difficult. What is the appropriate balance point between efficiency and the fundamental values of our society as expressed by the Constitution and its amendments? When do possible safeguards become more dangerous than the abuses they are supposed to guard against? How can a society devoted to the notion that the free flow of information is essential to the development of sound public policy make a deliberate decision not to collect certain kinds of information? What does society do in those cases in which protecting a specific category of information collides with other important principles such as the right to own property or the right of a free press to publish what it knows?

These are a few of the conundrums that immediately present themselves when a congressional committee, a state legislature, the courts, a federal agency, a private corporation or an institution such as a university or the American Civil Liberties Union begins trying to decide what actions it should take to protect the individual from domination by computer-powered bureaucracies. In the give-and-take of the legislative and judicial process, as discussed in the preceding chapter, these efforts have not always been successful. Sometimes remedies were blocked by powerful interest groups with opposing goals. Sometimes the solutions were ineffective. Frequently important hazards have gone unrecognized.

With all the failures, however, have come important victories. In 1972, the Massachusetts legislature passed a model law to regulate and control the use of information recorded by the police and courts about those who are arrested. In 1974, the U.S. Congress approved a law imposing a limited set of restrictions on the collection and distribution of some kinds of information by agencies of the U.S. government. In 1978, fearful of the potential for political repression, the Carter administration ordered the Internal Revenue Service to drop its plans to develop a $800 million computerized telecommunications network.

Judging the overall success of these various efforts is difficult, depending in part on whether the judge believes the glass is half full or half empty. Richard Neustadt, a Washington lawyer and former assistant to President Carter, expresses pride in the various steps taken during the Carter years to contain the sometimes overbearing reach of the computerized bureaucracies. To some knowledgeable persons, however, the apparent victories are mostly an illusion. James Rule, a sociology professor at State University of New York at Stony Brook, was an adviser to the Privacy Protection Study Commission. Professor Rule and three of his colleagues, in an analysis titled "The Politics of Privacy," attempted to summarize the gradual development of the issues of computerized bureaucracies and the remedies that have emerged. In their judgment, most of the political responses of the last decade lack real meaning because the underlying bureaucratic and technical imperatives leading organizations to collect more and more information have not been confronted.

What are some of the specific steps that society has taken since the beginning of the modern age of the computer to prevent these systems from being abused? Why were some reforms adopted while others were not? Who were some of the actors, the individual men and women whose knowledge and convictions led them to fight for specific curbs? Are there lessons in these successes, their authors and the environment in which they flourished that could provide helpful guides for fighting all the battles of the future?

The record suggests that many of the current areas of concern about the effects of the computer were identified a long time ago, at about the same time that America's large bureaucracies were beginning to harness them for their separate purposes. In 1955, for example, the late Thomas B. Hennings, chairman of the Senate Subcommittee on Constitutional Rights, asked his staff to collect information about how the constitutional rights of the American people were being abused by the federal government. Because the research and hearings of the Hennings subcommittee focused on blacklisting and other abuses of the McCarthy era, the staff very soon began to worry about the computerized data banks that were just beginning to replace the old manual file systems.

Journalists and writers were also among the first to focus public attention on the hazards inherent in computer-powered bureaucracies. In 1964, Vance Packard and Myron Brenton published separate books about some of the negative effects of computerizing America.

Among other subjects discussed by both authors were the credit reporting companies and how their slipshod investigative methods damaged individual consumers. The horror stories told by Packard and Brenton contributed to the political concern that a few years later would lead to congressional hearings and ultimately the passage of a law concerning this particular form of corporate surveillance.

In 1966, a second area of public concern about computers emerged when an intense debate developed within academic and government circles about the value and dangers and wisdom of establishing a National Data Center. The proposed center would collect, on a single computer, all the statistical information obtained by scores of different federal agencies about everyone in the United States. The proposal, under which information from such organizations as the IRS, the Census Bureau and the Social Security Administration would be unified, was greeted with widespread revulsion.

While the center was never formally recommended by the Johnson administration, it was warmly endorsed by the Office of Management and Budget of the president and by economists, planners and other top managers of the executive branch. Powerful public opposition, however, prompted the government to drop the plan to develop the National Data Center. The decision appears to mark the first occasion when a deliberate policy decision was made not to use the enormous speed and agility of the computer to centralize information because of the perception that such a step would be harmful to the American people.

Alan Westin published his book *Privacy and Freedom* in 1967. During the same year, almost unnoticed at the time, the federal government printed a second study that included an analysis and recommendation which later developed into a central part of the continuing debate about the use of computers in Modern America.

This second book was *The Challenge of Crime in a Free Society,* a report by the President's Commission on Law Enforcement and Administration of Justice. The primary purpose of the report was to present a detailed plan showing how the federal government, the states and local communities could combat crime by improving the performance of the police, courts and corrections agencies. One specific recommendation was that the states and the federal government develop a complex system of linked computers to store and transmit information about those who were arrested. As envisaged by the commission, the system also would report whether each defendant was found guilty or innocent and any sentence that was imposed.

The commission, however, did more than simply recommend a massive new computer system. Surprisingly, given the intense public concern about crime, the commission also warned about the hazards of such a system for society. "Whenever government records contain derogatory personal information they create serious public policy problems," the report said. "The records may contain incomplete or incorrect information. The information may fall into the wrong hands and be used to intimidate or embarrass. The information may be retained long after it has lost its usefulness and serves only to harass ex-offenders, or its mere existence may diminish an offender's belief in the possibility of redemption."

In a rather sophisticated analysis, the commission rejected the arguments that the computer only represented an incremental improvement in record handling. In the past, the commission found, "the inherent inefficiencies of manual files containing millions of names have provided a built-in protection. Accessibility will be greatly enhanced by putting the files in a computer, so that the protection afforded by inefficiency will diminish, and special attention must be directed at protecting privacy."

The next few years saw a flurry of activity on several different fronts. In 1968 and 1969, the House Government Operations Committee and the Senate Banking Committee held separate hearings on the need for legislation to regulate the credit reporting industry. During the fall of 1970, these hearings culminated in the passage of the Fair Credit Reporting Act. Supporters of the new law praised it as a measure that increased the rights of consumers by allowing them to inspect their credit records. Critics saw the law as an industry-backed statute that authorized and legitimized the investigative practices of the credit reporting companies.

It was during the same period that Senator Sam J. Ervin, Jr., who had become chairman of the Constitutional Rights Subcommittee after the death of Senator Hennings, began an extensive examination of how the federal government abused the privacy of its own employees and the impact and propriety of the blizzard of questions the government asked citizens on census forms and other kinds of questionnaires.

In the early Washington spring of 1971, Senator Ervin enlarged the scope of his earlier inquiries and began a lengthy and widely publicized set of hearings on federal data banks, computers and the Bill of Rights. Though the hearings touched on many different abusive uses of the computer, the subcommittee's examination of the U.S. Army's secret surveillance of civil rights activists and opponents of the war in Vietnam provided a shocking insight into some of the questionable activities of the spooked governments of Lyndon Johnson and Richard Nixon.

The first witness at these hearings was Arthur R. Miller, then a professor of law at the University of Michigan. Mr. Miller had just published *Assault on Privacy,* a detailed analysis of the dangers of modern bureaucracies, and his impassioned concern was informed and contagious.

"Let me start with three basic propositions. First, Americans today are scrutinized, measured, watched, counted and interrogated by more government agencies, law-enforcement officials, social scientists and poll takers than at any time in our history.

"Second, probably in no nation on earth is as much individualized information collected, recorded and disseminated as in the United States.

"Third, the information gathering and surveillance activities of the federal government have expanded to such an extent that they are becoming a threat to several of America's basic rights, the rights of privacy, speech, assembly, association and petition of government."

Senator Ervin, the exuberant chairman who a few years later was to lead the Senate investigation of most of the collected abuses of the Watergate era, interrupted the witness. "Once people start fearing the government, once they think they are under surveillance by government, whether they are or not, they are likely to refrain from exercising the great rights that are incorporated in the First Amendment to make their minds and spirits free," Senator Ervin said. "And what you are saying, as I construe it, is that the gathering of all this information on the activities of individuals which are lawful in nature and encouraged by the First Amendment is calculated to coerce the individual not to exercise the freedoms which are calculated to make their minds and spirits free. And that in the long run the government is going to suffer from the effects of this as much as the citizens are to suffer the loss of their freedoms."

It was the same year as this set of Ervin hearings, 1971, that the particular seed planted in 1967 by the President's Commission on Law Enforcement and Administration of Justice first bore fruit. After the publication of the commission report in 1967, the staff director of the commission, James Vorenberg, returned to the Harvard Law School, where he is a professor. Lanky and incredibly energetic, Mr. Vorenberg immediately became involved in trying to carry out the commission's recommendations in Massachusetts. One of these proposals was that each state form a central criminal justice planning committee to coordinate improvements in law enforcement. Such a committee was formed. Among the first matters considered were the linked questions of how to build a statewide criminal history information system and what restrictions should be placed on the dissemination of individual records.

"The studies we did found that the Massachusetts records were incredibly inaccurate—they still are—and that anyone could get hold of another person's records if he had a friend in the local police department," Arnold Rosenfeld recently recalled. Now forty-one and the deputy chief of the Massachusetts Defenders Committee, he peers at you through gold-rimmed glasses. Then Mr. Rosenfeld was working for the attorney general of the Commonwealth of Massachusetts.

"We developed legislation that we called the CORI Act, the initials standing for Criminal Offender Record Information. We handed it over to Governor Sargent's staff, and somehow they got it passed in the dark of the night. The law for the first time established the legal principle that criminal-history information should be protected. The only ones who could legally have access to such information were criminal justice agencies—such as the police or courts—and those other organizations that were certified by the Criminal History Systems Board."

Mr. Rosenfeld was named the first chairman of the board. "We got a big rush of requests for access to our records. All the federal agencies came in saying they wanted records. Under the CORI Act, we looked at the individual statutes of each agency to determine what their legal mandates were. The Labor Department came in. The law said they were authorized to have felony conviction information about union officials, not information about arrests, not information about misdemeanor convictions. We ruled they could have only felony conviction information. The Small Business Administration wanted the same access to information they had enjoyed for many years, but there was no provision authorizing them to do so in their charter legislation. The army recruiters wanted records. Again we checked the law and found no legal authorization for them to have it. We held that the SBA and army recruiters no longer could obtain criminal-history records in Massachusetts."

The rulings of the Criminal History Systems Board enraged the officials of the federal government located in New England. "The feds were really upset," Mr. Rosenfeld continued. "They had a regional council up here and the U.S. attorney for Massachusetts, Jim Gabriel, told the other members of the council that he would straighten out the problem. Gabriel came to see me and very forcefully told me about the supremacy of the federal government in these matters. He also called Governor Sargent and said that if the state did not reverse its stand that he was going to halt all federal contracts in the area."

The regional council wrote Governor Sargent on March 13, 1973, asserting that the actions of Massachusetts created an "undue burden on the federal government." The council requested that the governor promptly ask the Massachusetts legislature to amend the law and exempt all federal agencies from the certification requirements of the state Criminal History Systems Board.

"I have to hand it to the governor's staff," Mr. Rosenfeld recalled. "It hadn't even occurred to me that we had been given a wonderful political issue. Andy Klein and some of the others working for Sargent instantly saw that the federal demand was dynamite. The governor began making speeches about how we were not going to be pushed around by Washington."

The irony of a New England governor assuming the states' rights posture of the Old South did not escape those who worked around Francis Sargent at the time. But the Watergate scandal was beginning to trickle out of President Nixon's White House and the hearings of Senator Ervin two years before had established how the U.S. Army and other federal agencies under both Johnson and Nixon had been encouraged to undertake mass, computerized surveillance of the usually legal protests of civil rights activists and those opposed to the Vietnam War and other policies of the government.

"I think most of the staff and the governor himself were amazed at how much interest there was in the issue," said Andrew Klein, who had begun as a $75-a-week intern on Mr. Sargent's policy and planning staff a few months after graduating from Harvard College in 1970. "But the controversy over the criminal-history records came at the right time. It allowed the governor, a Republican, to talk about states' rights in a liberal way. The federal government at that moment was considered the bad guy, Nixon was in office, and Massachusetts and its governor were standing up for the rights of individual citizens."

On June 11, 1973, the Nixon administration ineptly escalated the war with Massachusetts. In a suit brought in federal court in Boston that day, the government said the effort to regulate federal access to the criminal-history records held by the Commonwealth of Massachusetts violated the U.S. Constitution.

Two days later, Andrew Klein drafted a letter designed to restate the conflict between the commonwealth and the federal government in concrete and easy-to-understand terms. The letter concerned a computer system that the FBI had just begun to build which at the time was envisaged as becoming a central repository of the criminal-history records held by the fifty separate states.

The letter dispatched to Washington on June 13 by the Republican governor contained a blunt but indirect reference to the bits and pieces of the Watergate scandal that had begun to emerge in the nation's press. "Recent revelations concerning the Department of Justice, the FBI and top government employees do not inspire confidence in Massachusetts that internal controls and self-policing by line operating agencies or administrators are sufficient to guarantee the integrity of something as sensitive and potentially abusive as a national criminal information computers system interfaced with the fifty states' systems," Mr. Sargent said.

"For this reason, I am hesitant to allow Massachusetts' state criminal justice agencies or the state criminal history system to participate in the FBI's National Crime Information System until such times as the Department of Justice or Congress provides sufficient guarantees to safeguard individual rights and the system's integrity against abuse."

The tiny seed of caution planted by the President's Commission on Law Enforcement and Administration of Justice in 1967 was becoming a flourishing tree. With the understanding that he would be held responsible if there was a negative reaction, Andrew Klein leaked the governor's letter to Michael Kenney, a powerful reporter and columnist on the *Boston Globe* who had written about the potential hazards of computers on several earlier occasions.

The editors put Mr. Kenney's exclusive story on the *Globe*'s front page the next day. "Power in Massachusetts often means having the *Globe* on your side," Mr. Klein explained. But the governor's position won him praise and publicity far beyond the boundaries of Massachusetts. *Time* magazine ran a short but flattering notice of his crusade. Out-of-state papers such as the *Washington Post* and the *Charlotte Observer* and liberal columnists such as Tom Wicker of the *New York Times* supported Governor Sargent's goals.

The elegant presence of Elliot Richardson provided a continuing overlay of irony to the dispute between the United States and Massachusetts, a dispute that served as an important focus in the national debate about what kinds of controls should be imposed on the distribution of criminal history records. In the first place, Mr. Richardson himself had been a victim of the misuse of criminal-history records. On several occasions his basic fitness to hold office had been brought into question when records showing he had been arrested for drunken driving were leaked to the press.

Mr. Richardson overcame the doubts created by the misuse of his arrest records and was elected attorney general in Massachusetts in

1966. While there, he helped establish the state planning committee that drafted the legislative proposal strictly regulating the distribution of arrest records.

But a few years later, Mr. Richardson went to Washington, where he held a number of top positions in the Nixon administration. It was while the former attorney general of Massachusetts was serving as the attorney general of the United States during the spring and summer of 1973 that the Justice Department brought suit contending that the regulation of the records by Massachusetts violated the Constitution.

One more curious footnote about the zigs and zags of Mr. Richardson's positions on what was then called the privacy issue. While serving as attorney general of Massachusetts he first had been an early player in the process leading to the passage of the CORI Act. As attorney general of the United States, he then authorized a federal suit against the CORI Act. In July of 1973, two months before he and the Justice Department abandoned its action against Massachusetts, a committee he had formed when he was the secretary of health, education and welfare published an influential report on automated personnel data systems. The report of the committee did not recommend any revolutionary solutions but is generally credited with contributing to the political momentum building in the United States for a federal law to regulate the reach of organizational computers.

Congress approved the Federal Privacy Act in December of 1974. The escalating crescendo of public outrage, including the anger created by the tangentially related abuses of President Nixon and his men, no longer could be contained by the essentially conservative forces of the permanent federal bureaucracy. The law, of course, was in large measure a monument to the focused diligence of Senator Ervin and his staff on the Senate Constitutional Rights Subcommittee and to the newly discovered privacy concerns of the Senate Government Operations Committee, which he also chaired. It in no way diminishes the important contribution of this unusual man to acknowledge that the legislation ultimately approved by Congress covered considerably less ground than he had originally proposed.

As originally drafted, for example, the Privacy Act's principles would have covered the information systems of private industry and of state and local governments, as well as those of the federal government. As approved by Congress, the law only applied to federal agencies and the private organizations it did business with. A second major reduction in the reach of the Privacy Act involved the dropping of a plan to create a permanent independent commission to monitor and regulate the development of significant new computerized information systems. Instead, Congress created a temporary group to study the data banks, automatic data processing programs and information systems of governmental, regional and private organizations, to recommend remedial standards and procedures and then to go out of business. One other major reduction in the sweep of Senator Ervin's original plan involved the elimination of federal law-enforcement and intelligence agencies from many but not all the requirements of the Privacy Act.

Despite the considerable reduction in the reach of the legislation, however, the Privacy Act that Congress actually approved might still have had a significant impact if it had been wholeheartedly implemented by presidents Nixon, Ford, Carter and Reagan. One provision, for example, requires that federal agencies collect only information that is relevant and necessary, a restriction which if enforced would prevent the demonstrated excesses of the military, the FBI, the Secret Service, HEW and other agencies. A second provision requires that, to the maximum extent feasible, federal agencies obtain information directly from the individual they are interested in. A third provision requires federal agencies to inform the individual why the information they are seeking is required, how the information will be used, under what statutory authority it is being solicited and what penalties would be imposed if the individual declined to respond. A fourth provision gives every individual the basic right to inspect and correct his records.

The United States prides itself on being a nation of laws and not men. And to an extent unknown to most other parts of the world, it is. But public policy is much more than the sum of the laws passed by the legislatures and the regulations published by the agencies. Because every agency enjoys wide discretion in how they choose to apply the law, individual men and women whose names are unknown to even the most meticulous newspaper reader are able to influence the process of government much more than usually is imagined.

Two and a half years before Congress approved the Privacy Act and about the same time as the Massachusetts legislature passed the CORI Act, one such unknown person who was to have considerable influence on one narrow but important area of government policy was hired by a small office in the Nixon White House. At the time he went to work as the law-enforcement consultant to the White House Office of Telecommunications Policy, William (Bill) McMahon was forty-two years old, a tall, wisecracking Irishman from northern New York. For two years he had been a New York state police trooper. For nine years he had been an agent, instructor and technical expert with the Central Intelligence Agency. For two more years he had been chief of the Technical Division of the Secret Service, the federal agency responsible for protecting the president and preventing counterfeiting.

It is not the résumé of a person you might expect to be worried about the possible development of a police state in the United States. But for the last ten years Bill McMahon has played an important behind-the-scenes role in an effort to prevent the Federal Bureau of Investigation from creating and controlling a centralized communications system through which all local and state police would converse. Such a system, he is convinced, would lead to the gradual weakening of the independent and locally controlled police agencies all over the United States, and ultimately to the creation of a national police force.

The substantive questions about the impact of the FBI plan are examined in the chapter entitled "Data Bases." Here we are examining how one anonymous individual working within the federal bureaucracies in Washington managed to confound what is generally regarded as one of the toughest, most determined agencies of the U.S. government.

Bill McMahon is now the owner of a campground and water-mill restaurant in western Maryland and a part-time consultant to the National Telecommunications and Information Administration. But from 1972 to 1976 he was a full-time adviser and technical expert within the White House office that advised President Nixon and President Ford on national communication policy issues.

The conversion of the former state trooper and CIA agent to underground apparatchik required a profound change in personal values. "I began driving a patrol car on the highways of western New York," he said. "I liked the work, but living in the barracks was tough for a married man and the pay was minimal. Then someone told me the CIA was looking for people. I literally had never heard of the agency at that point, but I drove down to Washington, knocked at an unmarked door and submitted my application. After a security check, I was accepted. My first assignment with the CIA was in New York City."

While growing up in upstate New York, Bill McMahon had worked as an electrical contractor. "Everyone in the CIA office was either a lawyer or an English major, so my everyday knowledge of electrical wiring made me a valuable asset," he said.

Very soon Bill McMahon was installing secret listening devices around New York and learning how to detect the bugs of the intelligence services of other nations. In addition to becoming an electronics warfare warrior, he also was briefly involved in a secret and totally illegal operation in which nearly one-quarter of a million first-class letters mailed between the United States and the Soviet Union were steamed opened, photographed and sent on their way between 1953 and 1973. His electrical skills, however, led him to CIA's Washington headquarters, where he became chief of the agency's engineering security branch. After the assassination of President Kennedy, the Secret Service followed the recommendation of the Warren Commission and began to enlarge its engineering staff. From 1966 to 1968, William McMahon served as chief of the Service's Technical Development Division. Then came a four-year stint in private industry, as director of the Washington Law Enforcement and Technology office of the Illinois Institute of Technology.

"I never gave much thought to the legalities of what I was doing in the CIA," McMahon recalled, puffing on his cigar. "But then in 1972, shortly after I went with the White House Office of Telecommunications Policy, I learned that the FBI had suggested that it should take over the management of a communications network that was run by the states and now is called the National Law Enforcement Telecommunication Service. It suddenly became very clear to me that if the FBI took over NLETS we would be heading toward a national police force," he said.

"At that point I wasn't thinking about privacy at all. What got me was what it would mean if the FBI took over NLETS. This is what got me off my hind feet. One of the things that got my dander up was the newspaper stories about the Justice Department trying to push Massachusetts around when it wouldn't jump through the FBI's hoop. I don't like bureaucratic bullies."

McMahon laughed and leaned back in his swivel chair. "I also knew what a real nice fellow I was and how I had done a bunch of pretty far-out things while working for the CIA. If you know you can't trust yourself, who can you trust?" he asked.

William McMahon is a man of very strong convictions. He also is extremely persistent. Once he decided the nation would be harmed by the FBI's ambitious plan to operate and control the central communication system linking local law-enforcement agencies, he began maneuvering from his obscure but powerful position as a staff member of a White House agency. His campaign took a number of different forms. In late 1972 and 1973, according to a summary chronology of the long-simmering dispute, he became actively involved in a successful campaign to provide NLETS with a federal grant to improve their service. The services offered by NLETS, a communication system operated by a consortium of the states, were directly competitive with the services the FBI wanted to provide.

The implicit opposition of the Office of Telecommunications Policy to the FBI was made explicit in May of 1973 when Charles J. Joyce, the assistant director of the White House Office, spoke at an NLETS conference. "We [OTP] believe that the control of the emerging National Law Enforcement Telecommunications System should be primarily in the hands of state and local authorities, where the primary responsibility for law enforcement resides," he said.

But the FBI kept seeking to enlarge its authority in a series of requests to the Justice Department and Congress. In January of 1974, FBI director Clarence Kelley sent a private message to William B. Saxbe, then the attorney general, requesting that the FBI be allowed to take over NLETS communication functions. Shortly thereafter, Clay Whitehead, the director of Mr. Nixon's telecommunications policy office, accepted the arguments of his law-enforcement expert. On March 4, Mr. Whitehead dispatched a letter to Mr. Saxbe setting out OTP's concerns over the FBI's ambitions. The official's concern was spelled out at a personal meeting between the two men the next week. Six months later, Mr. Whitehead's worries were restated by his successor, John M. Eger, in a letter leaked to the *New York Times*. Giving the FBI a green light, Mr. Eger warned the attorney general, "could result in the absorption of state and criminal data systems into a potentially abusive, centralized, federally controlled communications and computer information system." The resulting front-page story tended to focus the attention of the Ford administration that was desperately trying to get away from the surveillance abuse of the Nixon administration. Attorney General Edward Levi put the FBI plan on hold.

But the record indicates that William McMahon and several of his colleagues adopted tactics other than writing letters. One standard Washington method for delaying a decision you don't like is to generate an investigation. Soon the Office of Management and Budget, the General Accounting Office and several congressional committees were examining the possible long-term impact of the FBI plan. Though some of the staff members of these organizations were aware of the underlying issues, Bill McMahon never hesitated to lay out his views to those he decided should be educated about the dispute.

One of the congressional staff members that William McMahon came to know needed no instruction. This was Marcia MacNaughton, a lovely, soft-spoken Mississippi liberal who during the last quarter of the century has made herself a uniquely informed expert on how computers and computerized telecommunication networks are changing the United States. Her formal education was at Barnard College in New York and the London School of Economics. But in 1955 she joined the staff of the Constitutional Rights Subcommittee chaired by Senator Hennings and undertook an investigation of the impact of data bases. As the years went by, Ms. MacNaughton and other staff members such as Lawrence Baskir and Judy Futch kept enlarging the scope of their inquiry. In 1969, for example, the three staff members worked together preparing for subcommittee hearings on privacy, the census and federal questionnaires. Two years later, there were hearings on federal data banks, computers and the Bill of Rights.

The lengthy hearings, subsequent reports and proposed remedies were infused with the profound constitutional concerns of Sam Ervin. But they were based on a foundation of unusually thorough staff work. The staff drafted, mailed and tallied elaborate questionnaires designed to inform the subcommittee exactly how hundreds of federal agencies were using their computers. The staff conducted countless interviews with government officials, corporate executives and affected individuals about the operation and impact of computers. The staff prepared complex analyses and reports. Before each hearing, the staff developed detailed questions for each witness, thoughtful opening statements and easy-to-understand press releases. Finally, the staff undertook the intense political and legal research necessary before Senator Ervin and the other subcommittee members could agree on proposals to ameliorate the problems they were uncovering. For a period of more than ten years, Senator Ervin and his small staff were a formidable force, the leading edge of the congressional examination of the role of the computer in American life.

Then came Senator Ervin's 1973 appointment as chairman of the special Senate committee investigating the Nixon administration's involvement in the burglary of the Democratic national headquarters in the Watergate office building. One year later, Senator Ervin, still vigorous and alert at seventy-six, quit Washington to return to the private practice of law in Morganton, North Carolina. But Marcia MacNaughton had not lost her intense interest in tracking the vast power of the organizational computer. In 1976 she became an analyst with the Office of Technology Assessment, a small agency established by Congress to help it weigh the advantages and disadvantages of the machine on modern life.

Her first OTA assignment was director of a study requested by the House Ways and Means Subcommittee on Oversight to consider the long-term social effects of a very large computerized telecommunications system that the Internal Revenue Service had decided was needed to collect the nation's taxes. A few months after OTA in

March 1977 produced its preliminary assessment of critical issues raised by the IRS proposal, the Carter administration made an almost unheard-of decision: it decided that the potential hazards of increasing the ability of the IRS to collect and manipulate individual tax information outweighed the possible advantages the system would give to the tax collectors.

As Marcia MacNaughton was preparing her report on the IRS in a small OTA office near the Capitol, the public debate on the hazards of large government agencies, especially those armed with powerful computers, lurched off in a new direction. More than five years before, the Ervin subcommittee had made an extensive investigation of the assignment of army intelligence agents and computers to track the written and spoken words of civil rights demonstrators and those opposed to the war in Vietnam. Though the Army apparently halted its widespread surveillance with the first breath of publicity, Nixon administration officials vehemently denied that the program had violated the constitutional right of the American people to speak their minds and petition their government. And this view was upheld by a split decision of the Supreme Court in a decision that concluded that Senator Ervin and the other petitioners had not proved the surveillance had chilled the First Amendment rights of the American people to assemble and speak their minds.

But two days before Christmas of 1974 the character of the debate about surveillance underwent an important change when the *New York Times* published a long, detailed article by Seymour Hersh alleging that the Central Intelligence Agency had been a major player among the agencies snooping on citizens and developing computerized dossiers of their activities. Because a good deal of the CIA surveillance clearly violated a law prohibiting the agency from most kinds of operations in the United States, Sy Hersh's story added a major new element to the on-going controversy. Sensing an intense level of public concern, President Ford immediately formed a special commission headed by Vice-President Nelson Rockefeller to investigate the CIA. And within a matter of weeks, separate inquiries were underway by special committees of the Senate and the House.

Both the June 1975 Rockefeller Report on CIA Abuses and the far broader Senate Report on Intelligence Activities and the Rights of

Americans a year later upheld the charges of the *Times*. For more than a quarter century, the investigators found, important elements of the intelligence community had been operating outside the law. In several critical ways the careful system of checks and balances established by the founding fathers to assure that the American people might avoid the wounds of tyranny had faltered.

Without the knowledge and consent of Congress, for example, Attorney General Ramsey Clark had authorized the creation of the Interdivision Information Unit, a computerized system initially established to collect information about the activities of those thought to be instigating, spreading or preventing urban disorders. Within two years, however, the mandate of the IDIU had grown and it was receiving and storing more than 42,000 reports a year from the army and others about those opposed to the war in Vietnam and active in campus demonstrations as well as civil rights activists.

But collecting the information was just the first step. Computer tapes prepared by this Justice Department Intelligence Unit—which included the names of tens of thousands of people whose only crime was to criticize their government—were given to the CIA and the Internal Revenue Service. In the IRS, a special unit began auditing some of the suspects fingered by the IDIU. At the CIA, heavy pressure from the White House prompted Richard Helms to establish Operation Chaos. Mr. Helms approved the CIA's involvement in a computerized effort to track political dissent even though he wrote several letters at the time acknowledging that the program violated a law prohibiting his agency from engaging in "internal security functions."

A second problem with the executive orders is that this form of government regulation remains in force only as long as it suits the interests of the man in the White House. With the election of President Reagan, the somewhat parallel interests of Mr. Carter and Mr. Ford went out of style. The new president signed a new executive order considerably enlarging the discretion of the intelligence agencies to act as they see fit.

Mr. Ford and Mr. Carter tried to assure greater longevity for their shared views about the potential mischief that the intelligence agencies could stir up by recommending that Congress approve legislation giving their executive orders the status of law. Partly because of growing political concerns about the state of national security, partly because of the strongly conflicting values of most intelligence officials and those concerned with civil liberties, partly because of hard-to-resolve technical questions, Congress failed to act on the intelligence charter bills proposed by the two presidents.

One other aspect of the history of the recent effort to control the impact of the organized computer on the American people should be considered. Senator Sam Ervin was unable to win congressional approval of his plan to establish a permanent watchdog agency to keep track of all the new computer systems sought by government and business. But the Privacy Act of 1974 did establish a temporary commission to study the impact of corporate, institutional and government computers on individual freedom. In July of 1977, the Privacy Protection Study Commission issued its report.

In a quietly understated way the commission sounded an alarm. "In a larger context," the commission concluded, "Americans must be concerned about the long-term effect record-keeping practices can have not only on relationships between individuals and organizations, but also on the balance of power between government and the rest of society. Accumulations of information about individuals tend to enhance authority by making it easier for authority to reach individuals directly. Thus, growth in society's record-keeping capability poses the risk that existing power balances will be upset. Recent events illustrate how easily this can happen and also how difficult it can be to preserve such balances once they are seriously threatened."

The recent events mentioned by the commission of course referred to the abuse of the information powers of government by political administrators holding the investigative and computer power of certain parts of government primarily during the years that Lyndon Johnson and Richard Nixon were in the White House.

In addition to its broad warning about the future, the commission made hundreds of specific recommendations about fifteen separate areas including the use of mailing lists, the relationship between the citizen and the IRS, the use of social security numbers for other purposes, the citizen as the beneficiary of government assistance and the record-keeping practices of such institutions as banks, universities, insurance companies and employers.

As documented by the separate investigations of the Senate, the House of Representatives and a presidential commission, the range of criminal acts committed by various agencies of the intelligence community really was quite impressive. For several decades, the CIA had secretly and illegally intercepted thousands of first-class letters as they left the United States. FBI agents, searching for leads about persons suspected of disloyalty to the United States, committed a number of admittedly illegal burglaries. And, as related in greater detail in another chapter of this book, the National Security Agency for about a quarter of a century systematically violated a specific provision of law by obtaining copies of most of the telex messages entering and leaving the United States.

Considered together, the reports of the different congressional, executive and judicial bodies confirmed that the intelligence agencies to a remarkable extent had evaded the checks and balances that surround most institutions of the United States. Together, the reports generated substantial political pressures for broad legislation to outlaw the excesses of these increasingly computerized agencies. So outrageous was the behavior, in fact, that for a brief time a consensus developed that a law that prohibited this act or that activity was no longer sufficient. What was required, many seem to agree, were laws that spelled out the specific goals of the agencies while at the same time establishing that Congress, the president and the attorney general each were specifically responsible for assuring that the agencies lived within the boundaries of the statute.

Almost a decade after the extensive and official disclosures of the illegal and immoral acts of the intelligence community, however, the consensus has evaporated and the permanent procedural reforms that seemed so essential in the last half of the 1970s have been abandoned. In the immediate wake of the critical reports of the Rockefeller and congressional committees, Presidents Ford and Carter signed detailed executive orders that sought to define both the positive goals expected of the agencies and the activities they were henceforth to avoid. One serious drawback of these orders, admirable though they were, was that some of the activities they regulated were so sensitive that parts of the orders themselves had to be kept secret. The public was thus forced to accept the good intentions of the Ford and Carter administrations as an article of faith. Given the recent history of abuses, such faith did not come easily, especially to anyone who agrees with Lord Acton's rule that power tends to corrupt.

The commission report identified three separate but concurrent objectives it thought should guide the nation in making choices about the development of computerized bureaucracies. America, the report said, should seek to minimize the intrusiveness of record-keeping organizations, maximize the fairness by which these records are used to make judgments about individuals and give every citizen a legitimate, enforceable expectation of confidentiality about most of the government and business records that describe his life.

For the most part, the commission's recommendations were ignored. President Carter established a small staff—usually no larger than two or three persons—to draft legislative proposals to transform the recommendations of the Privacy Study Commission into law. After many months of study and hours of intense negotiation with the powerful voices of law enforcement in the Justice and Treasury departments, however, only a handful of proposals were ever actually sent to Capitol Hill. One of these bills, legislation giving bank customers a limited right to protect their bank records from federal snoopers, passed Congress. Several other bills proposed as a result of the Carter administration's so-called privacy initiatives were never acted upon.

The failure of the Carter administration, however, went well beyond its faltering attempts to find a consensus on what it wanted Congress to act on. First, there were occasions when the men and women around Carter failed to identify the pervasive problems created by the increasing intrusion of the computer into every nook and cranny of our lives. Second, there were times when the staff closed their eyes.

In the years ahead, for example, it is probable that two decisions made during the Carter years affecting the National Security Agency will prove to be enormously significant in the growth of the power of the government to dominate its citizens. On one occasion, in a decision made by Mr. Carter himself, the NSA was given a broad new mission to assist private corporations develop procedures to prevent information not previously thought important from falling into the hands of foreign governments. On a second occasion, as we have seen, the Carter administration allowed the NSA to take steps increasing its domination of cryptographic research conducted by scientists not working for the government. In both decisions, the small staff group specifically established by Mr. Carter to raise questions about actions that might undermine individual freedom was not consulted at all. Whether the exclusion of the staff from these critical decisions about the NSA was deliberate or inadvertent is not clear and, in terms of the outcome, unimportant.

In the case of the NSA, President Carter and his advisers appeared to have made several major information policy decisions without considering their potentially damaging impact on the freedom of the American people. There were other times, however, when Mr. Carter and the highest officials in his administration knowingly adopted policies that conflicted with principles laid down by the 1974 Privacy Act that the president repeatedly had endorsed during his election campaign. A prime example was the debate within the Carter administration over the program of Joseph Califano, when he was the secretary of health, education and welfare. The objective was to identify persons receiving improper government benefits by using a computer to compare the information contained in the individual personnel files of federal employees with the information collected about welfare recipients.

Mr. Califano announced the launching of what he called Project Match with great fanfare in November of 1977. He did so, according to the research of Jake Kirchner, an excellent reporter with the weekly newspaper *Computer World,* despite an August 17, 1977, memo from the HEW's general counsel suggesting Project Match might not be legal. The problem was a provision in the Privacy Act of 1974 that "requires each federal agency that maintains a system of records . . . not to disclose any record from that system to any person or to other agencies without prior written consent of the individual." Such notification, of course, would have been time-consuming and expensive and would have defeated the purpose of Mr. Califano's project.

A second memorandum, this one from the Civil Service Commission, raised a second problem. The commission was worried that a legal loophole placed in the Privacy Act by Congress was not large enough to allow Project Match to be driven through it. In adopting the so-called routine-use provision, the lawyers said, Congress meant that a federal record could only be utilized "for a purpose that is compatible with the purposes for which it was collected." They further noted that the routine-use provision "implies that information will not be disclosed without some indication that a specific violation has occurred or might have occurred."

Mr. Kirchner then added his own comment to that of the lawyers. The routine-use provision of the Privacy Act extends to a person's government files a protection that parallels the constitutional prohibition against unlawful search: the personal possessions of a person will not be subject to seizure unless there is some evidence suggesting he has committed or is about to commit a crime.

Project Match, of course, turned this principle upside down. None of the hundreds of thousands of government workers whose computerized records were matched against the records of welfare recipients were individually suspected of illegally accepting government funds. Instead, the government argued it had reason to suspect that a small number of individuals—whom it could not identify—might have received improper benefits.

Carl F. Goodson, the general counsel for the Civil Service Commission, explained why the Califano Project appeared to conflict with the Privacy Act. "It is evident that this information on employees was not collected with a view toward detecting welfare abuses. Secondly, and perhaps more significantly, at the matching stage there is no indication whatsoever that a violation or potential violation of law has occurred."

Despite the objections of the Civil Service Commission, the Defense Department, and the lawyers at HEW, Project Match was allowed to proceed. But because of criticism from Congress and the American Civil Liberties Union, the Office of Management and Budget committed itself to develop a policy on computer matching programs. A memorandum to the president from James T. McIntyre, Jr., then the director of the OMB, indicates Mr. Carter was personally aware of the serious implications of the conflict between computer matching and the constitutional principles reflected in the privacy law. One problem, Mr. McIntyre told the president, was "the use of personal information for different purposes than those for which the individuals were told the information was collected." A second problem was "the indiscriminate extension of these matching programs into areas of greater personal privacy expectations, e.g., tax information or political activities."

The lines in the policy dispute were very clear. There was the language of the Privacy Act. There was the general conclusion of the Privacy Protection Study Commission: "The ability to search through hundreds of thousands or even millions of records to identify individuals with peculiar characteristics of interest is at once the most important gain and the most important source of potential harm stemming from the automation of large-scale personal-data record-keeping systems." There was the specific warning of David Linowes, the chairman of the Privacy Commission. The computer-to-computer linkage of Project Match, he said, presented "the biggest threat to privacy today."

In March of 1979, the Carter administration issued its long-promised guidelines. Computer matching was permitted after the agency undertaking the match had cleared it with the Office of Management and Budget. A press release claimed that the guidelines balanced the government's need to maintain the integrity of federal programs against the individual's right to privacy.

But the words were hollow. A few months after the guidelines had been issued, the Office of Personnel Management, previously known as the Civil Service Commission, decided that releasing its computerized record of the individual files of federal employees to another federal agency would not violate the prohibition in the Privacy Act. The Personnel Management people rested their case on an exemption in the Privacy Act that said that records could be shared if such sharing was for routine purposes. Passing the individual files on to a second agency was not illegal, they contended, because "an integral part of the reason these records are maintained is to protect the legitimate interests of government. Therefore, such disclosure is compatible with the purpose of maintaining these records."

With the election of President Reagan, computer matching by the federal government has accelerated. And as this is written, an inter-agency committee is working on new guidelines to replace those approved by President Carter. Hugh O'Neill, a Privacy Act expert in government, said one of the goals of the new committee was to make the rules "consistent with our technology." He did not mention making the rules consistent with the law.

This is only one example of how technology influences the shape of the law and administrative practice of government programs that affect millions of Americans. The phenomenon is usually denied by technology apologists and computer salesmen even as they lure well-meaning administrators into a morass of new, interlocking computer systems in an often fruitless effort to save money and look good to the voters.

The history of how the Carter and Reagan administrations have encouraged the growing use of computer matching, despite provi-sions of law that would appear to prohibit it, is highly instructive when one is considering the question of what can be done to prevent political and other abuses with the help of the computer. The history tells us first how hard it is to deny technology. Once an individual or company or government has the technical ability to travel down a specific path, there frequently is an overwhelming compulsion to make that journey. The history further tells us that a simple legal prohibition is often an insufficient brake. Many laws cannot stand alone. In these areas the laws need at least three things. Most essen-tial is the continued, active and intelligent monitoring by members of Congress who know what abuses were meant to be corrected, who understand the machinery of the law and who will press for enforce-ment. Second, it needs the honest effort of executive branch officials who implement the law throughout government. Third, it requires the active participation of those citizens and groups who stand to gain from its enforcement.

Preventing the abuse of computer matching is especially difficult because the procedure is seen as offering government administrators very particular advantages. Mr. Carter and Mr. Califano convinced themselves that the appearance of efficiency and integrity that re-sided within computer matching programs was important to their personal political standing as well as to maintaining support for the medical, educational and welfare programs they sponsored.

From all appearances, the decision of the Reagan administration to actively encourage the increased use of computer matching re-quired none of the anguished weighing of values and obfuscation suggested by the memoranda of the Carter administration lawyers. Along with many law-enforcement officials and other permanent executives of government, Mr. Reagan and his advisers appear to live in a world where the desire for orderliness dominates other consider-ations. Perhaps because most of the members of the Reagan adminis-tration have so long held positions of corporate or political power, they find it hard to conjure up situations where the institutions they are associated with might some day turn on them. The implicit assumptions of the Privacy Act, the sure knowledge of the value of individual freedom and a firm conviction that any bureaucracy can become abusive, have not been the hallmark of the Reagan team or the permanent cadre of the federal government.

The more conservative elements of American life, however, cannot claim exclusive rights to the occasionally dangerous pursuit of order. The widespread abuses of government data bases, computerized tele-communication systems and federal investigators uncovered during the congressional hearings of the 1970s left tar on the administrations of every political coloration. The abuses, furthermore, were continu-ing evidence of the naive faith in government by a substantial number of U.S. citizens.

In a world where the obsession for order has become a driving force, acting to make sure that the computerized organizations of America do not create a stifling restrictive environment is not an easy task. But given cultural, political and business leaders who have the vision to identify the ills and the courage to prescribe the necessary medicines, much could be done.

There are in fact a variety of different approaches that can be used to prevent large, powerful organizations from abusing computerized information. There are *technical* methods to better secure sensitive information. There are *laws and procedures* that could be adopted to increase the chance that information will be used in a fair and open manner. There are *institutional* adjustments that would reduce the hazards of the computer by changing the size and shape and purpose of some of our larger organizations or setting up systematic checks and balances for them. Finally, there are *social programs* that could be pursued to increase public awareness of the potential dangers of the large computerized organizations or lessen the probability that computers may leave millions of Americans holding technically obsolete jobs.

Whether we have the wisdom to make the correct diagnoses and the will to spoon out the necessary medicine is not clear. But a good deal of systematic research has been undertaken to determine the ingredients of the various possible remedies.

There sometimes appear to be more *technical* solutions than problems. Computer experts are particularly addicted to this special form of wish list. Raise a problem about the potential danger of the computers controlled by the National Security Agency, the Federal Reserve Board or AT&T and the experts conjure up a gadget or system that if adopted could eliminate the hazard.

Small, relatively inexpensive computer devices, for example, could be mass-marketed that would present an almost absolute barrier to telephone eavesdropping. Similar small devices could be manufactured that would provide the same level of protection to all written information transmitted by electronic means. The equipment, by sharply increasing the technical skills and time required for various forms of eavesdropping, would in most instances eliminate the local police and private investigators from such activities.

The problem of protecting medical records is another area that could be solved by technology. Medical records maintained by doctors, hospitals, clinics, pharmacies, state drug agencies and psychiatrists contain enormous amounts of the most revealing kinds of information that most people believe should be sharply restricted. But in the age of the computer, medical records are widely exchanged by private employers, insurance companies and a variety of government agencies and can easily be obtained by individuals with no legitimate need for the information.

One possible solution offered by technology would be to give every individual the control of his own medical records. With cheap microfiche procedures now on the market, a detailed medical history could be recorded on small wallet-sized plastic cards that would be held by the individual. With this personal information always available when a person was applying for a job, was visiting a doctor or had been injured in an accident, there would be no need for institutions such as hospitals to develop the massive computerized data bases that always are subject to abuse.

One of the largest holders of medical records—and other categories of revealing personal information—is the chain of agencies that process social security, medicare and medicaid payments. In attempting to handle this very large case load while at the same time avoiding fraudulent payments, the Social Security Administration has purchased billions of dollars' worth of computers. Since 1974, however, a special branch of Congress called the General Accounting Office has issued thirty-two separate reports identifying various serious problems of this massive computerized system. The GAO said these problems have included improper development of systems and software, deficiencies in the acquisition and operation of equipment, and the failure to provide adequate protection and security for the millions of personal records held by the Social Security Administration.

Despite the flood of critical reports and the expenditure of hundreds of millions of dollars aimed at improving the administration of this giant conglomeration of government programs, the GAO in December of 1981 reported that automatic data processing operations of the Social Security Administration "continue to be plagued by serious problems." One area targeted for special criticism was what the GAO described as the administration's long-standing lack of concern about privacy. The individual records of all the millions of persons making their payments to the social security system, receiving their monthly checks at their retirement and obtaining specific payments under the medicare and medicaid programs "constitute a valuable national resource that must be protected against alteration, destruction, abuse or misuse," the GAO said. "Better controls, both manual and automated, are needed to prevent program abuse and malicious acts of violence resulting from unauthorized access to agency facilities, records and payment systems."

The history of the computerization of social security is instructive. Faced with the responsibility of administering more and more programs, the Social Security Administration turned to the computer as its savior. As the demand for complex services increased, the administration gradually added more computers, more terminals, more systems and more communication links. But rather than taking the time to develop specific new instructions to run this growing maze of machinery as it was being enlarged, the Social Security Administration chose to make incremental changes, many of which were not recorded.

As a result of these hundreds of undocumented changes, the General Accounting Office and the Social Security Administration agree, a complex patchwork of computer systems has developed which even the most dedicated government expert is unable to understand fully. Because of this unusual chain of events, the GAO reports that the task of processing social security checks and other payments is becoming less and less efficient and more and more costly. Equally important, the job of sorting out and correcting the system becomes more difficult with every passing year.

Thus the technical fixes so glibly proposed as solutions to the various hazards of the organized computer may not offer the promised protection. Of course voice scramblers and personal encryption devices could assure increased privacy for the individual citizen. Of course a medical record stored in an individual's wallet would be less subject to abuse than a huge collection of medical records held by an insurance company or hospital. Of course the Social Security Administration could improve the security protecting the records of millions of citizens. But who is going to pay for these technical modifications? Do the large institutions that would be affected by the changes perceive them to be in their interests? And if not in their stated or unstated interests, why would the large organizations that are so important in the operation of the United States encourage a technical fix that would require a modification of their existing procedures?

The social impact of even far-reaching technical changes, however, is usually minimal without parallel changes in society's legal structure. Government agencies, for example, must write new regulations. City councils, state legislatures and Congress must pass new laws. The courts must reconsider their thinking about many issues.

Such a broad range of changes in a legal structure as large and complex as ours is a never-ending and extraordinarily challenging endeavor. President Ford and President Carter, for example, both came to the White House after the public disclosure of widespread abuses in the intelligence agencies. Both men signed lengthy executive orders that were said to restrict the collection and distribution of information about the political activities of individual citizens by these agencies. The actual language of the orders is not known because the computerized techniques of the intelligence community are so sensitive that the orders must be kept secret. The U.S. Congress, also influenced by Watergate, approved a law intended to regulate how the federal agencies collect, store and distribute the information that comes to them mostly on the computer. City councils, granting charters to cable television companies, pass ordinances prohibiting the companies from distributing such information as what homes are watching which programs without a court order. A federal judge temporarily blocks state and city agencies in New York from requiring that private charitable organizations turn over computerized records about the families who are receiving their assistance.

The changes being wrought by the computer ultimately might even prompt the American people to demand a strengthening of the Bill of Rights. With the growing power and reach of all kinds of surveillance systems, for example, they might decide an extension and clarification of the areas protected by the Fourth Amendment is essential to maintain the freedom of all Americans.

Despite the large number and far-reaching range of regulations, laws and court opinions, there are many gaping holes in the fabric of controls that the American people have so far thrown over the computer. We have seen that recent efforts to develop charter legislation regulating the information-collecting activities of the National Security Agency, the Central Intelligence Agency and the Federal Bureau of Investigation have collapsed without producing a law. A proposal by the Carter administration to establish a limited expectation of privacy for medical records met a similar fate in 1981.

One important reason for the frequent inability of society to confront the hazards raised by the computers of large organizations is the incredible complexity of the issues. A second reason has been the vehement opposition of one of the affected parties. Many members of the intelligence community, for example, were bitterly opposed to any explicit limitation on powers they had exercised for many decades.

But even when an apparently successful effort has been made to adopt a rule to deal with a specific problem, it may often create a new and different problem that the rule makers did not anticipate. The City of Evanston, Illinois, for example, recently signed a contract with Cablevision of Chicago, a private corporation that has been selected to provide the residents of Evanston with cable television.

Section 12 of the contract between the city and Cablevision sets out an extraordinarily detailed group of provisions designed to make sure that the information collected about the living habits and thoughts of the subscribers is not abused by the corporation. But then comes Section 34, which deals with service calls and complaint procedures. "The company shall keep full records in connection with all inquiries, complaints and requests in connection with the system. Such records shall identify the person contacting the company and the person responding on behalf of the company, the subject matter of the contact, the date and time it was received, the resolution of the matter in question or the action taken by the company in connection with the contact, the time and date thereof, and such other information as may be deemed pertinent by the company."

The last line of this part of Section 34 is the interesting one, the Pandora's box of the electronic age: "These records shall be made available for periodic inspection by the city." The city fathers of Evanston could see the hazards of corporate misuse of the individual information collected and stored by the computers of Cablevision, but they apparently were unable to perceive how they or their successors could also become a part of the problem.

Institutional changes may also be required to minimize the harmful effects of computerization. The computer allows and encourages

the development of large bureaucracies. Given computerized reporting systems, the chief executive of a government agency, corporation
or other institution can supervise the performance of far more lieu-
tenants than he could in the age when personal inspection was the
only way a boss could keep track of the branch manager. Given
computerized filing systems, government agencies and private corporations can register and react to the various demands of vastly more
individuals than was possible in the age of the manual file. Given the
computerized billing and payment systems, the public and private
organizations can process far more individual transactions than was
possible in the age of the handwritten ledger.

It is not surprising, therefore, that we live in the age of the huge
multinational corporations like ITT, gigantic marketing companies
like Sears and powerful bureaucracies like the Internal Revenue
Service. Of course these three institutions and thousands of others
like them offer services that please the public. Or why else would they
survive?

But at a time when a significant number of voters can remember
President Eisenhower lying about the U2 spy plane, President Johnson's false promises about Vietnam and President Nixon's self-serving and dishonest statements about Watergate, there is also
considerable public distrust of elected officials and large bureaucracies. The distrust takes various concrete forms. Anecdotes about the
commercial and government computer systems that refuse to acknowledge error sprinkle conversations at parties. The sometimes
arbitrary decisions handed down by the IRS have become a favorite
target of congressmen looking for symbols of big government to
attack. Politicians have sought to tap this reservoir of public concern
with different but related strategies. President Carter is elected partly
on the basis of his promise never to tell a lie. President Reagan's
successful campaign includes repeated denunciations of the unbending and arbitrary rules of big government.

Given the steady stream of individual horror stories and the grim
intensity of the political rhetoric complaining about the exercise of
power by the computerized organizations of our country, the people
of the United States could decide that the mere existence of large
government and corporate institutions conflicts with the American

dream of individual freedom. Antitrust and tax laws could be modified to encourage the growth of small corporations, forestall the development of any more massive ones or require the breakup of existing giants. The campaign contribution laws that seem to give corporate America such a commanding presence in Congress and the state legislatures could be amended. The laws and executive orders granting considerable power to the police and intelligence community could be reconsidered.

Other forces, however, work against the adoption of procedural changes that would modify the structure of the large organizations of the United States. Despite their size and many individual flaws, some of the giants provide quite good service. AT&T comes to mind. Another force, fanned by the bureaucracies that would be affected by change, is the public perception of steadily mounting street crime and the growing power of the Soviet bloc. One other concern is the economic threat posed by a handful of very large government-backed combines in countries like Japan.

The result of these conflicting forces usually is inaction, a kind of societal gridlock that tends to favor the organizations already holding the reins of power. One illustration is sufficient. It is true that on at least three occasions during the last twenty years, sufficient political opposition developed within Congress and other centers of power to stop or delay the development of a major new computer system that a powerful arm of the government had decided was needed. The Internal Revenue Service was blocked in its plan to build the Tax Administration System. The FBI was blocked in its plan to build a central computerized data base containing information about most of the arrests made by local and state police. The Great Society planners of President Lyndon Johnson were forced to abandon their dream of developing a national data system that would centralize all the information collected about each individual citizen within a single computer.

But the three victories registered by the various individuals and organizations concerned about the long-term impact of these systems were somewhat accidental, the unexpected result of unusual alliances. And weighing against the few decisions not to proceed have been scores of decisions to develop powerful new computer systems.

Despite strenuous warnings about the serious hazards of a centrally controlled telecommunications network to process electronic funds transfers, for example, the Federal Reserve Board continues its inexorable drive to build just such a system. Despite similar deep concerns about the National Security Agency, it continues to increase its penetration and control of the most sensitive areas of telecommunications policy.

More important than the scoreboard of victories and defeats, however, is the failure of the United States to work out a way to consider the merits and demerits of every major new computer system before the sponsoring bureaucracy has committed millions of dollars and its organizational prestige to the project. After many years of study and consideration, Senator Sam Ervin decided the danger of massed data bases was sufficient to require the creation of a permanent counterweight, a commission that could serve as an institutional ombudsman for both public and private computer systems. He made the proposal despite a profound mistrust of new government agencies in the belief that such a counterweight was essential to the preservation of freedom. While similar bodies have been established in several European countries such as Sweden and Germany, the plan was opposed by many large institutions in the United States and was flatly rejected by Congress. To this day, in a period of steadily accelerating use of the computer, no mechanism has been devised to weigh the advantages and disadvantages of one of the most powerful instruments devised by man.

But even the profound change implicit in the creation of an *institution* that would review the use of computers by government agencies and private corporations would not be of sufficient compass to generate the social revolution that may be required by the arrival of the computer state. Everyone, from the most enthusiastic booster to the most fervent critic, agrees that the computer has brought, is bringing and will bring profound changes in the shape of our society. Many economists and other experts, for example, are convinced that the computer will alter the fundamental nature of work for a large segment of the American people and may lead to a substantial long-term decline among factory employees, office workers and white-collar professionals such as engineers.

The most optimistic observers do not believe there will be a net decline in available jobs, though they acknowledge that computerization will cause major dislocations in certain specific industries and areas. The loss of jobs among the auto workers of Detroit, they contend, will be offset by the creation of new jobs in new industries, perhaps in different geographic sections of the United States.

The social problems generated by these computer-generated changes in the work patterns of the American people may well represent the most serious challenge of the computer age. To develop training and other programs to even begin to cope with this challenge is going to require an unprecedented degree of cooperation between the schools, labor unions, corporations, and state and local governments of the United States.

Rodney A. Bower, the president of the International Federation of Professional and Technical Engineers, visited Europe several years ago to examine how such countries as Sweden, Germany and Great Britain were attempting to deal with the computerization of their economies. In a subsequent report, he said that virtually all the government and management officials expressed confidence that the new technologies, as had happened in the past with earlier forms of automation, would lead to the overall creation of jobs.

"But every employer we spoke to, be it a bank, a manufacturing company, or a communications organization, expressed interest in the new developments as means for increasing productivity and halting personnel growth in that organization," Bower explained.

"Well, the whole is the sum of its parts. If every single organization seeks to end employment growth, or even reduce total manpower, and populations continue to increase, where will new jobs come from in the future?"

The impact of the computers on employment frequently is startling. Harley Shaiken, a research associate at the Massachusetts Institute for Technology, reported at an AFL-CIO workshop that Chrysler engineers took fifteen minutes to design the geometry of the steering gear for the 1982 Dodge. In 1956, before the introduction of computer-assisted design equipment, the same job took three months. He further noted that a government study in France and an industry study in Germany predicted that at least 30 percent of the office jobs in those countries in such areas as banking, insurance and government would be eliminated by 1990 because of the computer.

A report prepared by a British trade union, the Association of Scientific, Technical and Managerial Staff, found that seven Japanese manufacturers reduced their combined work force from 48,000 to 25,000 workers between 1972 and 1976. During the same period, production increased by 25 percent.

A broader view of the impact of computers on the world auto industry was provided by Arthur J. Cordell, science adviser to the Science Council of Canada, at a conference in Iowa in 1982. "The automated automobile factories of North America are twice as efficient as their less automated counterparts in the United Kingdom, while the most automated factories in Japan are twice as efficient as the North American auto plants. Thus in the United Kingdom, the auto industry produces about fifteen to seventeen cars per man-year; Japan's industry produces almost seventy cars per man-year."

The social problems created by the computerization of work are monumental. Which workers are going to be retrained for new jobs? Who is going to pay for retraining? Does the government in fact have an obligation to provide everyone a job? What about a guaranteed annual income? Most people define themselves in large part by their work. I am a shoemaker. I am a gardener. I am a writer. I am an engineer. I am a lawyer. Assuming that the computer reduces the total hours of work needed to keep our society running and reduces the need for blue- and white-collar workers who also are skilled craftsmen, will the psychological health of millions of Americans be damaged?

Devising effective strategies to ameliorate the economic and psychologic wounds that many believe inevitably will be inflicted by the computerization of America is going to require extraordinary wisdom. Developing a national consensus to transfer the strategies into concrete programs will require great political skill. It also may require a fundamental change in our values.

Thomas R. Donahue, an official of the AFL-CIO, discussed one such change he thought would be necessary. "I think it's time that America's corporations are judged not on their bottom-line profits alone, but rather on their responsibility toward their workers and the communities in which they operate," he told a 1979 conference.

"Why can't we say that XYZ Corporation had a bad year because it ended the year with fewer employees than the year before? Why can't we say that the Apex Corporation had a bad year because it closed its plants in Akron or Columbus and left three hundred workers without jobs? That's surely a greater failure than a drop of one or two cents in the dividends that year. Until we get those kinds of social measures, until we teach Americans to measure our corporations in that fashion—we won't solve the problem of adjusting to new technology."

Another change that may be required is for the United States to abandon its hostile view toward social planning. Coordinated programs involving a variety of different government and private organizations and possibly millions of workers will have to be established. Schools will have to change curriculums. Welfare agencies will have to change eligibility requirements. The federal government will have to consider changing the tax laws to provide corporations with incentives to find new jobs for obsolete workers. Unions will probably have to change some of their most cherished goals. All these projects and other developments will have to be integrated in ways that will make coordinated programs available to the affected blue-collar, white-collar and professional workers as different segments of the economy and different areas of the country are hit by different waves of computerization.

But the level of social coordination that apparently will be required to deal successfully with the possible dislocation of large segments of the American population may require a decision to grant the nation's social planners extraordinary power. One man who has thought a great deal about the use and abuse of power is Samuel J. Ervin, Jr., the retired senator, still alert and active and practicing law in the small town of Morganton, North Carolina.

Ervin sat behind a large antique desk in his small office in the modern glass and steel building down the street from the old stone courthouse where his father practiced law in the foothills of western North Carolina. He was wearing a bright electric-blue jacket, a blue tie and checked trousers. The only real sign of the burden of his eighty-six years were the gnarled arthritic fingers on the hand that occasionally stabbed the air for emphasis.

"I think that if history teaches us anything, it teaches us that no man or set of men can be safely trusted with unlimited or unsupervised power. For that reason, I think the greatest threat to freedom is big government. James Madison says that, you know, in *The Federalist Papers*. In effect he says the concentration of power in one individual or one body or one group is the very essence of tyranny. James Madison also said something I don't see quoted very often when he was talking to the Virginia convention that ratified the Constitution. He said that people had lost more power from the insidious and quiet usurpation of power by those people in authority than they had at the hands of any dictator."

Sam Ervin shifted in his chair. The small electric heater clicked off and on as it warmed the office against the blustery winter wind. "The Privacy Act, if enforced," he continued, "would be a pretty good thing. But the government doesn't like it. Government has an insatiable appetite for power, and it will not stop usurping power unless it is restrained by laws they cannot repeal or nullify. There are mighty few laws they cannot nullify.

"The unfortunate thing is that so many people in high places don't have time to study problems," he said in reply to a question about the social impact of the growing use of computers. "Most legislators, it seems, are too busy with other things to understand where the threat lies."

But it is not just those in high places who have to learn where the threats lie. The American people must observe and learn and understand. They must not allow the complexity of these machines and the vast reach of the organizations that are harnessing them to obscure their vision. They must work together to devise a multitude of solutions to the prickly forest of problems that have been nurtured by the computer.

There are grounds for optimism, there are reasons for pessimism. In a floundering way, the people of the United States have already taken a number of important steps to tame the savage beast they perceive within the cool machinery of the computer. Laws have been passed by Congress and many state and local legislatures. Regulations have been written to restrict the use of computerized data for socially acceptable purposes. The development of several large computerized data systems that had the backing of powerful organizations has been stopped or slowed in the name of humanity. The easy cynicism of the technologist who insists that nothing can be done to stop technology is thus unfounded.

But there are enormous gaps in the laws that have been passed and the regulations that have been written. And for every computerized system whose development has been stopped because of concern about its harmful impact, scores of other systems have been set in place with little or no examination of the questions that surround their operation. The point is, we can act if we choose to act or we can passively allow ourselves to be blinded by our ignorance.

Chief Justice Charles Evans Hughes put the responsibility where it belongs. "You may think that the Constitution is your security—it is nothing but a piece of paper. You may think that the statutes are your security—they are nothing but words in a book. You may think that elaborate mechanism of government is your security—it is nothing at all unless you have sound and uncorrupted public opinion to give life to your Constitution, to give vitality to your statutes, to make efficient your machinery."

A
Future

I do not believe that the kind of society I describe
necessarily will arrive, but I believe . . . that something resembling it could arrive.

—George Orwell

Manhattan. A cold winter day in the year 2020. Peter Strauss, a
marketing executive with the Chase Manhattan Bank, looks down
from the window of his sunny Lexington Avenue apartment at the
nearly deserted streets below him. The icy wind has discouraged
the few shoppers who on pleasant days still prefer to wander through
the polished boutiques and elegant wine stores and brightly lit deli-
catessens that dot the spotless neighborhood where many of America's most powerful executives, bankers, scientists and artists have
chosen to live and work and play.

Strauss, who was born in 1970, muses about the years when he was
growing up in the same area on the East Side of Manhattan. Then
the streets were choked with people, he remembers. Mink-coated
men and women looking for designer jeans. Earnest young lawyers
trudging to the Wall Street-bound subways. Flip youngsters, dressed
in the blue blazer uniforms of their high-pressure prep schools,
laughing and shouting as they jumped on the crosstown bus. Gloomy
couples waiting patiently in long lines to see the latest movie from
Japan or Italy or France. And partly because the shoppers then still
paid for many of their purchases by currency, there was also an
occasional robber.

But now, with every apartment, office, supermarket, store and bank in Manhattan tied together by a mysterious strand of light-filled glass, a modern cornucopia of information, there is almost no reason to ever venture on the street, especially on an icy day in February.

Peter Strauss pushed the memories aside, idly wondering why he had always been so interested in the past, in history, in the incredible rush of technology and commerce that in just a few decades had so changed the process of life in the United States and the values of the American people. Turning from the window, he sat down at the large flat table that had become such an important part of his life. He touched a discreet button and a panel in the table slid back, revealing a key board. At the same time, a large abstract painting on the far wall slid noiselessly aside to reveal a telescreen and a built-in recording system snapped on. The equipment was the unified communication terminal of the Information Company, the successor to the New York Telephone Company.

Peter announced his name and his personal identity number. After checking to make sure his voice and number were properly recorded in the national data base, the natural sounding voice of the Information Company, actually a speech synthesizer, asked him what he wanted. Speaking in a low tone and at a natural pace, he asked the computer to give him the balance sheet of his account in the National Electronics Funds Banking System. A second later, the Information Company's computer dipped into the Banking System's computer and flashed Strauss' financial sheet on the tele-screen. He was surprised to see that the utility bill, which had been automatically deducted from his account three days before, was considerably higher than deductions of the last few months. Then he remembered that the Utility Commission had granted the power company a rate increase the week before.

He then asked the Information Company computer for the departure time of all jets flying to Los Angeles that afternoon. A listing of all available flights replaced his financial statement on the screen. Tapping a few numbers on the key board, he ordered and paid for his ticket on the noon flight.

The trip to Los Angeles was for the bank, to explore whether Chase Manhattan should consider merging with a large West Coast computer company. For a moment Strauss thought about detouring to San Francisco to see his former wife, a painter who had recently received a lifetime grant from the National Department of Fine Arts. They had not lived together for many years, but had remained friends. He rejected the idea. The federal banking inspectors who automatically received and scanned the travel, financial and Information Company records of all bank executives might not approve. He knew the inspectors would not openly criticize a personal detour —as long as he paid for it himself—but that the trip would be regarded as a bit romantic and therefore mildly suspicious. Of course there was no way he could travel anywhere without the automatic construction of a detailed record of his journey.

Glancing at the digital clock that was projected on the lower righthand corner of his telescreen, Peter Strauss realized it was time for his scheduled meeting with his boss, the Chase Manhattan vice-president for marketing. Speaking to the invisible microphones, he announced the call for the meeting and gave the identifying number of his supervisor. Within a few seconds, the two men were brought together by an advanced teleconferencing system in which the holographic presence of each banker was transmitted to the home of the other in such a realistic manner that despite their knowledge of the technology, the two men almost immediately forgot they were actually forty-five miles apart. Peter's boss, Andrew Clurman, was in fact sitting in his house in New Canaan, Connecticut.

"Good morning, Andrew, did the ice storm do much damage out there?" Peter asked, tacitly acknowledging the distance which the technology so glibly denied. After a moment of small talk about the storm, the two men got down to the subject of the meeting: the bank's long-standing practice of making substantial campaign contributions to each of New York's two senators.

"Listen, Andrew," Strauss said, "the bank began making these contributions a long, long time ago, before we were around. From the stuff I've read, the senators at that time actually had some power —they could help you or hurt you. But now these two jokers, Garcia and Cohen, and the whole Senate, for that matter, have about as much influence as a dummy in the window of Bloomingdale's."

Peter Strauss' father had been an editor with the *New York Times* back when it was an independent newspaper rather than a computerized news service and a division of the Gulf Oil Corporation. Unlike the homes of most of his boyhood friends, his home had been full of newspapers, books and magazines. With a perspective on history quite rare to people in his generation, Peter Strauss was able to see that Congress was a shadow of what it had once been. He correctly perceived that the power of the president and executive branch to control the instantaneous national polling system—to frame the questions that were asked and paraphrase the answers that were given—had reduced Congress to a ceremonial institution with no real constituency.

"They still make a lot of noise, fight like hell to get the perks of office, but they have lost their power to do anything for the bank," Peter Strauss argued. "I think we should just stop pretending that Congress is anything more than a cave of winds and cut the cord."

Clurman acknowledged agreement with a silent nod. "I think you're right, and I'll take it up with the executive committee at our tele-meeting next week," he said.

The two men had completed their business. Peter Strauss waved good-bye to his boss and asked the control computer to end the meeting; the holographic presence of Andrew Clurman evaporated from his apartment like magic.

It was time to go to Los Angeles. Peter Strauss again spoke to the empty room, this time ordering a cab to take him to LaGuardia Airport. A few minutes later the cab was waiting by the entrance of his apartment. The driver already knew the destination because it had been printed out on the little screen connected to the meter. The two men had little reason to begin a conversation and they did not. When they reached the airport, Peter Strauss shoved a wallet-sized plastic card into the small computerized device located in the passenger's compartment of the cab and then tapped out his personal identity number, the fare and amount of the tip. The information was transmitted by radio to Peter Strauss' bank, where the proper deductions were made from his account and instantaneously deposited in the separate accounts of the cab company and the driver. Because currency could be lost or stolen, and a computerized communication net had been laid down in most of the cities and suburbs of the United States, it was almost never necessary to carry pocket money.

The same cold day in the year 2020. A few miles to the north of Peter Strauss' warm apartment on Lexington Avenue, the scarred outer door of an old brownstone tenement house flaps in the wind. The hallway is strewn with rubble and garbage. The sharp smell of urine fills the air. The stairs sag. A thin trickle of water drips from the landing above. Somewhere on the upper floors of the tenement, a water pipe has burst.

Two flights up, the muffled sound of clanking steel. Behind a door, partially protected from vandals by a thin sheet of metal, Bill Peterson fastened down the old Fox lock, a complicated arrangement of security bars.

Years before, the New York City Police Department had almost completely abandoned the Bronx—the huge, ugly, half-burned-out area to the north of Manhattan. The littered lots, the boarded-up windows, the abandoned cars, the garbage-strewn gutters, the grimy sidewalks were appalling. But somehow the powerful forces of life continued to display themselves. Even in the cold, the street-wise fleet-footed kids played their games, the young laughing mothers proudly held their babies, the pitiless street gangs strutted around their bonfires, the powerful hoodlums in their plumed hats and fancy capes somehow recalled the courtiers of medieval Italy. The sound of competing radios filled the air. The backyard clotheslines flapped with their strings of cheap, brightly colored clothing.

Bill Peterson, like Peter Strauss, had been born in 1970. Because his father had been a gambler, a successful merchant in one of the few businesses open to him, an executive in the illicit numbers game who of course shared his earnings with the police, Bill Peterson was one of the few residents of the Bronx to still hold any job, let alone one with the government.

Every day, six days a week, Bill Peterson cleaned the toilets and swept the hallways of the single heavily fortified outpost that the New York City Police Department still maintained in the Bronx. The job did not pay much, and along with virtually all the other men and women in the Bronx he could have chosen to receive about the same amount of money from the welfare department without the necessity of actually working. But along with the police job came an extra benefit that welfare did not provide: a plastic tamperproof identity card that allowed him to pass through the guarded and computerized checkpoints that had been erected on all the bridges, tunnels and subways that led to the sanitized island of Manhattan.

Bill Peterson finished the elaborate procedure of barricading the door against the marauding junkies. He then turned to Sally Higgins, the pregnant young woman who shared the small flat with him. Sally sat with an old olive-drab army blanket around her shoulders. A smile flashed across her face as Peterson pulled four large candy bars from the sagging pocket of the worn tweed topcoat he had pulled from a trash can two years before.

"I went across the river today," he explained. "I was walking along 59th Street and it was so cold that the man had left his stand to warm up a bit," he said, holding the stolen candy in each hand. "Jesus, it was cold." Sally had not been to Manhattan for ten years, ever since the city government adopted the pass requirement, so she could barely remember the clean streets, beautiful display windows and shiny cars. But she was grateful for the treat. The thick, sweet, crunchy chocolate sharply contrasted with her normal diet.

Sally was relieved. Early that morning, after Peterson had gone to work, she had made a quick trip down to the government-operated grocery store where she had drawn her weekly ration of cheese, powdered milk, dried eggs and ketchup. The bundle of supplies had been shoved at her through a small opening cut in the heavy metal grill after she had slipped her plastic computerized food card into an automatic scanner. Then Sally had returned to the apartment she shared with Peterson. The hours after he normally returned from his job had been full of worry for Sally. But it was too dangerous for a woman to go anywhere in the Bronx without very good cause, and there was nothing she could do but wait.

Sally was only twenty years old. Unlike Peterson, she only had gone to school, or what passed for school, for five years. After that, she lost contact with her mother and began wandering the streets with a gang of extraordinarily tough kids, all under twelve. Lacking any skills required of even moderately successful people in the year 2020, she had never held a job. Without any work record or experience, without a lease or mortgage, without any money, the Information Company quite appropriately never even considered giving her the complex electronic equipment that made Peter Strauss' life so convenient and comfortable.

Sally could not read. Even if one of the Information Company's terminals had been available to her, she could not have used it. While the terminal was designed to respond to voice instructions, and thus partially obviate the need for traditional literacy, operating it assumed a mechanical proficiency far exceeding the almost nonexistent skills that Sally had learned while wandering through the streets of the Bronx. With no ability to read, no books, no newspapers, no history, Sally had no knowledge of the country or world beyond her few short years in the Bronx.

But Bill Peterson, like Peter Strauss, could read and did have memories. He remembered when there were no checkpoints, when a special identity card was not needed to enter Manhattan. He also remembered when the Bronx still had a small voice in the political decisions made at City Hall in Manhattan, or Albany and even Washington. An exceptionally brilliant child, Peterson had surmounted the casual, almost nonexistent public schools of the eighties and had won a scholarship to Columbia College. But then in 1990, his second year, he was arrested during a demonstration of the five black students then attending Columbia. He was charged with assaulting a police officer. Peterson had of course been much too smart to offer any resistance when the police broke up their pitiful protest, and the case was soon dismissed. Without a lawyer to bring a suit against the State of New York, however, there was no way to remove the damaging information from the computerized criminal-history files. Once affixed to his name, the assault charge meant the end of his nearly impossible dream to leap the powerful social currents that like the East River so completely separated the people of Manhattan and the Bronx.

While the arrest record had made it impossible for him to keep his scholarship and continue college, it ironically was not an obstacle a few years later when, because of the old partnership of his gambler father and the Bronx police commander, he was given the job of sweeping out the station house. The police, after all, understood that the charge of assaulting a police officer, especially when not prosecuted by the district attorney, was an indication of political concern, not criminal behavior.

These two snapshots of America in the year 2020—the one showing a superficially glossy but limiting world of high technology, the other a despairing underclass—are not the only possible futures available to the United States. After all, there are few things as risky as attempting to predict the course of history, particularly of a country as large and vibrant and energetic as the United States. The public school systems of our central cities, for example, could learn how to use the computer to inspire and teach and uplift the hordes of disheartened, embittered and sometimes violent children they now often try to cage.

The revised school systems, working with industry, labor and the federal government, could provide the children of the slums and the blue- and white-collar workers made unemployable by robots and high-speed word processors with the necessary skills to find new creative jobs.

The FBI and the state and local police departments could be forced to curb their seemingly insatiable appetite to collect and store and share more and more information about more and more people and keep their investigations aimed only at the genuine outlaws.

The incredible access to the information of the world that a computer terminal can provide a trained person could create a new age of gentle reason and art, a second Renaissance of the human spirit. But there are powerful forces at work in the early 1980s that could shape our society into a dark and joyless army and not the exciting, playful, creative and purposeful family of artists, scientists, students, craftsmen and philosophers of our dreams.

The pervasive fear of crime, the unrelenting demand for more security, the corrosive impact of trying to make society's decisions on the basis of a numerically determined idea of efficiency, all these may be inching our country by small, almost invisible, steps toward a final destination that many of us, perhaps even most of us, would prefer to avoid. This gradual drift toward authoritarianism suggests that in addition to taking steps to curb the crime, terrorism and subversion of individual lawbreakers, society also must be alert to the overreaching ambitions of large organizations.

There have been other times, of course, when the reaction to a mood of fearfulness has threatened our country. But this time the men and women who direct our government, our corporations and other large institutions have armed themselves with the computer, that powerful instrument of organization that can be used for good or ill, and sometimes for both at the same moment.

Within the next decade or so, these computers will spin dozens of new communication networks across the face of America. One massive computerized network, for example, will substantially change the way we pay for almost everything we buy. A second network will significantly alter the way we receive information such as airplane schedules, entertainment and news. A third system will greatly enhance the easy availability of all information that comes to the attention of law enforcement. A fourth national system, quite likely, will greatly increase the power of the IRS to collect, store and transmit detailed financial information about every person in the United States.

Anticipating the future is difficult in any case. But attempting to understand the potential impacts of systems as large and powerful as these is unusually challenging. The task of perceiving the effects of these particular systems is especially difficult because of the lack of obvious villains—government officials or corporate executives who knowingly are plotting to create a dismal world where the bureaucracies have grown too large, too arbitrary and too powerful to serve our individual needs.

Certainly George W. Mitchell, sitting in a small unpretentious office at the Federal Reserve Board in Washington, does not appear to fit this mold. Mr. Mitchell is officially retired now, no longer a member of the governing body of one of America's least known and most powerful institutions, the Federal Reserve Board. But as vice-chairman of the board from 1973 to 1976, a member from 1961, and now as the board's consultant on electronic funds transfer (EFT), the cheerful economist with the bright blue eyes and wavy white hair and gold-rimmed glasses has been a key advocate of a financial development that many experts believe represents the single most serious threat to American liberty.

Mr. Mitchell contends that such worries are, as he put it in his forthright way, "a lot of goddammed nonsense. Sure, I suppose that a computer might someday be able to become a threat in this area. It is theoretically possible. But a lot of things are theoretically possible that never are going to happen. If you are engaged in an illicit business like drug peddling or robbing the Internal Revenue Service or whatever, then you should use cash and not checks or electronic payment systems of the future. But if you are an honest citizen, nobody gives a damn about your account."

Others disagree. The Privacy Protection Study Commission, for example, was created by Congress a few years ago to make an overall investigation of what steps are required to maintain the individual rights guaranteed by the Constitution. After two years of study, the seven members of the commission unanimously concluded that, given the likely improvements in computer technology, government operation of electronics funds transfer was "dangerous" and posed "an unparalleled threat to personal privacy." A few months later, the White House Office of Telecommunications Policy under President Ford opposed plans for a national EFT center because such a center would give the federal government "a highly effective tool for keeping track of people and enforcing 'correct' behavior."

But under the law, the Federal Reserve Board is unusually autonomous and the objections of congressionally created commissions and executive branch officials, no matter how vigorously phrased, do not necessarily carry any weight. Furthermore, there are powerful economic forces at work that tend to encourage the board's natural inclination to develop an extraordinarily ambitious communication system. And once this system is in place, it will in fact give the board an unprecedented ability to collect and monitor details about many of the millions of daily financial transactions that together mark the ebb and flow of the American economy.

What is electronic funds transfer, or EFT? Simply put, EFT is any network or group of networks in which the processing necessary for any economic exchange is accomplished by brief electronic messages.

As such, EFT systems reduce or eliminate the need for the movement of paper in the form of either checks or currency.

After decades of talk, the Federal Reserve Board and the banking industry are beginning to actually develop a number of different EFT systems and applications. One example of such a system is widely known as the automatic teller machine, or ATM. An ATM, as presently used by many banks, allows a customer to withdraw cash and transact other business with the bank on a twenty-four-hour basis. As this is written, there are about 9,000 ATMs operating in the United States. By 1985, the number of installed ATMs are expected to reach 18,000, double the machines operating today, and by 1995, many experts believe there will be 50,000 ATMs.

As the reach of the separate ATM networks broadens, there ultimately will be a need for central, regional and perhaps even national switching points, a juncture where the competing ATM systems can swap information. The Federal Reserve Board, already providing a similar service for the banks, sees itself as the natural proprietor of such a switch for the banking needs of both individual citizens and corporations.

An example of an EFT application, in contrast with the EFT system, involves the decision of many corporations and government agencies to pay employees or beneficiaries by electronic means rather than by check. Consider the Social Security Administration. In 1977, 5 million Americans, 16.7 percent of all recipients, received their monthly social security payment thanks to a blip in the computer that subtracted a few hundred dollars from the U.S. Treasury and added the same sum to the bank account of the appropriate senior citizen. Five years later, such payments had more than doubled and 11.1 million Americans, or 33.3 percent of the total recipients, had abandoned the paper chase.

A second indication of the shift from a paper to an electronic economy in the United States is the sharp decline in the use of currency—greenbacks and coins—in relation to gross national product. Between 1955 and 1980, the use of currency in relation to the GNP had declined by about 50 percent, dropping from 6.9 to 4.2 percent in just twenty-five years.

The movement away from currency and the growth in use of

checks and electronic transfers has been encouraged by the policies of the Treasury Department. On July 14, 1969, the Bureau of the Mint announced that it no longer would print $500, $1,000, $5,000 and $10,000 bills. In addition to halting the printing of the large-denomination bills so handy for anonymous transactions, the Treasury Department also asked the Federal Reserve banks to withdraw them from circulation any time they entered the system. Such bills are now mostly held by collectors.

The fundamental forces moving the United States toward a broad acceptance of electronic funds transfer, however, are economic. George Mitchell, the Federal Reserve Board's EFT guru, said one such force is the cost of processing paper.

Very little work has been done in the United States on how much it actually costs a bank to handle an individual check, Mitchell explained. But in the late 1970s, a detailed analysis was done in the United Kingdom that concluded that 60 to 70 percent of bank resources—people, branches and equipment—are consumed in processing checks.

Mr. Mitchell said that because of the similarities between the two countries it was reasonable to apply the British findings to the United States. "In 1980 U.S. commercial banks spent $24.6 billion for salaries, wages and employees benefits, $7.3 billion for occupancy and equipment, $14.6 billion for all other operating expenses. Applying the U.K. experience to these data, payment services involving cash and deposit transfer cost U.S. commercial banks something on the order of $25 to $28 million in 1980. This means the cost to the banks was in the range of 65¢ to 80¢ for every check."

Like all bankers, Mr. Mitchell is committed to the principle that there is no free lunch. This conviction in turn leads him to believe that the real expenses of processing currency and checks will exert an enormous and continuing pressure on the banking industry to change "the U.S. payments system from paper and its transport to electronics and telecommunications."

Mr. Mitchell's certainty about the future of EFT has found concrete expression in the decision of the Federal Reserve Board to launch a major program to restructure its communication system, which currently is hard-pressed to process about half of the 35 billion checks written each year in the United States.

The new system is called FRCS-80, a set of initials standing for Federal Reserve Communications System for the Eighties. During its seven-year lifetime, the system may cost the banks who support it about $250 million. But the planners, who began working on the system in 1975, are convinced that the expenses of developing FRCS-80 will be offset by the reduction in the cost of transferring payments throughout the nation's economy.

Mr. Mitchell said the board's decision to move ahead with FRCS-80 was based on three assumptions. First, the system should be flexible enough to accommodate the significant increase in EFT payments expected in the next ten years. Second, the proposed system should also be able to satisfy the board's internal needs for providing additional services to banks, the Treasury Department and other government agencies. Third, FRCS-80 should provide a standard nationwide approach through which all types of depository institutions could access and use the network for the electronic transfer of both funds and securities.

What do all the separate but intricately related developments within the Federal Reserve Board and the banking industry mean to the individual consumer within the next decade or so? The answer is the same whoever is talking. Even the most avid supporters of the banking industry and the Federal Reserve Board agree with the critics of these institutions that the computerization and centralization of banking will mean that more information will be collected and readily available about more and more Americans.

One of the latest studies of the electronic funds transfer environment was made for the Office of Technological Assessment, a research arm of Congress, by a group of computer and communication experts associated with the University of California at Irvine.

The conclusions of the Irvine group are sobering. The increased use of EFT, as a substitute for cash, means more transactions could be monitored through electronic networks, the group said. As the speed of the various computerized banking systems increases, the potential for instantaneously learning the activities of an individual grows. The development of regional and national interchanges, coupled with faster computers, could allow instantaneous monitoring of an individual's activities beyond the local level. The increasing concentration of information of all types, including EFT, savings, demand deposit, mortgage and other loans, in a single computer-based file, or a system of files linked by computers, will make personal information easily retrievable at less cost and with greater speed.

The group further concluded that the legal framework and technological momentum of the EFT systems were increasing the potential hazards. The requirements of the recently passed EFT Act, coupled with the information requirements of the banks for the correction of errors and the reversal of mistaken transactions, will expand the amount of information associated with each transaction. As the range of services available through EFT grows to include general accounting and tax systems, the potential for access to even greater amounts of personal information increases. As EFT terminal networks grow beyond present limited geographic areas, the places at which or through which a breach of confidentiality could occur also increase in quantity and remoteness.

Mr. Mitchell does not argue with most of these judgments. But like many supporters of EFT, he has enormous faith in the integrity of the present governors of the Federal Reserve Board and the banking fraternity in general. He therefore rejects as outlandish the suggestion that the gradual installation of a national network of EFT systems—under the guiding hand of the board—is a matter of serious concern.

John Eger was the acting director of the White House Office of Telecommunication Policy under President Ford. Now a Washington lawyer, he is a cautious, conservative man. A few years ago, in an article published in the *Catholic University Law Review,* he described his view of EFT. "A detailed monitoring of the information carried on such a system could easily generate data on a user's buying habits, political activities, physical movements and nearly every other aspect of his personal life," he said.

Mr. Eger contended that history has repeatedly taught us not to place total reliance on the continued goodwill of large bureaucracies. The lawyer recalled as an historical analogy the IRS—an agency that originally was created as an independent body whose records were only to be used for income tax purposes—and how all the presidents from Franklin Roosevelt to Richard Nixon had violated the law and used tax records for secret political purposes.

But the electronic funds transfer system is not the only computerized network that soon will fundamentally alter the way we live. A second system, one that will reach directly into the homes of millions of Americans, has also begun to creep across the face of the land. An intimation of just one of the far-reaching effects of this second system was presented to the American people during the 1980 campaign for the White House.

Within a hundred minutes after the nationally televised debate between Ronald Reagan and Jimmy Carter, three-quarters of a million Americans used their telephones to flash a thumbs up/thumbs down verdict on the confrontation to an electronic voting booth set up by AT&T for the news division of the American Broadcasting Company. It was the world's largest and fastest public opinion poll.

Though the ABC survey was conceptually and technically flawed, it was a one-shot example of what well may become a daily exercise in the not-very-distant future when two-way interactive television systems have been established in most parts of the United States. Despite its somewhat misleading name, such systems are not two-way in the sense that they allow the operator to peek into a subscriber's home, only in that the subscriber is able to answer questions or place orders via the wire that brings the television picture into the home. Politicians, news organizations and marketing companies, for example, already are harnessing Qube, a prototype of such a computer system in Columbus, Ohio, to harvest public feelings about a variety of issues ranging from national energy policies to the appropriate role of the homosexual in America.

The ability to collect and tabulate almost immediately the reactions of millions of Americans to a specific event or problem could ultimately work to reduce the cynical feeling of alienation that today seems to infect so many Americans. But it could just as well lead to a serious weakening of individual rights, the destruction of many of the existing institutions of representative government and the gradual erosion of the confidence, independent judgments and leadership of public officials.

Two-way interactive television, the communications revolution
that presents such starkly contrasting opportunities for good and
evil, is a computer-powered system that now gives the family that is
hooked to it a way of instantly answering the multiple-choice questions they are asked or a method of ordering the goods and services
they are offered.

At the present time the home terminal of this electrical umbilical
cord is a small plastic keyboard about the size of a thick paperback
novel that is attached to the family television set. When responding
to a question, for example, the subscriber "touches in" on one of a
series of buttons, the central computer swiftly calculates the percentage of the audience that prefers the various options, and an answer
is displayed on the home screen.

The system also allows the subscribing family the option of wiring
their home with sophisticated security and health monitoring devices
and greatly expanding the entertainment, news, educational and
information programs that are piped into the living room.

Two-way interactive television has been the subject of rather
dreamy blue-sky speculation for more than a decade. But now, with
500,000 wired homes expected within the next three or four years
and many millions more by the late eighties, the wave of the future
is about to crash on the beach of reality.

The opportunities for two-way interactive television to enrich
America's cultural life, improve the responsiveness of government
bureaucracies and even solve the national energy crisis by eliminating the need to drive to the shopping center or town meeting have
been eloquently celebrated by executives selling the system and optimistic futurists such as Alvin Toffler. The perils, however, have been
largely ignored. Some problems:

Instant Polling: As already noted, the technical ability of two-way
television to continually monitor the pulse of the body politic creates
an almost irresistible desire to engage in the measurement of impul-
sive political judgment. If ABC News is willing to ask the American
people who won a presidential debate, why won't ABC News or
some other organization decide to ask the nation whether the United
States should immediately start dropping bombs the next time some
nation decides to seize a group of American diplomats? And how

would such unreflective and necessarily ill-informed opinion influence the actions of the politician then occupying the White House or the response of the country holding the hostages?

Personal Privacy: With a fully developed two-way system, a large number of significant details about the life of the subscribing family will be funneled through the system's computer. The information collected by such a computer might well include messages sent by electronic mail to a stockbroker or travel agent, various banking transactions, books ordered at the local bookstore or library, hours devoted to various pay-per-view programs including soft-core pornography, and the comings and goings of those subscribers who signed up for security services. Though such details are now frequently recorded by separate organizations, the concentration of the data in the computer of one privately owned company clearly presents a much enlarged snooping hazard.

Collective Privacy: Even if laws and procedures are developed to provide each subscriber with an ironclad guarantee that individually identifiable information will never be improperly shared, neighborhood patterns of book reading, television watching, banking and electronic shopping will give commercial and political marketing experts a powerful new tool to burrow into the psyches of unsuspecting customers. When the information collected by the computer of the two-way television system is merged with the information collected on a tract-by-tract basis by the Census Bureau, the super salesmen will be able to target their ever-more-refined pitches only at those who have indicated they are most susceptible to them.

Information Deprivation: The basic two-way service offered by the new information providers is not expensive. But obtaining all the extras can be quite costly. The rate for the full range of services offered by the system in Dallas, for example, currently is $47 a month. As such systems become more and more essential in the delivery of cultural, educational and political information, will the ability to purchase the service further widen the gap that already separates the poor from the rest of society? Behind this issue lies a complex debate about whether two-way television systems should continue to be owned and operated by traditional business organizations or whether they ultimately should be considered a regulated utility.

Blurring: With the enormous increase in the number of channels entering the home of subscribers, many new kinds of programs are possible. One program offered on an experimental basis in Columbus is called the "infomercial," a combination of the objective documentary and paid commercial. Some consumer experts fear the marriage of the two forms could increase the distribution of misleading and confusing information. Lurking behind this problem is the broad question of editorial responsibility. Should the owners of two-way cable systems be considered similar to newspaper publishers and granted the First Amendment rights and obligations given newspapers? Or should cable systems be likened to the telephone company and be required to carry any message that an individual wants to send?

Regulation: A traditional American response to a serious social problem is to establish a new government agency to deal with it. In this case, however, where easy-to-destroy values such as freedom of speech and privacy are at stake, the cure might well end up being more deadly than the disease. Curiously enough, that possibility has not stopped Sweden, France and several other European countries from recently establishing strong government agencies to inspect and license the very computerized information bases that need protection. The prospect of a similar fox being asked to guard the chicken coop in the United States may well be the ultimate ironic threat of the revolution now occurring within the nation's communications system. The swiftly dimming but nevertheless powerful memories of the Watergate years remind us that government agencies sometimes abuse their powers.

All the talk about the potential problems inherent in the broad changes occurring in communications irritates Gustave M. Hauser, a major figure in the commercial development of two-way interactive television. "Tony Oettinger, the Harvard professor, got it right at a seminar in Cambridge last year," he said. "Perils, perils, perils. If we keep worrying about all the perils, we're going to be paralyzed."

Mr. Hauser, a Harvard-trained lawyer and former senior executive in the independent telephone industry, now is the co-chairman, president and chief executive of Warner Amex Cable Communications, Inc. It is Warner Amex, a subsidiary of the entertainment conglomerate Warner Communications and the American Express Company, that has pioneered the commercial development of two-way television in Columbus and now is installing similar systems in Houston, Cincinnati, Pittsburgh and Dallas.

The considerable technical capabilities of Qube's system, which other companies have been forced to match in the current scramble for territorial franchises, has excited Scott Kurnit, the tall, bearded and faintly Mephistophelian program director for the Warner Amex system in Columbus, Ohio. "I think interactive television can be an enormously beneficial social instrument," Mr. Kurnit said during an interview in his cluttered Columbus office. "I think the unrelieved passiveness of traditional television broadcasting has had a significant negative impact on the American family and the American community. Interactive television will allow people to have fuller, freer lives, to communicate with each other, to learn how to work with each other. The system lessens isolation because it almost requires the family or community to consult with each other before deciding important issues raised by the system."

Qube, Warner Amex's version of two-way interactive television, offers two other television services in addition to allowing a subscriber to answer questions or order products. First, Qube's 29,000 Columbus subscribers have an enormous number of programs available to them, approximately 720 hours' worth in every 24-hour day. Second, because of the design of the system, separate programs can be offered to different groups of subscribers. A highly specialized medical course, for example, cannot be seen by the regular subscribers, but only by the physicians who have signed up for the training. A second example of the ability of the system to restrict usage to a particular group has occurred during televised town meetings, where only subscribers living in the affected township could express their views by "touching in" their responses to the questions put to them by their mayor.

"The idea, our goal, is to offer sufficient programming so that every member of our community can satisfy his separate needs every moment of the day," Mr. Kurnit said as he flipped through the thirty channels currently available to Columbus subscribers. There was the channel providing a twenty-four-hour-a-day news program, another showing round-the-clock movies, a third featuring old television shows with their commercials removed, a fourth carrying children's programs and another channel offering soft-core pornography. The special pay-per-view features—such as a major boxing match or the Ohio State University football games not on regular television—were of course not visible that weekday afternoon.

In addition, once every month Qube offers interested viewers a chance to take part in a discussion about books. The program is unlike any discussion show on conventional television, however, because the audience frequently is asked to answer multiple-choice questions about the book under discussion that evening and is given an opportunity to vote on which one of five books should be the subject of next month's program. Any member of the audience, furthermore, can telephone into the program while the discussion is underway and propose an appropriate question or call for a change of subject matter; the proposal will immediately be put to the audience. One final wrinkle. After the book for the next month's discussion has been selected, the audience is given an opportunity to press a button that results in the central computer recording their individual names and addresses so that the Columbus Public Library can automatically send them a loaned copy of the book in the mail.

"The book club is in many ways the most interesting and exciting use of interactive television now on Qube," said Tom Harnish, a thirty-five-year-old former navy pilot. Both Mr. Harnish and his wife, Judy, are officials of a Columbus-based nonprofit organization that operates an on-line computer network used by more than 2,300 libraries. Neither are noticeably uncomfortable with America's high-tech society. But sitting in the second-floor den watching as the Qube MC led an early evening interactive discussion about a book on government regulation, both indicated they had some reservations about Qube.

"One aspect that worries me," said Mr. Harnish, puffing on his pipe, "is what happens to those who are not able to pay the basic fifteen or twenty dollars a month for Qube, the possibility that we may be creating a new kind of underclass. I remember I once worked in a hospital in Baltimore where medical treatment was pretty easy to get as long as you had a telephone. But you would be surprised at how many people living in a big city are so poor or disconnected that they don't have a telephone."

A second criticism voiced by Mr. Harnish is that there is precious little interactive television now being offered by Columbus cable system. "They bill Qube as two-way interactive, but there aren't very many hours of interactive each week and some of the programs so labeled tend to ask trivial questions, such as whether you wear eyeglasses."

Gustave Hauser, the Warner Amex executive, at first brushed aside a question concerning the extent of Qube's commitment to interactive television. "No, no, no," he replied when asked how many hours of such television were scheduled each day, "you can't judge it that way. Television is not based on tonnage, it's based on quality. The number of hours are irrelevant. You can put a dog in front of a camera and you have a show, but you don't have a program."

After further pressing, however, Mr. Hauser said Qube was now programming "several hours of interactive television each day. But some days we might do none. It depends upon what we want to spend our money on. Everything is a question of economics. I can't schedule eighteen hours of interactive every day. It requires too many people. Everything is relative to economics and the economics is changing because there will be advertising and other sources of revenue, particularly if we do market-research programs."

The question of economics—what the subscribers and advertisers are willing to pay for—of course affects every issue concerning two-way television. But because the service is totally new, developing at a tremendous speed and impacting on American life in ways that are now only dimly perceived, it is hard for the public to know what safeguards are worth buying. Two years ago, in a speech before the Union League Club of New York City, Charles D. Ferris, then the chairman of the Federal Communications Commission, tried to alter the public perception about the value of personal privacy. "The fundamental problem I see with the coming information age," he warned, is that it "will rob us of one of our more important rights in a free society, the right to privacy."

When American families are wired for two-way television and its ancillary services, he went on, "a computer will have a record of what they buy and how much they spend. It will know whether they pay their bills quickly, slowly or not at all, and it will know where their money comes from. It will know whether they watched the debates or the football game or a controversial movie. It will know when they came home the previous night (and probably in what condition, depending on how many alarms they accidentally set off). It will know how many people are in their houses and in what rooms. In other words, it will know more about them than anyone should."

Charles Ferris expressed his warning in the future tense. But there already has been the first ominous nibbling at the two-way interactive data base. The incident began in early 1980 in Columbus when Domenic Suriano and Dean L. Farling were arrested on charges of pandering to obscenity. The two men were employees in an adult movie theater that was showing two sexually explicit films, *Taxi Girls* and *Captain Lust.* Upon learning that one of the movies had recently been shown on the pornography channel offered by Qube, the defense attorney for the men subpoenaed the company's computerized records. He hoped the records would show that the running of the film in the theater did not violate the standards of Columbus.

The company resisted providing the defense attorney with individual records. For the whole community, however, it provided data showing that 10,655 homes had paid to watch the pornographic movie in question when it was shown over the Qube system, and that on the average about one-quarter of the Qube subscribers watched the pornographic material when it was offered to them.

On June 9, 1980, the jury found the defendants not guilty. When reporters happened to glance at the empty jury room after the trial, they found the phrase "contemporary community standards" written on the blackboard. The jury apparently agreed with the defense that the theater manager and his assistant could not be charged with obscenity when the Qube computer showed that a significant part of the community did not object to sexually explicit movies.

What's to be done? Many knowledgeable experts believe that mechanical or legal safeguards can be developed. "In my own view, privacy is something of a wash," said Harry M. Shooshan III, the former chief counsel of the House Communications Subcommittee. "Of course there are problems, but there also are ways technology can enhance personal security."

Charles L. Jackson, a partner with Mr. Shooshan in their recently established Washington consulting firm, formerly was the chief engineer of the House Subcommittee. "The technology gives us an opportunity to enhance privacy as well as undercut it," Mr. Jackson said during a conversation in the small firm's new office. "As the system is being built, you can choose the ends that will be served. I do not believe that reliance on the technology by itself creates the hazard to privacy. The question is what are the goals and values of the people who are creating that system."

But Mr. Jackson acknowledged that privacy was a subtle issue. "Somehow we want an assurance that someone who is a political dissident—whether it's John Anderson or Abbie Hoffman—can live his life without fearing his political opponents will someday be handed a detailed report on his private behavior."

Mr. Hauser emphasized the concern he felt about the privacy of Qube customers. "I am concerned, others are concerned, we should all be concerned," he said. But the executive, like many lawyers, saw the savior in the law, rather than in technology. "If there is an abuse, there will be a regulation. I am delighted to have any regulation that is appropriate. Why don't we see what the public wants before we start regulating the business? Why don't we build the system and then worry about the things we don't like in it? The people who want to regulate in advance are the people who are going to prevent progress."

While the seriousness of the privacy threat and what should be done generates considerable disagreement, there appears to be a more generally shared concern about the inherent dangers posed by the ability of interactive television to conduct instant polls.

"There, there lies the potential for a real problem," said Mr. Shooshan. "The media dominates the political environment too much today. If a mayor can take a poll over two-way television about any issue he wants, he can significantly erode the powers of an elected city council or the intent of state referendum laws that require a certain number of signatures before an issue can be put on a ballot for a direct decision by the voters."

"Instant polling is an area of enormous peril," said Sidney W. Dean, the chairman of the New York City Club's Ad Hoc Committee on Cable Television and for seven years a member of the city's advisory committee on the same subject. "Instantaneous surveys on public policy issues are frightening for a number of reasons. First, there is no time for thoughtful consideration of the issue. Second, from my long experience in marketing research, I know that the hand that writes the questions usually begets the answers."

An incident in early 1982 demonstrates the irresistible attraction of the instant polls and their considerable impact on the political process. In late February of that year President Reagan gave a speech to the Organization of American States in which he announced an important new United States policy toward the nations of the Caribbean. The day after the speech, the article on the Reagan administration's effort was the lead story in the *New York Times*. The paper's editors also ran several other stories on the initiative, one of which bore the headline "A City Swings Sharply After Reagan Speech." The gist of the story was that the percentage of Columbus viewers favoring the president's position in the Caribbean had jumped from 35 percent before the speech to 64 percent after it.

"It means either he's very persuasive or they're very malleable," a spokesman for the Cable News Network was quoted as saying.

Even though the last paragraph of the story properly noted that the survey was "a non-scientific tally rather than a true poll," the decision of the *Times* editors to run it completely belied the disclaimer. So did the headline. Even the sophisticated editors of the *Times* were unable to resist the allure of this seriously flawed story.

How many readers understood that the poll only measured the views of the fairly small fraction of Columbus residents who were Qube subscribers and happened to be watching television when the president made his speech? How many knew that unlike a standard poll, where the makeup of the respondents roughly parallels the ethnic, economic and social makeup of the nation, the Columbus poll very well may have included a disproportionate number of children, women, or white middle-class homeowners?

Robert W. Ross is the young, aggressive and highly articulate senior vice-president for law and government affairs of the National Cable Television Association. "The consequences? All the consequences are positive," Mr. Ross replied to a question about the ultimate impact of the industry he was representing on the American people. "Information is like nuclear power. You can harness it for good or you can harness it for evil. It depends upon what kinds of regulatory structures are set up and how the regulations are applied."

But as he talked, Mr. Ross quickly qualified his first cheerful assessment. He was particularly concerned about what he ironically called "the era of plebiscitary democracy," which he defined as the time when a politician could say "push button 3 if you agree with me and 17 million hit button 3 and the decision is made to lock up the Nisei."

Mr. Ross recounted his experiences as a twenty-one-year-old ensign in Vietnam, where he believes the existence of nearly instantaneous communication links with Washington robbed him and the rest of the officers of the appropriate authority to make decisions. "If the day comes when an elected official has the ability to swiftly determine how his constituents feel about any issue he is dealing with, it is my guess that the individuality and self-confidence of that official will be undermined," he warned. "A congressman is there to represent his constituents, not just to do his own will. On the other hand, it is simultaneously important for politicians to exercise their own judgments about the rightness of something rather than responding to the pressures of the mob or the emotions of the moment."

The fundamental constitutional, philosophical and economic perils raised by the installation of two-way interactive television in the homes of a significant number of Americans require the most careful analysis. But Ithiel de Sola Pool, a professor at the Massachusetts Institute of Technology, is concerned about the possible response of society once the threats are identified.

"No democracy would tolerate the notion that a reporter's notebook be licensed and subject to inspection by those he is writing about," Professor Pool warns. "No democracy would tolerate that a political party's campaign plans be treated the same way, nor that our correspondence with our friends abroad should be compulsorily opened up. But that is exactly what many countries are requiring for computer files. What then happens when a reporter keeps his files on his home computer or when a political party produces its plans on an intelligent word processor or when we write our friends by electronic mail?"

Professor Pool noted the laws recently passed by several European countries. "A Luddite fear of the computer is leading to a reversal of several centuries of struggle for the protection of personal freedom," he warned darkly.

At a time when technological changes are placing large and frequently unanticipated pressures on society, choosing the right course is hard business. Harry Shooshan recalled the telling comment of Lord Devlin about the dangers of our difficult and subtle times. "If freedom of the press or freedom of speech perishes, it will not be by sudden death. It will be a long time dying from a debilitating disease caused by a series of erosive measures, each of which, if examined singly, would have a great deal to be said for it."

There are so many signs pointing to the broad use of EFT and two-way interactive television that predicting these developments is not difficult. While there are disagreements about exactly when the systems will be in place and precisely how they will affect our society, the United States certainly is moving toward a world where a substantial number of our homes will be directly connected to one or more electronic networks capable of providing a level and variety of services far more elaborate than is currently available over the telephone.

But there are other aspects of the future and the computer that are harder to grasp, where there are fewer road signs. What will it mean, for example, when a machine is devised that can truly understand human speech? At the most obvious level, even a crude and imperfect form of automatic speech recognition will reduce the barriers that separate humans from machines. When men and women speaking in their natural voices are able to routinely instruct a machine to stop or start, or dictate directly to a typewriter, the potential power of all humans will be incredibly enhanced. But the power also will be transformed. Will humans become more machinelike or machines become more humanlike?

Machines that can respond to various kinds of spoken instructions represent a fundamental change in the relationship that has existed between humans and their inanimate tools since that moment when prehistoric man first picked up a stick to dig honey from a beehive or grabbed a jagged bit of rock to slaughter a deer. The change is so enormous, in fact, that trying to grasp its implications requires an extraordinary, perhaps impossible, leap of imagination.

During most of history, men and women have adjusted their lives to the demands of the machine, whether it be a plow, a steam engine or an automobile. Will the computer modify the demanding, unbending nature of machines? Or will the computer, like most machines before it, stamp its imprint on man? For a large number of Americans, the question already has been partially answered. Who has not fruitlessly argued with the police computer that sent them someone else's parking ticket, the utility company computer that sent them incorrect electric bills, or the credit reporting computer that mistakenly rated their bill-paying habits?

The machines of the first part of the Industrial Revolution changed the way we used our muscles. The machines of the second part seem to be changing the way we think. Here is one example a bit beyond the rigid orthodoxy of most of the computers operated by the bureaucracies that shape our lives. Very soon, computers are going to be taught to talk. But because their vocabularies for the foreseeable future will remain quite small and consist of simple and easy-to-define words, the exchanges with these latest computers will necessarily be narrowly focused. As the talking computers come to play a more important role in the powerful institutions of society, will the limited vocabulary of the engines of these bureaucracies tend to dangerously simplify public debate on the subtle, complex and even ambiguous issues that confront the American people? Will it be possible for government officials, corporate executives and the public to make difficult ethical and moral decisions when the computers that inform and teach us have a relatively limited vocabulary?

Research to develop computer systems that can understand human speech has been intense. A few years ago, the Advanced Research Projects Agency of the Department of Defense spent $15 million attempting to devise such a device for the military. While most scientists viewed the ARPA project as only marginally successful, scientists at Carnegie-Mellon University in Pittsburgh did devise a system called Harpy. Harpy, they said, was able to comprehend five different men and women reading sentences drawn from a 1,011 word vocabulary with only a 5 percent error rate. One drawback: it cost $5 for every sentence that Harpy "translated" from the spoken word to the written.

Private companies like AT&T, IBM, Xerox and the Stanford Research Institute have also been seeking to devise speech recognition systems. At Bell Labs, the research arm of AT&T, the research has been aimed at a less ambitious goal than attempted by the military. Bell Laboratory scientists have been trying to develop specific ways a relatively simplified speech recognition system might help improve the usefulness and at the same time reduce the costs of telephoning. In one project, for example, a computer system was devised whose basic vocabulary consisted of the letters of the alphabet. The purpose was to determine if a method could be devised for a person to look up telephone numbers by dialing information and then spelling out the name of the person they wanted to call.

In a second experiment, a computer system with a somewhat larger vocabulary was devised which enabled an individual to call in and determine the names of the airlines offering flights to a number of specific cities and the time and day of such flights. Though the person calling the computer was required to follow a quite specific format, it correctly understood the questions put to it over a conventional telephone line more than 85 percent of the time. In a third project, the engineers devised a computerized system to handle the billing when an individual wanted to reverse the charges on a long-distance call.

But the experiments, at least the ones that have been announced, are still only experiments. So far no research teams have publicly claimed that they have devised a computerized system that can understand human speech. Too many words have different meanings in different contexts. No machine has yet been created that can recognize irony or sarcasm. And a few truly knowledgeable computer experts such as Joseph Weizenbaum argue that in some very important ways a machine can never "understand" a human, that human thought and expression is so complex and subtle that only a human being can provide the context that gives meaning to a sentence spoken by another human being.

There are persistent rumors, however, that the National Security Agency, the secret eavesdropping arm of the United States government, has developed a system that scans the tape recordings of international telephone calls and automatically flags those messages where one of the callers uses certain trigger words such as the name of the president or a highly sensitive subject like plutonium. Because of the towering barrier of secrecy that surrounds the NSA, determining whether the agency actually has developed such an ability simply is not possible. But from the experiments we know have been conducted by AT&T and other groups, it is not unreasonable to assume that the NSA has such equipment to monitor some telephone calls.

The development of language recognition systems that could record conversations and automatically identify those intervals when the speakers were discussing certain specified subjects of interest would have a major impact on the way we live. At the present time, electronic eavesdropping in the United States is far more limited than most Americans think. This is partly because federal law prohibits wiretapping and bugging except in very special circumstances. The far more important deterrent, however, is that wiretapping and bugging cost too much money.

Every year, the Congress votes to provide the Federal Bureau of Investigation with more than $600 million to enforce the federal law. But even the FBI cannot afford to order its highly trained agents— many of whom make more than $40,000 a year—to eavesdrop on conversations unless they are of the highest importance. People talking at their normal speed, calling a doctor, arranging for a baby- sitter, checking with a friend about where to meet for dinner, can devour an enormous amount of an agent's time. The extremely low cost of labor in countries such as Russia and India is a major reason why the governments of these two countries can afford to eavesdrop on a huge number of telephone lines.

But a computerized voice recognition system would dramatically alter the economics of eavesdropping. When a system is devised that allows an FBI agent or private detective to focus on only the sensitive or suspicious conversations and automatically screen out the routine and innocuous ones, then eavesdropping will become a far more widespread and troubling problem than it is today, no matter what is prohibited by law.

The computer thus may lead to more wiretapping and bugging by reducing the economic barriers to eavesdropping for agencies and organizations that can afford to purchase voice recognition systems. But the computer will not only knock down the obstacles that tend to protect the words we speak. More importantly, it someday may increase the vulnerability of the thoughts we think.

Though the subject is extraordinarily complex, the research of Dr. Steven A. Hillyard and Dr. Marta Kutas of the University of California at San Diego is provocative. With the help of a computer, the two researchers believe they have identified brain-wave patterns that in a limited sense allow them to understand what people are thinking. More specifically, the researchers apparently have discovered that one pattern of brain wave is generated when a test subject is presented with a surprising situation and an entirely different brain wave when the subject is presented with nonsense.

In one set of experiments, the reactions of test subjects were compared when they heard a sentence presenting a conventional thought and when they heard a sentence that unexpectedly ended in nonsense. According to the researchers, the nonsense sentence provoked a unique brain pattern four-tenths of a second after the subject heard it. "I like my coffee with sugar and cream," for example, did not prompt the creation of the special brain wave. But with the change of only one word—"I like my coffee with cream and cement"—the computerized instruments of Hillyard and Kutas spotted the unique signal.

Dr. Hillyard is planning to do experiments in which the incongruity of the last word will be made progressively more subtle, thus testing a person's verbal skills in a way that is impossible to match by any other objective test. He and his colleague hope such tests some day may prove useful in identifying children with reading disabilities and indirectly determining their language skills.

Computer systems that can distinguish between when a person is surprised or confused by nonsense, however, might possibly be used for less benevolent purposes. Official investigators traditionally have been confronted with an almost absolute barrier when it came to determining a subject's motive for committing a given act. Certainly, the show trials of the Soviet Union in the thirties and the confessions of American soldiers captured in Korea and Vietnam show that many individuals can be subject to sufficient psychological pressure to force them to "confess" to any crime. But such pressure, while encouraging an individual to say what the investigator wanted to hear, may prevent the individual from describing his true emotion. Could the increasingly sophisticated brain-wave-measuring system of researchers like Hillyard and Kutas provide the answer to this problem? History tells us that once such a system becomes available, even if it provides data of questionable validity, there will be corporations and law-enforcement agencies who use it.

Paralleling the development of computers that in some sense understand speech or provide a possible technique for defining the motives of individuals is an even more amorphous and potentially terrifying possibility: a world where scientists have perfected a machine that can think as well as, and possibly better, than scientists. To many, the subject of artificial intelligence is absurd. The most common objection is that a computer, no matter how big its memory or fast its processing, will never match a human because a computer requires instructions to think.

It is true, of course, that all machines must be given instructions. But the objection seems to lose some validity when you remember that humans too are given instructions; that the rules of life are impressed on their psyches by their mothers and fathers, wives and husbands, friends and enemies, children and grandchildren.

Many are not satisfied with this parallel. They argue that no computer will ever be able to make the intuitive leap of imagination that seems to be required for the creation of all great works of art and science. But again, the objection does not seem entirely valid.

Certainly the specific evolution from the background and training of a Ludwig van Beethoven or a Madame Curie to the Ninth Symphony or the nature of radioactivity, is impossible to trace. On the other hand, all great artistic and scientific achievements do in fact grow from what the late Christopher Evans eloquently wrote were "the seeds of experience planted in the fertile substrate of the brain."

Furthermore, computers in recent years have in fact leapt the boundary that the critics argue separates man from machine. Evans, the experimental psychologist and computer scientist whom we have met before, discussed the question of original thought in the last book he wrote before his death. "If a person demonstrates a skill which has never been demonstrated before and which has not been specifically taught to him by someone else, or in an intellectual domain provides an entirely novel solution to a problem, then they can be said to have done something original or had an original or creative thought," he wrote. Evans then described one instance when a computer developed a completely novel proof for the ancient theorem that the base angles of an isosceles triangle are equal. "Quite apart from the fact that the proof had not before been known to man," Evans commented, "it showed such originality that one famous mathematician remarked, 'If any of my students had done that, I would have marked him down as a budding genius.' "

Because comprehending the potential impacts of highly intelligent machines is very difficult, many experts in the area have tended to dismiss their significance. It was not very many years ago, for example, that deep skepticism was expressed about the possibility of ever designing a computer program to play chess. This was done. Then the doubters questioned whether the computer could ever be taught to play chess with a novice who understood only the tactical rules of how each man moved, not the strategic ebb and flow of one of the world's most complicated games. This was done. Now several programs have been devised which enable the computer to regularly defeat all but the very best chess players in the world.

The gap between man and machine is narrowing. With every major industrial nation in the world spending millions of dollars a year to increase the size, flexibility and speed of computers, many knowledgeable experts are convinced that the day they will match or surpass many of the abilities of the human brain is quite close. Because virtually all of the research funds to enhance the computer are provided by large organizations like the Department of Defense, AT&T and IBM, it seems likely that the first applications of what the Japanese call the fifth generation of computers will be to assist these groups achieve their varied goals and not necessarily to nurture the development of individual freedom.

The question of how these enormously powerful computers will be used by society was a matter of concern even to computer enthusiast Christopher Evans. "One gloomy possibility is that the intellectual resources of machines will be misused," he wrote. "They could be tapped by criminals, by forces hostile to society or even by groups concerned with defending society at all costs, and, in one form or another, used against human beings."

Evans thought government security forces and secret services would be first to recognize the potential of highly intelligent computers for outsmarting the opposition, with the military tacticians a close second. "Police forces, too, will find artificial intelligence enormously attractive, for criminals' movements can be 'predicted,' and their crime anticipated to some degree."

While perceiving benefits in these uses, Evans also expressed deep concern. "Nevertheless we should all hope and pray that the day of dictatorships and authoritarian governments is done before substantial advances are made in artificial intelligence and certainly before artificial intelligence machines come into being. Any regime supported by the power of intelligent machines would be more secure and more terrible than any all-human equivalent."

Does this warning bring us full circle, to the cold Manhattan winter of the year 2020, to the glossy high-tech world of Peter Strauss and the filthy, disorganized slum of Bill Peterson and Sally? Will the bureaucracies of the next few decades, buffeted by powerful economic, political and military fears, mobilize their ranks or computers for dark and crabbed purposes? Or will the individual men who run these bureaucracies choose a path where computers are used to help more and more individuals achieve their full potential?

Selected Bibliography

GENERAL BOOKS

Boden, Margaret A. *Artificial Intelligence and Natural Man.* New York: Basic Books, 1977.

Bowden, B.W. *Faster Than Thought: A Symposium on Digital Computing Machines.* United Kingdom: Pitman and Sons, 1953.

Danzinger, James N., William H. Dutton, Rob Kling, and Kenneth L. Kraemer. *Computers and Politics: High Technology in American Local Governments.* New York: Columbia University Press, 1981.

Dertouzos, Michael L., and Joel Moses. *The Computer Age: A Twenty-Year View.* Cambridge, MA: MIT Press, 1979.

Donner, Frank J. *The Age of Surveillance.* New York: Alfred A. Knopf, 1980.

Ellul, Jacques. *The Technological Society.* New York: Vintage Books, 1964.

Evans, Christopher. *The Micro Millennium.* New York: Viking Press, 1979.

Hoos, Ida R. *Systems Analysis in Public Policy: A Critique.* Berkeley and Los Angeles, CA: University of California Press, 1972.

Information Technology: Some Critical Implications for Decision Makers. The first in the series of management of change studies directed by the Conference Board. New York: The Conference Board, 1972.

Kraemer, Kenneth L., William H. Dutton and Alana Northrop. *The Management of Information Systems.* New York: Columbia University Press, 1981.

Levine, Emil H. *Information Science: Law Enforcement Applications.* Cincinnati: Anderson Publishing Co., 1979.

Marchand, Donald A. *The Politics of Privacy, Computers, and Criminal Justice Records.* Arlington, VA: Information Resources Press, 1980.

Martin, James. *The Wired Society: A Challenge for Tomorrow.* Englewood Cliffs, NJ: Prentice-Hall, 1978.

Moore, Doris Langley. *Ada, Countess of Lovelace, Byron's Legitimate Daughter.* United Kingdom: John Murray, 1977.

Nora, Simon, and Alain Minc. *The Computerization of Society.* Cambridge, MA: MIT Press, 1980.

Orwell, George. *1984.* New York: New American Library, 1961.

Rule, James, Douglas McAdam, Linda Stearns, and David Uglow. *The Politics of Privacy.* New York: New American Library, 1980.

Sanders, C.W., G.F. Sandy, J.F. Sawyer, and A. Schneider. *Study of Vulnerability of Electronic Communication Systems to Electronic Interception.* Volumes I and II. McLean, VA: Mitre Corporation, January 1977.

Smith, Robert Ellis. *Privacy: How to Protect What's Left of It.* Garden City, NY: Anchor Press/Doubleday, 1979.

Strassels, Paul N., with Robert Wool. *All You Need to Know About the IRS.* New York: Random House, 1979.

Toffler, Alvin. *The Third Wave.* New York: Bantam Books, 1981.

Weber, Max. *Essays in Sociology.* Translated by Hans H., Gerth and C. Wright Mills. Oxford: Oxford University Press, 1946.

Weizenbaum, Joseph. *Computer Power and Human Reason: From Judgment to Calculation.* San Francisco: W.H. Freeman and Company, 1976.

Westin, Alan F., and Michael A. Baker. *Databanks in a Free Society: Computers, Record-Keeping and Privacy.* New York: Quadrangle/New York Times Book Company, 1972.

Wicklein, John. *Electronic Nightmare: The New Communications and Freedom.* New York: Viking Press, 1979.

Wiener, Norbert. *The Human Use of Human Beings: Cybernetics and Society.* Garden City, NY: Doubleday, 1954.

GOVERNMENT PUBLICATIONS

Federal Information Sources and Systems 1980. A Directory Issued by the Comptroller General. 1980 Congressional Sourcebook Series. Washington, D.C.: U.S. Government Printing Office, 1977.

Long, Susan B. *The Internal Revenue Service: Measuring Tax Offenses and Enforcement Response.* Washington, D.C.: National Institute of Justice, September 1980.

Personal Privacy in an Information Society. The Report of the Privacy Protection Study Commissioner. Washington, D.C.: U.S. Government Printing Office, July 1977.

Records Computers and the Rights of Citizens. Report of the Secretary's Advisory Committee on Automated Personal Data Systems. U.S. Department of Health, Education and Welfare. Washington, D.C.: U.S. Government Printing Office, July 1973.

U.S. Congress. House. Committee on Government Operations Together with Additional Views. *The Government's Classification of Private Ideas.* Thirty-fourth Report, 96th Congress, 2nd Session, 1980.

U.S. Congress. House. Subcommittee of the Committee on Government Operations. *Privacy of Medical Records.* Hearings, 96th Congress, 1st Session, 1979.

U.S. Congress. House. Subcommittee on Labor-Management Relations of the Committee on Education and Labor. *Pressures in Today's Workplace.* Volumes I–III. Oversight Hearings, 96th Congress, 1st and 2nd Sessions, 1979.

U.S. Congress. Senate. Ad Hoc Subcommittee on Privacy and Information Systems of the Committee on Government Operations. *Privacy: The Collection, Use and Computerization of Personal Data.* Joint Hearings, 93rd Congress, 2nd Session, 1974.

U.S. Congress. Senate. Committee on Government Operations. *Materials Pertaining to S. 3418 and Protecting Individual Privacy in Federal Gathering, Use and Disclosure of Information.* Committee Print, 93rd Congress, 2nd Session, 1974.

U.S. Congress. Senate. Select Committee to Study Governmental Operations with Respect to Intelligence Activities. Final Report, 94th Congress, 2nd Session, 1976, Books I–VI: Book I. *Foreign and Military Intelligence,* Book II. *Intelligence Activities and the Rights of Americans,* Book III. *Supplementary Detailed Staff Reports on Intelligence Activities and the Rights of Americans,* Book IV. *Supplementary Reports on Intelligence Activities,* Book V. *The Investigation of the Assassination of President John F. Kennedy: Performance of the Intelligence Agencies,* Book VI. *Supplementary Detailed Staff Reports on Foreign and Military Intelligence.*

U.S. Congress. Senate. Select Committee to Study Governmental Operations with Respect to Intelligence Activities. Hearings, 94th Congress, 1st Session, 1975, Vols. 1–6: Vol. 1. *Unauthorized Storage of Toxic Agents,* Vol. 2. *Huston Plan,* Vol. 3. *Internal Revenue Service,* Vol. 4. *Mail Opening,* Vol. 5. *The National Security Agency and Fourth Amendment Rights,* Vol. 6. *Federal Bureau of Investigation.*

U.S. Congress. Senate. Subcommittee on Constitutional Rights of the Committee on the Judiciary. *Privacy, the Census and Federal Questionnaires.* Hearings, 91st Congress, 1st Session, 1969.

U.S. Congress. Senate. Subcommittee on Constitutional Rights of the Committee on the Judiciary. Hearings, 92nd Congress, 1st Session, 1971, Parts I–II: Part I. *Federal Data Banks, Computers and the Bill of Rights,* Part II. *Federal Data Banks, Computers and the Bill of Rights Relating to Departments of Army, Defense and Justice.*

U.S. Congress. Senate. Subcommittee on Constitutional Rights of the Committee on the Judiciary. *Surveillance Technology—1976.* Staff Report, 94th Congress, 2nd Session, 1976.

U.S. Congress. Senate. Subcommittee on Consumer Affairs of the Committee on Banking, Housing, and Urban Affairs. *Fair Financial Information Practices Act.* Hearings, 96th Congress, 2nd Session, 1980, Part II—Credit.

U.S. Congress. Senate. Subcommittee on Intelligence and the Rights of Americans of the Select Committee on Intelligence. *Foreign Intelligence Surveillance Act of 1978.* Hearings, 95th Congress, 2nd Session, 1978.

Index

About the Author

DAVID BURNHAM has been a reporter for UPI, *Newsweek,* and CBS, and has worked for over ten years for the *New York Times* in both New York and Washington. His articles about police corruption in New York City, based partly on information from Frank Serpico and David Durk, led to the formation of the Knapp Commission and reform of the police department. While working on a story about health and safety problems at the Kerr-McGee plutonium factory in Oklahoma, Burnham arranged a meeting with Karen Silkwood, a worker at the plant. Ms. Silkwood died under mysterious circumstances in a car crash on her way to that meeting. Over the years Burnham has won numerous awards, including the George Polk Award for Public Service, the Society of the Silurians Award for Reportorial Enterprise, the Page One Award for Crusading Journalism of the Newspaper Guild of New York and the Golden Typewriter Award of the New York Press Club. Burnham now lives in Washington, DC.